Family Art Therapy

THE FAMILY THERAPY AND COUNSELING SERIES
Consulting Editor
Jon Carlson

Family Art Therapy

Foundations of Theory and Practice

Christine Kerr

Janice Hoshino

Judy Sutherland • Sharyl Thode Parashak • Linda Lea McCarley

Routledge
Taylor & Francis Group
New York   London

Routledge
Taylor & Francis Group
711 Third Avenue
New York, NY 10017

Routledge
Taylor & Francis Group
2 Park Square
Milton Park, Abingdon
Oxon OX14 4RN

International Standard Book Number-13: 978-0-415-95464-8 (Hardcover)

Library of Congress Cataloging-in-Publication Data

Family art therapy : foundations of theory and practice / Christine Kerr ... [et al.].
    p. ; cm. -- (The family therapy and counseling series)
  ISBN 978-0-415-95464-8 (hardcover : alk. paper)
  1. Family psychotherapy. 2. Art therapy. I. Kerr, Christine, Ph.D. II. Series.
  [DNLM: 1. Art Therapy. 2. Family Therapy. 3. Family Relations. WM 430.5.F2 F19807 2007]

RC488.5.F3242 2007
616.89'1656--dc22   2007005574

Visit the Taylor & Francis Web site at
http://www.taylorandfrancis.com

and the Routledge Web site at
http://www.routledge.com

Contents

Series Editor's Foreword

"Every artist dips his brush in his own soul, and paints his own nature into his pictures."

Harriet Ward Beecher

As a student I always loved art classes but was not very creative or talented at this type of expression. No matter how much I tried, my flowers always appeared wilted and my cars looked more like boats. Once I accepted my lack of artistic ability, I concentrated on learning to appreciate others' art. As a graduate student I learned about projective techniques and was fascinated by watching people draw houses, trees, and persons. It became very clear just how each person would project himself or herself onto the paper.

I was very excited for this book to be completed. The integration of family therapy and art therapy can provide many advantages for the practicing therapist. The combination of art and traditional talk therapy provide for new avenues of understanding and intervention. Placed in a family context, this creates a venue for deep therapeutic intervention. Art allows each family member to communicate using his or her own symbols to represent the family's functioning. The artwork not only communicates but also provides a projective assessment for the therapist to use in tailoring treatment. By focusing on the family and not on the individual members, an accurate picture of each member's true self becomes possible.

The visual record helps non- or less verbal family members participate. It allows the family members to reach the deeper levels of being that are only available through experiential understanding. Restructuring communication patterns makes it possible to balance the family system in a healthy fashion. Resistance and defensiveness are frequently eliminated.

I found this book to not only be a helpful professional text but to be a deeply personal statement about the contributors. The chapter authors share their skills and knowledge in both art and family therapy, along with themselves. The words and insights tell as much about the contributors as their ideas. I applaud each of them for their effort in bringing this important therapy to a wider professional audience.

Jon Carlson, Psy.D., Ed.D., ABPP
Series Editor

Foreword

Family Art Therapy is a celebration of family therapy theories and their wedding to art therapy. The amalgamating process is viewed through case histories. This book sets the stage by reviewing art that portrays family life throughout the ages. It begins with the ancient Egyptians, continues through the various periods in history and concludes with the Western art of the twentieth century. These images reveal the state of the family and the roles various members play. This first chapter ends with an art therapy case history of a 9/11 widow and her son. Together, they create a picture of a mother and young child hugging each other. Thus, the importance of the art in family work is introduced. Although pictures of the past reveal important information, we are reminded that our clients today are also making metaphoric records of family life in the twenty-first century.

Systems theory and family therapy are explored. Descriptions of the early family therapists are all inclusive. Theoretical approaches are fully and clearly delineated; then each paradigm is incorporated into the family art therapy modality.

A comprehensive history of family art therapy is included. It is interesting to read the information on the pioneering art therapists and their descriptions of "how" they got started on the innovative path to family art therapy. The directives that each clinician uses during the initial stage of treatment is listed. It shows the similarities and differences in their evaluation styles.

In the sixties and early seventies, clinicians who claimed they were "eclectic" in their treatment approach were often therapists who reached out to multiple ways of working because they did not understand or were not grounded in any family theory. It was out of desperation that they grasped at anything they could think of at the moment.

It was late in the twentieth century that essential educational changes were made. Schools, especially those in states where licensure was south, instituted stringent family art therapy requirements. As a result a solid foundation was established. The American Art Therapy Association is also credited with important improvements in this regard.

The Conclusion in *Family Art Therapy* is unique. Each author contributed personal and reflective statements. In the process of creating this text, a remarkable bonding effect took place. A profound kinship was formed; one filled with support and caring. The authors found themselves to be a part of "a family of writers." This collaborative effort enriched the life of each person.

I found this involvement unusual. As a coeditor for the book *Adult Art Psychotherapy*, there were no personal connections, except with my coeditor. Each author sent in a chapter and was engaged on a one-to-one basis. They never had the opportunity to meet as a group. I believe that is the usual method of putting a book together with a number of writers. By contrast, when I read this book's conclusion, I envied the family dynamics involved in their joint effort.

My career as a family art psychotherapist has been gratifying and rewarding. There are fourth generation families that I see on an occasional "as needed" basis. I believe this is a testimony to the effectiveness of the family art therapy modality.

In my practice, parents seldom come requesting family therapy. The tendency is to view their child as the designated patient. When they are told the entire family will be treated together, they are surprised. Initially, they tend to be resistant. However, after the evaluation session I share my observations regarding their communication system. They are astonished and impressed by the insights gleaned from "just drawing together." As a result, they agree to continue with this mode of treatment.

Family Art Therapy is an important book for all clinicians. It contains information on an amazing number of family and family art therapists. The documentation is monumental and impressive. Writing styles are consistently excellent, clear, informative, and interesting. Long-time family art therapists will read this book and be reminded or may discover additional options for their family work. It will be especially helpful to students and to the new generation of art therapists because it gives them a broad spectrum of choices to think about and to put into practice.

Helen Barbara Landgarten,
DAT, ATR-BC, HLM, MFT

Acknowledgments

In their respective chapters, the family art therapists who have written chapters in this text have given acknowledgment to those who assisted them in contributing to this book. I would like to express my sincere gratitude to those who have supported me in the *overall* writing of this book. First and foremost, I would like to thank Dr. Janice Hoshino, ATR-BC LMFT, for her considerable efforts in research as well as her contribution of essential chapters to this book. Her wisdom and friendship have been inspirational. Second, I would like to acknowledge those who have served on the Educational Program Approval Board (EPAB) committee. This committee of women, with their unique expertise, agreed to share their work, their clinical insights, and their energy. Their unique and important contributions to this text have made this book rich and an important addition to the field of family art therapy. Last, I would personally thank Naomi Schwartz, ATR-BC, LCAT for her constant diligence and friendship and Sharon Murray ATR-BC, LCAT, for her continuous care and academic scholarship.

In closing, I would like to thank my husband, Gary T. Kerr, LCSW-BC, ATR-BC, LCAT. We have been treating couples and families for some time now. We always treat these families together as cotherapists. He often says, "*I need you.*" I must say *I need him as well.* Though we have very different personalities and therapeutic styles, we complement each other. Can you imagine after 30 years of marriage we as co-family therapists find the best in each other? We try to help families also find *the best in each other* and to *heal.*

Introduction

CHRISTINE KERR

Family therapy textbooks are plentiful for the beginning family therapist, the educator, and the seasoned clinician. In many textbooks, the vast number of theoretical paradigms, as well as applied clinical vignettes, provide those who are interested in skills advancement with numerous resources. Within the field of traditional family therapy, there are extensive family therapy theories and depth within any one given schema. Various family models of traditional family therapy have evolved and become differentiated since the 1960s, the classification of which continues to undergo change and reevaluation.

Classic family therapy theory can and is currently being integrated within art psychotherapy treatment. What is unique to the practice of clinical art psychotherapy is the use of action-oriented art processes that can work in tandem with traditional family therapy verbal dialoguing. Consequently, art interventions have the potential to parallel many of the theoretical paradigms of conventional family therapy. Much like traditional family therapy, family art therapy does not focus on the individual alone but treats the nuclear family, specific family dyads and often the family intergenerationally. The art therapist and the family therapy practitioner, both of whom work with families, should have an understanding of the variety of theoretical viewpoints and associative art interventions to interactively and integratively meet the affective and developmental needs of client families.

As art therapy educators and authors in this book, we discussed the need for a comprehensive, updated family art therapy text. Noting that Helen Landgarten authored the seminal family art therapy text in 1987, we concluded that a restructured family art therapy text could draw together an overview of classic and postmodern theories with applied art techniques. Other books that have been written on family art therapy after this date have either focused on specific client populations or have integrated limited family therapy theory with the art therapy process.

It is important to note that many of the theoretical constructs found in art therapy were largely psychoanalytical. However, as systems theory emerged within the larger field of psychology and social work, art therapy education likewise included systems theory within its educational curriculum. A paradigmatic shift from traditional art therapy approaches to a systemic, cybernetic approach in education and clinical practice began to surface. Out of this paradigm shift emerged those practitioners trained in art and action-oriented nonverbal processes that began to clinically incorporate the use of art in therapy with couples and families.

Consequently, we proposed a family art therapy text that would bring together the classic and postmodern family therapy theories and techniques (Anderson, 1991; Bowen, 1972; Duhl & Duhl, 1981; Framo, 1982, 1992; Haley, 1967; Gergen, 1985; Ginsberg, 1989; McGoldrick & Gerson, 1985; Minuchin, 1974; Satir, 1971, 1983; Whitaker, 1976) with practical clinical approaches from the field of art therapy. Unlike other introductory texts in family art therapy, this edition hopes to not only summarize where and how this field has developed over the past 25 years (Kwiatkowska, 1978), but also to present where the field of family art therapy is going. As the field broadens and is more inclusive of disparate theoretical points of view, so should the family art therapist be able to develop a breadth of knowledge that incorporates classic family therapy theory with postmodern approaches.

WHY INCORPORATE ART INTO FAMILY THERAPY TREATMENT?

What are the potential benefits of family art therapy? The art process offers a variety of meaningful experiences for families in treatment. It has been stated many times by those in the field of art therapy, that art interventions *can* reduce defensiveness and may unlock deeper levels of experiential understanding for both individuals and families in treatment (Landgarten, 1987; Linesch, 1993; Riley, 1993; Rubin, 1984; Wadeson, 1980). Family problems are often tenacious and resistive to change because they are embedded in powerful but unseen structures. The art process can often bypass well-entrenched defenses that manifest themselves as obstacles to the family members' interpersonal understanding of each other. Additionally, the art process may allow the possibility for family members to articulate emotions and thoughts through a visual means, which unlike verbal dialogue allows individual self-expression to be made permanent through the art product.

Second, when the art-making process is combined therapeutically with verbal treatment, the art directive may allow the family therapist an opportunity to analyze communication patterns by providing a visual record of the family's structure, subsystems, and boundaries. The efficacy of this evaluative phenomenon is found in the abundance of clinical data that economically can be transferred from the visual art product into clinical assessment and treatment (Burns & Kaufman, 1970; Kwiatkowska, 1978; Landgarten, 1987; Linesch, 1993; Malchiodi, 1998; Oster & Gould, 1987; Riley, 1993; Rubin, 1984; Wadeson, 1980).

A third benefit of art making in family treatment is the potential of the art-making process to facilitate needed energy for families that appear deadlocked in anger and hopelessness. Families seeking treatment are often entrenched in failure and impotence (Linesch, 1993). Noting that the process of making art is by definition a creative and potentially an energizing endeavor, art making promotes not only needed energy for the family but may allow the family to experience a sense of accomplishment as they engage in art making. For this reason, the process of creative art making can be liberating and highly proscriptive.

A final benefit of the art process in family treatment involves an increase "in relationship building for family members" (Linesch, 1993, p. 6). In family therapy, attempts at genuine dialogue between: (a) husbands and wives; (b) mothers, daughters, and sons; (c) fathers, daughters, and sons; (d) brothers and sisters; and (e) extended family members are often plagued by rigid configurations of both behavior and ritual. However, the nonverbal nature of the art process can offer a means for liberating bound and redundant interpersonal styles that often make relationships stale, rigid, and dysfunctional.

THE CHAPTERS

The chapters in this text provide the student, educator, and clinician with a timeline that is formulated to sequentially delineate the historical context of traditional family therapy theory along with innovative art tasks that complement each theory.

Chapter 1, "Family Art Images in Historical and Social Perspectives," thematically explores the rich archival database of historical family art images, found across numerous artistic genres and in past and present societies in Western culture. From the perspective of art history scholarship, these works of art offer enormous validity and interpretative value for the use of family art images as a therapeutic tool in family treatment. This chapter will support this assumption and offer the reader an overview of the evolving Western family over time.

In Chapter 2, "The Development of Family Therapy and Family Art Therapy," the reader is introduced to basic cybernetic and systems theories. Key family therapists are highlighted, as well as the underpinnings of family therapy language and theory. This includes (a) the family as a system, (b) characteristics of functional and dysfunctional family interaction, and (c) the family developmental life cycle. Within these foundational constructs of classic family therapy theory, family art therapy is introduced to the reader. Included within this introduction is an historical overview of family art therapy and key interviews with notable family art therapy clinicians and authors. Additionally, the rationale for using art-based evaluations and assessments in addressing family dysfunction is also presented.

Chapter 3, "Object Relations and Attachment Theory: Creativity of Mother and Child in the Single Parent Family," is based on early mother and child intervention. This chapter gives a brief overview of object relation's theory/attachment theory and its application to the art therapy process. Additionally, this chapter formally introduces an exciting freestanding teen program that is based on pre-art, art, drama, and play therapy. This program addresses the mother/infant relationship within an object relation's theoretical construct.

Chapter 4, "Bowenian Family Therapy and Family Art Therapy," presents the core concepts and theoretical constructs of Murray Bowen (1972). Murray Bowen was the first family therapist to develop a complete theory concerning the therapeutic relevance of *the intergenerational projective process*. This concept describes the transmission of the family's emotional process through multiple generations. According to Bowen (1978), in every generation the child most involved in the family's emotional life moves towards a lower level of *differentiation of self*, while the least involved child moves towards a higher level. This led Bowen (1972) to develop a systematic approach to family therapy that emphasized *family of origin work*, which includes not only the nuclear family but also the family intergenerationally. Art therapy case vignettes highlight this technique as a vital and innovative tool in tapping into this key construct. Additionally, personal *self-work* for the art therapy trainee are presented in this chapter. The chapter highlights the importance of a family training model that integrates the technical components of the visual arts with family of origin exploration.

In Chapter 5, "Structural Family Art Therapy," the core concepts of Salvador Minuchin (1974) are presented. Minuchin's theory and contribution to the field of family therapy is notable. Minuchin's (1974) structural view focuses on how families are organized and what rules govern their transactions. His core concepts and therapeutic guidelines for diagnosis and treatment have often been regarded as one of the most influential and most widely practiced family systems in the history of family therapy. Art therapy interventions and case vignettes elucidate and complement Minuchin's (1974) core theory and techniques.

Chapter 6, "Experiential Family Therapy and Art Therapy," focuses on the work of Fred and Bunny Duhl (1981); Virginia Satir (1983); Satir and Baldwin (1983), and Carl Whitaker (1976). Experiential family therapy is influenced by existential, humanistic, and phenomenological theories. The central premise in this family therapy orientation is a commitment to: (a) self-actualization of the individual and family, (b) personal self-expression, and (c) congruency between feelings and behaviors. Emanating from this tradition is the inclusion of a host of innovative techniques and structured exercises to help the family expand their repertoire of emotional experiences. Within this tradition, family art therapy was born with the work of Hanna Kwiatkowska (1978) at the Institute for Mental Health in Washington, DC.

Chapter 7, "Adlerian Family Art Therapy," is based on the theory found in *individual psychology* as conceptualized by Alfred Adler and Rudolf Dreikurs (Dreikurs, 1986). Individual psychology is a theory that evolves to meet the challenge of understanding human behavior in the social field.

Chapter 8, "Filial Art Therapy: A Rogerian Approach," supports the work of humanistic traditions found in the work of Carl Rogers and relationship enhancement therapy (Ginsberg, 1989). Core concepts of both of these approaches are addressed. Additionally, *filial therapy* is presented as an innovative child-centered family therapy approach. Within a filial art therapy approach, the family is engaged in a psychoeducational process that focuses on learning principles and skills needed to provide child-centered, home-based art therapy sessions. This approach originated in the early 1960s to engage the parents as the primary agents of change. Second, this approach has benefited from historical effectiveness for dysfunctional families with young children (Ginsberg, 1989; Guerney & Guerney, 1985).

Chapter 9, "Narrative Art Therapy within a Multicultural Framework," explores the current postmodern theories within the field of family therapy that focus on cutting edge models within the expanding field of multicultural theory. Multicultural theory is often an acronym for expanding the definition of multiculturalism to include ageism, disabilities, religion, ethnicity, sexual orientation, socioeconomic status, indigenous populations, national origin, and gender. By presenting both social constructivism theory and the narrative revolution, this chapter displays how the creative arts therapies are integral to fully increasing the clinician's attention to the values behind our assumptions about families and their functioning, within the total spectrum of our worldviews. Clinical case vignettes that give a broad spectrum of cultural experiences within family work and the art therapy experience address this most important area.

Chapter 10 is the "Conclusion." We as authors wished to have a special space to more personally reach out to our audience to speak to our love of family work and especially family work and the art process. As authors, we wanted to keep this chapter as unrestricted as possible to give you as readers some of our wisdom and mentoring from the family work we have provided for our client families over many years. The art process is universal, the family is universal. There is a melodic and symphonic resonance in the understanding of both of these creative configurations.

REFERENCES

Anderson, T. (1991). *The reflecting team.* New York: Norton.

Bowen, M. C. (1972). Becoming a family therapist. In A. Ferber, M. Mendelson, & A. Napier (Eds.), *The book of family therapy.* New York: Science Hour.

Bowen, M. C. (1978). *Family Therapy in Clinical Practice.* New York: Jason Avonson.

Burns, R.C., & Kaufman, S. H. (1970). *Kinetic family drawings: An introduction to under-standing children through kinetic family drawings*. New York: Brunner/Mazel.

Dreikurs, S. (1986). *Cows can be purple: My life and art therapy*. Chicago: Alfred Adler Institute.

Duhl, B. S., & Duhl, F. J. (1981). Integrative family therapy. In A. S. Gurman & D. P. Knisknern (Eds.), *Handbook of family therapy*. (pp. 465–472). New York: Brunner/Mazel.

Framo, J. L. (1982). *Explorations in marital family therapy*. New York: Springer.

Framo, J. L. (1992). *Family of origin therapy: An intergenerational approach*. Philadelphia: Brunner/Mazel.

Ginsberg, B. (1989). Training parents as therapeutic agents with foster/adoptive children using the filial approach. In C. Schaefer & J. Briesmeister (Eds.), *Handbook of parent training: Parents as co-therapists for children's behavior problems* (pp. 442–478). New York: John Wiley & Sons.

Guerney, L., & Guerney, B. (1985). *The relationship enhancement family of family therapies*. In L. L'Abate & M. A. Milan (Eds.), *Handbook of social skills training and research* (pp. 226–241). New York: John Wiley.

Haley, J. (1976). *Problem-solving therapy*. San Francisco: Jossey Bass.

Kwiatkowska, H. Y. (1978). *Family therapy and evaluation through art*. Springfield, IL: Charles C. Thomas.

Landgarten, H. (1987). *Family art psychotherapy*. New York: Brunner/Mazel.

Linesch, D. (Ed.). (1993). *Art therapy with families in crisis: Overcoming resistance through non-verbal expression*. New York: Brunner/Mazel.

Malchiodi, C. A. (1998). *The art therapy sourcebook*. Los Angeles: Lowell House.

McGoldrick, M., & Gerson, R. (1985). *Genograms in family assessment*. New York: Norton.

Minuchin, S. (1974). *Families and family therapy*. Cambridge, MA: Harvard University Press.

Nichols, M. P., & Schwartz, R. C. (2004). *Family therapy: Concepts and methods* (6th ed.). New York: Gardner Press.

Oster, G. D., & Gould, P. (1987). *Using drawings in assessment and therapy: A guide for mental health professionals*. New York: Brunner/Mazel.

Riley, S. (1993). Illustrating the family system: Art therapy as a lens for viewing the family's reality. *The Arts in Psychotherapy, 20*, 253–264.

Rubin, J. A. (1984). *The art of art therapy*. New York: Brunner/Mazel.

Satir, V. (1971). The family as a treatment unit. In J. Haley (Ed.), *Changing families* (pp. 20–26). New York: Grune & Stratton.

Satir, V. (1983). *Conjoint family therapy* (3rd ed.). Palo Alto, CA: Science and Behavior Books.

Satir, V., & Baldwin, M. (1983). *Satir step by step*. Palo Alto, CA: Science and Behavior Books.

Wadeson, H. (1980). *Art psychotherapy*. New York: John Wiley & Sons.

Whitaker, C. (1976). The hindrance of theory in clinical work. In P. J. Guerin Jr. (Ed.), *Family therapy: Theory and practice* (pp. 104–105). New York: Gardner Press.

CHAPTER 1

Family Art Images in Historical and Social Perspectives

CHRISTINE KERR

INTRODUCTION

This chapter explores and thematically analyzes an archival collection of family art works. These selected art images are found across numerous artistic genres, from past and present societies and cultures. From the vantage point of art history, these works of art may offer interpretative evidence that *the family* in art history has been a substantive theme. Additionally, by exploring this archival collection, the family therapist and family art therapist may further understand that the family is an evolving social institution. This social schema has uniquely developed transhistorically and through many enculturations.

In the first portion of this chapter, the discussion focuses on the value of this archival collection to family art therapists and to other professionals who work within the family therapy field. In the second portion of this chapter, recommended methodologies for interpreting and analyzing historical family art are discussed in order to acquaint the reader with processing qualitative data to glean major themes, typologies, concepts, and propositions. In the later portion of this chapter, the reader is introduced to a brief overview of family life in selected time periods. A representative compilation of art is presented that corresponds to the *life of the family* over "historical time and space" (Leedy, P. & Ormond [2001], 7th Edition. Upper Saddle River: New Jersey: Merrill Prentice Hall). In the final pages of this chapter, the discussion focuses on a single family therapy session that employed family art history images from Western culture, to help a mother and her son work through grief issues after the national disaster of 9/11 in New York City.

WHAT IS THE VALUE OF FAMILY ART REPRESENTATIONS?

According to Fleck (1983), Glick, Clarkin, and Kessler (1987), Lovejoy (1991), and Murstein (1974), anthropological data suggests that the origins of humans may not lie in "the development of a material culture or as a result of bipedality but in the development of the family either as groupings, kinship patterns or nuclear family systems" (Glick et al., 1987, p. 25). Within the context of historical, social, and cultural perspectives of Western civilization, the term *family* appears to unite the Western world with earlier civilizations. Although the structure of the family has altered to conform to the social and cultural mores of the times, the prevalence for humans to seek out social relatedness and familial kinship patterns extends historically over time and among most cultures.

Social researchers such as Bronfenbrenner (1979) and Hareven (1978) have argued that the family is a longstanding institution. Hareven warned against generalizing the term, *family*, or to treat this topic as a discrete field of inquiry. Rather, from a sociological, anthropological, and historical perspective, the examination of the family should address a variegated network of both present and historical roots. Some of the family kinship patterns are clearly preserved in art history. Individual works of art note social and cultural shifts. What is of significance for the contemporary family art therapist is the possible clinical implications for our work with clients and their families. As family art therapists and family therapists, we may use these images not only to help our clients make affective associative reference to the art, but also to educate them. Anderson (1989) noted that, "art is the spirit container of the human life force ... and also the cultural container of societies over time" (p. 45). Thus, examining historical family images is relevant to our work as family art therapists because archival images elucidate those human values and associations applicable to the evolving theme of the family within Western culture. This archival collection clearly denotes that family systems have been influenced by a wide spectrum of evolutionary norms and socially constructed shared values and assumptions. Second, these images act as a chronology of the family through time, differentiation, social unrest, and states of familial closeness and distancing. Within the context of a current family therapy session, these visual images may be used to help our own client families to further associate their own family's emotional process.

WHAT ARE TRADITIONAL HISTORICAL METHODOLOGIES?

Huizinga (1968) argues, "an understanding of history is like a vision, or rather like an evocation of images past to present" (p. 296). History is a transcript of the restless and ever-flowing stream of events and the inexorable changes in human life and its institutions. History studies the language, customs, art, philosophy, and lives of those who command the attention of their contemporaries. Historical research looks at the current and countercurrents of past and present events and at human thoughts (Leedy & Ormond, 2001). Historical research attempts to examine the relationship of *past to present* in the hopes of discerning dynamic relationships. It is the task of the historian to not merely relate *what* events happened but to present a factually supported rationale to explain *why* the event happened.

According to Denzin and Lincoln (1994), traditional historical archival data generally relies on documentary sources, although researchers occasionally study artifacts in conjunction with documentary evidence. These two resources are called *primary data*. It bears mentioning that within academic circles there has been considerable debate concerning the use of visual imagery as primary data (Martinez, 1996). Martinez further comments on this academic tradition when he states, "In the world of academia, few historians consult images in their research, and when images appear in scholarly history publications in most cases the images play a secondary role to textual research material" (p. 97). This preference for textual documentation in traditional historical scholarship emanates from the belief that if textual material is properly analyzed, history becomes objective reality.

There is an additional impediment within traditional historical research qualifying the usage of visual images in historical and social analysis. Most traditional historians remain unfamiliar with a visual vocabulary that allows careful synthesis of the visual image to the interpretation of history. To adequately use a visual language requires not only the capacity to appropriately process the language of the arts, but also a clear understanding of the more subjective disciplines of psychology, sociology, and anthropology (Arnheim, 1969; Bryson, 1991; Haskell, 1993). As art therapists and family art therapists we are acutely aware of the accuracy of this statement and of the utility of the visual image, which offers a myriad of ways of not only processing information but also "helps us order our world and explain the past" (Martinez, 1996, p. 34).

HOW DO YOU PROCESS HISTORICAL VISUAL IMAGES?

There are numerous paradigm structures to process visual data. One epistemological and methodological posture is to look at visual data from the perspective of *historical time and space* (Clive, 1989; Edson, 1986; Floud, 1980; Leedy & Ormond, 2001). This form of research strategy and interpretation qualitatively analyzes *the historical time* the artwork was produced, or temporal *when* of an *event*, whereas *historical space* refers to the wider relationship and significance of *why* a single work of art relates to the larger social context in which it was produced.

Noting that a single piece of artwork can be complex, the structure and method of interpretation must be as rich and diversified as the data itself. Adams (1996) argues for a holistic perspective in processing visual archival data and for a combination of structural analysis, formalistic analysis, and a connoisseurial approach.

Structuralism

"Art is constituted by cultural signs, which, when decoded, identify the breadth of its role in society" (Adams, 1996, p. 149). Structuralism attempts to look at artwork as it intrinsically relates to kinship patterns and global social blueprints. Additionally, Adams (1996) argues that the structuralist approach to analyzing artwork emerged after 1950 in Europe, "when intellectuals became disillusioned with Marxism and existentialism" (p. 133). In this approach, the artistic style and or personal attributes of the individual artist are minimized. What is of importance in this type of analysis is the social interpretation and social context in which the image resides. Consequently, interpretative analysis looks at the work of art as part of a larger geopolitical and social construct.

Formalism

From a formalistic approach, the researcher looks at art by examining and analyzing the formal elements or *visual language* found in the artwork (Feldman, 1987; Gilbert & McCarter, 1988; Holly, 1984). These formal elements are line, shape, space, color, light, and dark. According to Fry (1956), this form of inquiry is often ahistorical and focuses more on the artistic composition or design of the art piece.

The artist's visual language refers to many artistic and design elements. The element of line may refer to the type and directionality of the marks made by the artist. Some lines begin as dots and can go off in any direction: straight, broken, thin, dark, or light. The element of shape is often referred to as contour. Shapes can be recognizable objects or people. Artistically, shapes may be rendered in a manner that is either lyrical or suggestive (Fry, 1956). The element of shape often provides the dimension of illusion in a piece of artwork. Through the artist's attention to scale, placement, and plane, the elements of line and space can provide depth and dimensionality to the artwork (Feldman, 1987).

Color usage often influences the affective overtones of the artwork. Color can be used to augment realism in a drawing or to create a surreal overtone. Often color creates a sense of energy or motion. When color is applied to a piece of canvas or paper, the artist may manipulate the color to create light or even transparency. By the use of color application, the artist manipulates the overall density of the artwork's composition by selecting the amount of applied pigment (Gilbert & McCarter, 1988).

As part of the element of design, the artist employs the formal aspects of balance, order, proportion, and rhythm (Adams, 1996; Feldman, 1987). Balance is often achieved by the arrangement of images in either a symmetrical or asymmetrical manner. The element of proportion is achieved through the repetition of *what is in the drawing*. Proportion is often influenced by the use of artistic patterning and rhythm (Gilbert & McCarter, 1988). Motion in the drawing is often said to give the artwork "kinetic life" (Adams, 1996).

Connoisseurial

The connoisseurial approach is embedded deeply in the cultural traditions of Western art history. In this approach the analysis of the art is based upon the art's intrinsic attributes, such as *genuineness* and *evocative* qualities. The philosophic traditions of aesthetics underlie this methodological approach. Western philosophers determined that a work of art could be studied and judged based upon its beauty or how it pleases the viewer (Arnheim, 1969). Noting this point, Adams (1996) argues that interpreting the evocative and aesthetic value of the art often takes into account the *time* and *place* in which the image was made, the prevailing cultural themes, and the style of the particular artist or artistic genres.

Additionally, the connoisseurial approach includes the study of iconographic and symbolic values that might be found in the art piece. Most artistic creations attempt to impart some message or theme to the viewer. "Works of art, symbols or emblems that represent a person, idea or concept are often used in order to assist observers in understanding ideas, meanings which the artist wishes to portray" (Berensen, 1962, p. 75). These values give artwork a poetic quality and are often embedded in the artwork (Adams, 1996; Berenson, 1962; Hirsch, 1976; Trossman, 1986).

When the artwork is analyzed in this manner, it is necessary to remember the artist's creative process as a series of steps, both conscious and unconscious. As the artist sets out to create an image, he or she is often influenced by personal experience and universal images and symbols found throughout history (Garber, 1968). As art therapists we are aware that most artistic creations attempt to impart some underlying message to the viewer.

THE COLLECTION OF HISTORICAL FAMILY IMAGES

White (1991) argues that a family is an intergenerational social grouping, organized and governed by social norms regarding descent, kinship patterns and affinity, reproduction, and nurturing and socialization of the young. From this definition, several implications follow that are relevant to this chapter. Specifically, this definition of the family views the nature of the *family* as intergenerational. This implication appears to indicate that the family within a group norm has a parent-child relationship. According to White (1991) "without the presence of such a relationship, the group is not a family" (p. 38). This assumption has a direct bearing on the selection of art pieces that have been chosen to be analyzed in this chapter. All of the family art works were selected based on the depiction of a family unit; specifically artwork that depicted at least one parent and at least one child.

THE ANCIENT EGYPTIAN FAMILY

The family in ancient Egypt was an ordered society. The establishment of a family and children was central to the daily life of ancient Egyptian culture. "The Egyptian loved his home above everything else. By comparison with neighboring peoples, his way of life and civilization was of a greater order" (Sameh, 1964, p. 8). The culture was deeply rooted in nationhood as well as spirituality. The Egyptians' sense of discipline, and commitment to the land and their religion might have been the outcome of frantic dynastic revolutions, religious conflicts, and foreign domination. Silverman (1997) states "the topography of the land imposed social order as a fundamental necessity, without which Egypt could not have survived" (p. 10).

The family structure in ancient Egypt was fixed. Functionally, the husband and wife had little possibility of role or task rearrangement. The wife was solely responsible for the nurturance and education of the children. According to Silverman (1997), "setting up house and taking a wife were synonymous" (p. 79). The head of the household was the husband and always male. Kinship patterns were patriarchal, where the oldest male son exercised hegemony over other married sons and sisters. Only personal property of the wife could be bestowed to either a son or daughter after the husband was deceased (Sameh, 1964; Silverman, 1997).

Religious beliefs permeated daily Egyptian life. The religious devotion to the divine husband and wife, Osiris and Isis, epitomized the ideal family. Social relatedness provided the family with emotional, financial, and daily requirements. In fact, the quality and strength of relatedness was directly linked to the family's capabilities in successfully entering the afterlife (Sameh, 1964; Silverman, 1997). According to the Egyptian's belief system, the right to eternal paradise had to be secured during mortal life. Maintaining an orderly and harmonious family life was a prerequisite for a successful transition into the afterlife. It is important to note that art in traditional tomb paintings often depicts the husband, wife, and children in close proximity to each other, often tenderly holding hands or demonstrating an emotional relatedness to the overall family activity (Stokstad, 1995).

A Structural Perspective: Tomb Painting, Egypt 20th Dynasty

Figure 1.1 shows a domestic scene that was painted in the tomb of Inherka during the 20th dynasty (approximately 1500 BC). From ethnographic accounts, this mortuary practice of depicting Egyptian daily life provides a rich visual depiction that underscores social memories, social bonds, social structures, and the use of material culture to symbolically elaborate the Egyptian religious values (Binford, 1972; Chesson, 1999). The structural analysis of family artwork chronicles the social hierarchy of this particular family grouping. According to Stokstad (1995), this type of wall painting was often commissioned to meet the demands of wealthy patrons. These tomb decorations

Figure 1.1   A father and his naked children with partly shaved heads and the sidelock of youth. Wallpainting. 20th Dynasty, c. 118. Tomb of Inherkha, Deir el-Medina, Tombs of the Nobles, Thebes, Egypt. E. Strouhal, Werner Forman/Art Resource, New York.

focused on the daily life of socially prominent families. Schematically, the composition of this painting depicts the family in a harmonious and orderly fashion. The parents are seated. This use of this manner of composition lends a rather formalistic quality to this portraiture. Its formalistic rendering may underscore the family unit's central role in daily life, as well as the importance of harmonious family relations to ensure entrance into the afterlife.

A Formalistic Perspective: Tomb Painting, Egypt 20th Dynasty

From a formalistic perspective, the parental figures are depicted in profile. This profile perspective is in the classic style of ancient Egyptian art. Human figures in Egyptian art were rendered according to the Egyptian Canon of Proportions (Spenser, 1982). This means each artist followed the same regulations in depicting figures, using a grid to ensure precision. Because Egyptian art held strong religious purpose, the Canon of Proportions was necessary to ensure that the art fulfilled its funerary function. Additionally, in order to retain its significance in the afterlife, representations of human figures needed to be drawn in this stylized manner (Carr, 1995; Hall, 1994; Stokstad, 1995). Additionally, both the central male and female figures are rendered according to "the Egyptian ideal" where the eyes are drawn with a frontal view in contrast to the profile perspective of the human figure (Hall, 1994). The stylization of this painting appears to denote order and proportion, which may herald the patrimonial kinship pattern of the husband and father. This assumption is further evidenced by the female figure being seated behind the male.

A Connoisseurial Perspective: Tomb Painting, Egypt 20th Dynasty

From a connoisseurial perspective, the intrinsic attributes and overall poetic quality of this painting may suggest a high kinetic value. The kinetic value suggests an active and engaged family life. The visual rhythm of this everyday family scene is played out between the numerous family members playfully interacting with each other. For example, the mother symbolically gestures towards her husband. Her left hand emerges to lie gently against his shoulder. These expressions of endearment have an implied inference of mutual affection and tenderness towards each other and their offspring.

The children depicted in this painting are smaller in stature than their father and mother. They appear to be moving in all directions. From a structural perspective this may suggest the parents' supportive role in providing guidance and discipline to their children. The orderliness and dignified posturing of the parents stand in sharp contrast to the children's activity in the painting. What may be gleaned from this dichotomy is the suggestion of the seriousness of the parents' roles in juxtaposition with the playfulness of the children. Also, the children's kinetic depiction suggests both their attachment to and their disengagement from their parents. The children are playfully involved with their parents but simultaneously engrossed in youthful exuberance. Though family roles pictorially appear circumscribed, the children maintain a kinetic value and appear protected by more affectively contained parental figures.

From an iconographic perspective, the inclusion of a winged bird being offered by the seated child to another sibling symbolically suggests an offering of eternal life. The Egyptian *Ba*, denoted by a bird, is often seen in tomb paintings. *Ba* is the personality of the deceased. It leaves the body after death and returns every night to the tomb of the deceased (Carr, 1995; Hall, 1994; Spenser, 1982). The reed platter is another important Egyptian symbol that denotes the family's wealth and abundance in life. As noted in the painting the father is lovingly touching the oldest son's shoulder. The son wears a beaded necklace symbolically suggesting the passing of the family's lineage to his son.

THE GRECO-ROMAN FAMILY

The Greek family in antiquity (approximately 500 BC) deemed the social status of woman decidedly inferior. The concept of an egalitarian marriage seems not to have existed in many ancient cultures. This inequity resulted in women being poorly educated, financially disenfranchised from property or political pursuits, and subservient in social activities outside the boundaries of child rearing and procreative functions (Murstein, 1974). Though marital relationships were monogamous, there was a public acceptance and male patronage of the prostitute class, know as the *hertraine*. These women were presumably well educated and well versed in civic affairs (Gardner, 1986). The Roman family in antiquity was also patriarchal, similar to the ancient Greek family. However, the ancient Romans developed the concept of *Patria Potesta* or complete control of the father over his children. Johnston (1969) states that the Romans "carried Patria Potesta to greater lengths" (p. 77). They believed that the father had absolute power over his children, he punished what he regarded as misconduct, and he alone could exchange property.

The Roman family in antiquity differed moderately from its Greek counterpart in their regulations pertaining to marriage. Within different social classes, both Greek and Roman marriages were highly segregated and proscribed. The ancient Romans held marriage in high esteem, with the betrothal or *sponsalia* often taking place at a very early age between a young boy and girl (Bradley, 1991). This emphasis on betrothal within social class underscored the Romans' religious belief in the worship of ancestors. Bradley (1991) states that one of real strengths in the sanctity of marriage and the family was the Romans' belief in ancestor worship. According to Gardner (1986), pious Romans believed that the soul existed apart from the body, not in an afterlife but at the place of burial. For the soul to be at peace, it was the responsibility of the family to bring offerings of devotion to the burial site (Gardner, 1986). Descendents from one generation to the next were responsible for continuing the devotion to ancestors. This religious practice directly influenced their nuclear family by placing emphasis on the importance of intergenerational lineage and role assignment of family members (Bradley, 1991; Johnston, 1969).

One of the central themes in ancient Roman families was harmony between the husband, wife, children, and household servants. This was called *Concordia*. The concept of *Concordia* endeavored to maintain equilibrium between the family's public and private lives. However, this concept is different from our modern expectancies of emotional relatedness. Often emotional ties among family members were distant and socially isolative (Johnston, 1969). Bradley (1991) states, "the opinion of familial relatedness is rather passive in its associations, implying a state of tranquil and stable unanimity but it actually had little romance or intimacy" (p. 7).

Children within the ancient Roman family were viewed as a continuation of the sacred lineage of the ancestors. Consequently, their legitimacy within a social class was fiercely preserved. Though the children in ancient Rome were undoubtedly loved and nurtured, "ancient attitudes towards children are singularly paradoxical … parents in classical antiquity undoubtedly loved their children … yet their treatment of them was often severe, even brutal" (Bradley, 1991, p. 140).

A Structural Perspective: Greco-Roman Stone Wall Relief

The stone wall relief from the Greco-Roman era, Figure 1.2, is of a family and six children. This relief was found in a Roman cemetery. As in the art selection from ancient Egypt, this stone wall relief suggests a relational pattern among family members. Similar to the previous tomb painting, this stone wall relief denotes degrees of merger, as well as aspects of differentiation among the parents and their offspring. Additionally, the definitive roles of family members appear clearly circumscribed. From a structural perspective, the emphasis in this relief is on hierarchical positioning. This may suggest the great care that Roman society placed on lineage and social differentiation within and outside the family. It is important to note that the father is predominant in this stone relief. This clearly can be associated with the highly patrimonial nature of the Roman family in antiquity (Johnston, 1969). Second, the social construct of *Concordia* is suggested by the heightened formality of this wall relief. The overall affective tone suggests a more reserved and segregated family life.

Figure 1.2   Greco-Roman stone wall relief.

A Formalistic Perspective: Greco-Roman Stone Wall Relief

In Figure 1.2, the family appears formalized and less naturalistic than the Egyptian tomb painting. The hierarchical position of the family grouping is strongly suggested by the formal aspects of composition and proportion. The depiction of the father appears much larger than the wife or his children. The family appears to be gazing entirely at the father. The children appear as if in procession, moving towards the father. Although the family grouping is rendered on the horizontal plane, the father remains the central focal point. The artist has made a clear suggestion that the relief is to be viewed from the perspective of the father, which references the strong patriarchal influence of *Patria Potesta* in this ancient society.

A Connoisseurial Perspective: Greco-Roman Stone Wall Relief

From a connoisseurial perspective, there are important symbolic inclusions in the stone wall relief. Both the father and mother hold scepters. This may suggest the solemnity in which lineage and tradition are handed down from one generation to another. Although the scepter has many symbolic values, the more generic interpretation is an emblem of royalty or divine authority (Hall, 1994). The inclusion of this symbol further supports the patriarchal nature of the Roman family, as the father holds the largest scepter and appears to be motioning to a figure to receive it. It may be suggested that the scepter indicates the preferred pattern of passing authority from the oldest male to the son. Last, the inclusion of a column appears in the forefront of this relief. The column is indicative of funerary columns, commonly used to intern the dead. The oldest male appears to be leaning on the column as he approaches his father. This is suggestive of the family religious orientation towards the belief that the oldest son continues the practice of ancestor worship.

THE RENAISSANCE FAMILY

The Renaissance (early fifteenth to mid-sixteenth centuries) denoted an epoch of economic growth in Western Europe, with a marked and radical break from the past medieval societal and religious constraints. During this period in Europe, the ideals of classical Greece and Rome were revisited. The philosophic traditions emphasized humanism and placed a renewed interest in the arts. The spirit of naturalistic inquiry tried to understand the natural world phenomenologically, giving detailed observations to both man's work and the environment he lived in.

The term Renaissance is taken from the French word literally meaning rebirth (Klapisch-Zuber, 1985). The political, economic, and philosophical traditions of this movement engendered considerable transformations in family customs and rituals. One of the most significant changes was the migration of families into urban cities. Second, there was an emphasis on classical education for both males and females. There was greater value given to women, a lasting result of the glorification of the "lady" from the Middle Ages (Murstein, 1974). Conversely, women still found themselves under the authority of their husbands in reference to commerce and inheritance rights.

There was also an increased interest in child rearing, with an emphasis on the child's individuality and cultural training. Klapisch-Zuber (1985) draws conclusions from Renaissance art and iconographic themes that the "advent of the modern family in its urban setting was clearly evident in the artistic and political temperament of this period" (p. 95).

The Christian heritage of the prior medieval culture was incorporated into the Renaissance's social and religious values. During the 13th century, the *Cult of Mary* was a religious and artistic phenomenon (Murry, 1973). This movement reflected a reinterpretation of the traditional role of mother and child. Klapisch-Zuber (1985) states that the most striking aspects of Tuscan art in the fourteenth and fifteenth centuries are the artistic interpretations of the traditional themes of mother and child and family life. Art thematically reflected the life of the saints and the Virgin but also emphasized the intimate and human qualities of daily family interaction (Murry, 1973).

A Structural Perspective: Rembrandt's *The Return of the Prodigal Son*

In Figure 1.3, Rembrandt's *The Return of the Prodigal Son*, the artist is depicting the religious allegory of the lost son returning home to his father's forgiveness. Rembrandt painted this piece during the baroque period. However, the humanistic qualities that clearly prevail throughout this piece can be related directly to the philosophical traditions that grew out of Renaissance naturalism. This is noted in the intimate connectiveness of each subject painted, as well as in the vitality of the execution of a religious theme, which strongly embraces our deepest family experiences.

From a historical perspective, the baroque style originated in Rome and is associated with the Catholic Counter Reformation lead by the Catholic Church against the Protestants. According to the Council of Trent (1545–1563) and the Catholic Church, late-Renaissance and baroque artworks were instructed to be as clear and intelligible as possible. Artists were encouraged to paint realistically, in order to stimulate piety among the populous. This is in part the reason that Renaissance artwork turned towards naturalism.

In Figure 1.3, there is a depth of expression in the piece. Here the relationship between the father and son poignantly draws the viewer into the depth of emotion experienced between them. The father and son demonstrably embrace each other by compassionately forming an intimate physical bond. This attention to emotionality and naturalism is indicative of the philosophical traditions embedded in Renaissance thinking.

Figure 1.3   Rembrandt van Rijn (1606–1669). *The Return of the Prodigal Son*, 1668–1669. Oil on canvas, 265 × 205 cm. Hermitage, St. Petersburg, Russia. Scala/Art Resource, New York.

A Formalistic Perspective: Rembrandt's
The Return of the Prodigal Son

From a formalistic perspective, Rembrandt adhered to the classicism of the Renaissance's emphasis on composition, unity, and harmony. Distinctively unique to both the Renaissance and the baroque period is the technique effecting spatial relationships. The end result is a powerful technical statement. Rembrandt's technical virtuosity is evidenced by his use of chiaroscuro. This Italian term literally combines words for light and dark. Additionally, when used effectively, the light and bright areas of the painting are contrasted with the dark and shaded areas. The illumination of the overall painting results in a translucent and transcendental visual experience (Bryson, 1991). The figures in both Renaissance and baroque art are merged through chiaroscuro, which blends the edges of each form. This creates a mystical union of all the figures/elements. Renaissance art treats each figure in isolation, and they appear as discrete objects. Color contrasts, outlines, contours, or hard edges contribute to this linearity. The figures in the art piece seem projected out into the viewer's space, so the viewer becomes actively involved in the energy of the scene.

A Connoisseurial Perspective: Rembrandt's
The Return of the Prodigal Son

This piece of artwork speaks to the emotions of forgiveness, human connectedness, and spirituality. Not only is the viewer drawn into a personal family moment of reconciliation between a father and son, but also, the three men in the foreground of the painting bear witness to the reunion. The evocative quality of genuineness is inherent in this work. Stokstad (1995) states, "emotionalism refers to the powerful and immediate emotional response that many baroque and Renaissance works were deliberately meant to evoke in the viewer including astonishment, horror, sorrow, piety and intense empathy" (p. 753).

THE ADVENT OF THE INDUSTRIAL AGE
AND THE MODERN FAMILY

As Western civilization moved into the modern era, there was a gradual erosion of the private life of the family. According to Lasch (1977), the family was previously a self-contained unit providing for the emotional, financial, and spiritual needs of each of its members. As early as the late nineteenth century and most definitely into the early twentieth century, many families moved from an agrarian existence to the cities and the factories.

To fully understand the times, it is important to note that this era consisted of an unprecedented belief in systems. An enthusiasm for big-scale planning and developing elaborate schemes to solve social and moral problems and create wealth spread into many fields of human endeavor. Boston, Pittsburgh, New York, Chicago, Cleveland, Baltimore, St. Louis, and San Francisco exploded in size because of industrial innovation. Mobile steam-powered equipment could now level hills and turn vast wetlands into tracts of buildable real estate. New, city-sized neighborhoods, uniform and orderly in layout (though not always sanitary or well built), could be constructed in months. Similar technology brought in millions of people from the country-side and overseas to live in these new towns and work in milling, mining, and mass production.

The literary arts felt the impact. American realism (as promulgated by William Dean Howells and Henry Tanner) was intentionally aimed at this new tide of middle-class readers, eager to read about life as they knew it: life in contemporary cities and small towns, and the aspirations and struggles of people like themselves in an era of mobility and social dislocation (Stokstad, 1995).

During the late-nineteenth-century migration to industrial areas, the family's adaptation to economic influences concomitantly influenced its social and interpersonal functioning (Gladding, 1997; Lasch, 1977). One of the most marked shifts in family life was a decrease in daily social exchange and interplay (Goldenberg & Goldenberg, 1997). The rise of industrialism created an atmosphere in which family members spent less time in the home. Industrialization often forced numerous family members to work long hours separated from home life. Often families needed to geographically relocate to find work. Established cultural and familial relationships were often disbanded due to the miles distancing relatives and neighbors. A second transformation was that the industrial-age family no longer was solely self-sustaining (Goldenberg & Goldenberg, 1997). The influence of social programs in the early twentieth century often attempted to bridge this deficit.

A noteworthy transition in the era was the change from educating offspring in the home to the advent of the public school system. Early in the twentieth century, children were expected to leave their homes on a daily basis to attend school. Schooling became less vocationally oriented. There was an emphasis on liberal arts instruction. Although the family still held the main responsibility for the support and socialization of the children, there was a gradual trend toward a shared responsibility with the educational system and auxiliary social institutions (Carter, McGoldrick, & Ferrano, 1989).

Another outcome of the industrial age was the changing status of women. Before the industrial age women were denied the opportunity to vote and hold public office, and were not always guaranteed a formal education. Women were often disparaged for working outside the home. Only by the end of World War II had a reversal taken place and a majority of women were gainfully employed outside the home. As women were afforded more political, legal, and social freedoms, the family social blueprint began to change. Gladding (1997) states that as a result of the heightened visibility of women after World War II, marriage shifted from a structural perspective to one that was process focused. In the structural perspective of the marriage the union was by encompassed rules and cultural norms that were proscribed and nonnegotiable. Glick et al. (1987) comment on traditional marriage that the focus of marriage was functional in that each partner was expected to fulfill role obligations. Marital failure was synonymous with role failure, which was easy to determine because there was good cultural agreement about what husbands and wives should do.

In the process-focused marriage, marriage was viewed from the emotional perceptions of the individuals interested in the partnership. Glick et al. (1987) have defined this type of marital union as "companionate marriage" (p. 34) The essential concepts in companionate marriage are the necessary prerequisites of "love" and "choice" (Glick et al., 1987, p. 34). The concept of choice within marriage is a relatively recent historical shift. Marital partners are expected to "be in love" and "be happy" (Gladding, 1997). If these expectancies were not achieved, the marriage was dissolved. Consequently, the actualization of romantic love was elevated from merely a social or economic concern, to a prerequisite for considering the marriage proposal or maintaining the union (Gladding, 1997; Glick et al., 1987; Goldenberg & Goldenberg, 1997).

A Structural Perspective: Tanner's *The Thankful Poor*

Henry Tanner's *The Thankful Poor* was painted in 1894. Tanner was born in Philadelphia in 1859. As a teenager, Tanner began by painting everyday scenes and in 1879 joined the Philadelphia Academy of Fine Arts. He then moved to Paris in 1891. Illness brought him back to the United States in 1893. At this time, Tanner's subject matter for his painting turned to genre subjects of his own race.

Tanner attempts to make both a political and social statement in this painting. Although the theme of the *reverent poor* was a popular one in European academic art of the period, in this piece Tanner has put it to new use (Stokstad, 1995, p. 1093). Tanner brought this theme to the United States to make a social statement about racism and prejudice (Mathews, 1969). In 1893 most American artists painted African American subjects either as grotesque caricatures or sentimental figures of rural poverty (Mathews, 1969). Well after the American Civil War, racial prejudice and intolerance for ethnic and cultural diversity was extensive.

It may be suggested that Tanner's objective in the presentation of this African American family was to elevate and emphasize the intrinsic emotional life of the African American family. It is important to note that many early studies of African American families by mainstream researchers up until the mid-twentieth century adopted a pejorative, deficit view that characterized African American families as disorganized, deprived, and disadvantaged (Stokstad, 1995). In the last 20 years, an African psychology movement has developed that views the psychological behavior of African American families by emphasizing "the spirituality, wellness, collective unity, extended family systems and strong kinship bonds" of this elemental part of American society (McGoldrick, Pearce, & Giordano, 1996, p. 67).

A Formalistic Perspective: Tanner's *The Thankful Poor*

In Figure 1.4, Tanner's work specifically depicts the African American family's emphasis on spirituality and kinship. What is notable from a formalistic perspective are the elements of simplicity and clarity in this composition. The composition emphasizes the two figures seated at a table. The loose brushstrokes combine realism and an illusionary quality simultaneously. The theme evolves from a perspective of either day or night; with the light and dark

Figure 1.4 Henry Ossawa Tanner, *The Thankful Poor.* 1894. Oil on canvas. Private Collection. Art Resource, New York.

philosophic mood working in tandem with the subtle hues of the painting. There is realism and poignancy to this painting. Tanner's use of light and gentle brushstrokes augments this realism as he treats this subject matter with reverence.

A Connoisseurial Perspective: Tanner's *The Thankful Poor*

From a connoisseurial perspective, the overall poetic quality thematically documents the spiritual nature of this family bond and counters "the stereotype of the African American in art" (Stokstad, 1995, p. 1092). The symbolic function of the praying hands and the empty bowl serve to elucidate the overall thematic tones of this social statement. According to Hall (1994), the inclusion of the hand position of clasping together or one hand grasping another signifies intense grief. Originally viewed as a mourning gesture, this pictorial gesture has appeared over the centuries as a sign of lamentation (Hall, 1994; Stokstad, 1995). The inclusion of an empty bowl may suggest a reference to economic and financial hardship of the African American family. Hall (1994) states that this symbolic reference is an "attribute of beggars" (p. 59).

A Structural Perspective: Henry Moore's *Family Group*

In the final selection, Henry Moore's *Family Group*, (1950), shown in Figure 1.5, the family is depicted in a three-dimensional sculpted form. In this gentle, abstract, and softly surrealistic sculpture, Moore has attempted to assert his modern vision of the American family. Capturing in an organic yet classical three-dimensional format, this post-World War II sculpture depicts a family grouping and almost "comforts the post World War II viewer, anxious about the human capacity to endure" (Stokstad, 1995, p. 1074). It is relevant to note that World War II had a profound effect on both the European and American artist. The post-war sculptors initially reacted to the destruction and death experienced during the war with harrowing images in crushed iron and other metal (Stokstad, 1995). Others, like Moore, considered themes of regeneration and survival.

Formalistic Perspective: Henry Moore's *Family Group*

As stated previously, this sculpture's organic yet classical lines predominate this selection. Moore has attempted to "reinvigorate the classical tradition with the strength and power of primitive art" (Benston & DiYanni, 1998, p. 1075). The overall gestalt of this sculpture depicts the family as both dif-

Figure 1.5 Henry Moore, *Family Group*. Bronze (cast 1950). A. Conger Goodyear Fund. The Museum of Modern Art, NY Digital Image. © The Museum of Modern Art/ Licensed by SCALA/Art Resource, New York.

ferentiated and undifferentiated. The hierarchical positioning neither favors a patriarchal nor matriarchal schematic. It may be argued that this is a result of the greater status of woman after World War II. This is a notable contrast to Egyptian and Greco-Roman family images. This piece maintains a unilateral expression of egalitarianism where all figures appear proportioned. There is a fluid and almost heroic quality to this piece.

A Connoisseurial Perspective: Henry Moore's *Family Group*

The parents raise their child as if in proud presentation to the viewer. The destruction and disillusionment of previous world wars stands in sharp counterpoint to the strength of this visual statement. The three-dimensional attributes of this sculpture may be viewed as a contextual abstraction of both the transformation of the human family in the twentieth century as well as a tribute to the human family's innate social bonding capabilities. Moore has captured the essence of the family from its remote origins to its potential future. The strength of this sculpture is reminiscent of early tomb reliefs; however, the egalitarian quality and the poetic nature of this piece addresses the family in the twentieth century.

FAMILY ART THERAPY SESSION

No brief case description can fully capture the journey that this widow and her teenage son embarked on after the tragedy of 9/11. After the fall of the twin towers on 9/11, this wife had lost a husband and this son had lost a father. The mother began her own therapy with grief counselors who were available after this catastrophic event. Her son was reluctant to commit to any type of therapeutic intervention. In the second year following 9/11, the son often became angry at home and disruptive at school. Though both mother and son had an extensive support network their relationship was in crisis. The complexities of their grief and the ways in which they interacted with each other produced moments of deep private sorrow and psychological withdrawal.

According to a study in the *Journal of Neuropsychiatry and Clinical Neuroscience,* Roxane Cohen Silver, a professor of psychology and social behavior at the University of California Irvine, polled more than 2,700 adults after the attacks and found that psychological stress, anger, and disruptive behaviors were common (Silver, 1989). However, those who denied the severity of the situation were much more likely to have continued psychological problems. Trauma survivors need to find a way to work through their experiences to achieve a sense of understanding how the trauma has affected them. In general, cognitive-behavioral therapies (CBT) are an effective treatment approach to help traumatized individuals understand and manage the anxiety and fear they are experiencing.

Cognitive-behavioral interventions have proven very effective in producing significant reductions in symptoms of posttraumatic stress disorder

(PTSD) (generally 60% to 80%) in several civilian populations (Davidson, 1996). Additionally research suggests that brief, specialized interventions may effectively prevent PTSD in some subgroups of trauma patients. These brief interventions may include (a) education, (b) various forms of relaxation therapy, (c) *in vivo* exposure (repeated confrontations with the actual traumatic stressor and with situations that evoke trauma-related fears), and (d) cognitive restructuring or techniques for replacing catastrophic, self-defeating thought patterns with more adaptive, self-reassuring statements (Catherall, 1992; Davidson, 1996; Figley, 1989; Friedman, 2000; Zampelli, 2000).

The mother and son began family art psychotherapy in conjunction with the mother's individual psychotherapy. Both the individual therapist and this author felt that helping this family replace negative thoughts and emotions with more adaptive and self-assuring experiences could be achieved by family art therapy. Barton and Alexander (1981) and Morris, Alexander, and Waldron (1988) point out "that members of unhappy families tend to attribute their problems to negative traits in other family members" (Nichols & Schwartz, 2004, p. 260). The goal in family art psychotherapy treatment was to tap into "core beliefs" of this family prior to the events of 9/11. Though grief counseling was always at the forefront, this mother and son needed to process how the tragedy of 9/11 had created enormous cognitive distortions and concomitantly, a negative behavioral change in their relationship.

Mary Cassatt: Mother and Child

At an early session in art psychotherapy treatment, this mother and son were invited to look through many pieces of historical art that thematically suggested "the family." Out of numerous historical works of art, this mother and son chose this Mary Cassatt piece (shown in Figure 1.6) as a catalyst for their own unique reproduction (see Figure 1.7). Their decision was not an easy one. Therapeutically, their reluctance may have stemmed from their own grief issues, as well as jointly held cognitions of what their family unit had been prior to 9/11 and how they were both adjusting in the present. This Mary Cassatt painting is of a mother and child lovingly embracing each other. Perhaps in choosing this painting, they intuitively knew that they would have to begin looking at their negative perceptions of each other as they processed their individual grief and loss.

In this session both the mother and son contributed to the charcoal drawing (Figure 1.7). The son offered suggestions about the positioning of the figures and the shading in the drawing. For the most part they worked in tandem and often in silence. Yet even in their silence, there was a clear indication of their coming to terms with who they were together as a family unit, still very much processing their grief.

The son shaded in the mother's face. It may be suggested that he was reluctant to fully embrace her at this *moment* or, perhaps, metaphorically "*see her.*" The mother was insistent in clearly outlining her son's face in the draw-

Figure 1.6   Mary Cassett, Mother and Child.

Figure 1.7   Mother and son family drawing, October 1, 2002.

ing. The lines drawn were carefully executed and precise. Both the mother and son wanted the picture to reside on a pillow; an available frame was chosen to encapsulate their drawing efforts. It may be suggested that the pillow symbolically represented a needed comfort zone they had achieved by engaging in their own rendition of a mother and child drawing. The gilded frame encapsulated their shared experience. Additionally, the frame may symbolically suggest a perceived need for permanence to mark their efforts. In colored pencil, the son carefully drew the American flag and placed the charcoal drawing on top. Both the mother and son were reluctant to formally title the picture. Throughout subsequent sessions, they both spoke about the drawing effort of this session as a beginning experience of reconciliation.

CONCLUSION

Art images have enormous possibilities in helping us order our world and explain the past. Drawings, paintings, and sculpture from the past to the present may chronologically provide an overview of Western culture's concept of the family over *"historical time and place."* For the family therapist and family art therapist it appears prudent to understand how the family has changed over generations, cultural shifts, and social adaptations. As artists, it is relevant that we take the time to examine these images to further understand their potential therapeutic utility as practicing family therapists.

REFERENCES

Adams, L. (1996). *The methodologies of art.* Boulder, CO: Westview Press.

Anderson, T. (1989). Interpreting works of art as social metaphors. *Visual Art Research,* 2, 42–51.

Arnheim, R. (1969). *Visual thinking.* Berkeley: University of California Press.

Benston, J. R., & DiYanni, R. (1998). *Art and culture: An introduction to the humanities.* Englewood Cliffs, NJ: Prentice Hall.

Berenson, B. (1962). *Rudiments of connoisseurship.* New York: Schocken.

Binford, L. (1972). Mortuary practices: The study and their potential. In L. Binford (Ed.), *Archaeological perspective* (pp. 208–243). New York: Seminar Press.

Bradley, K. (1991). *Discovering the Roman family: Studies in Roman social history.* London: Oxford University Press.

Bronfenbrenner, V. (1979). *The ecology of human development.* Cambridge: Harvard University Press.

Bryson, N. (Ed.). (1991). *Visual theory: Painting and interpretation.* London: Polity Press.

Carr, C. (1995). Mortuary practices: Their social, philosophical, religious, circumstantial and physical detriments. *Journal of Archaeological Method and Theory, 2,* 105–200.

Carter, B., McGoldrick, M. (2005). The Expanded family life cycle: Individual family & Social Perspective (3rd ed.), Upper Saddle River: NJ: Allyn & Bacon / Pearson Education.

Catherall, D. (1992). *Back from the brink: A family guide to overcoming stress*. New York: Bantam.

Chesson, M. S. (1999). Libraries of the dead: Early Bronze Age charnel houses and social identity at Urbani Bah edh Draj. *Jordan Journal of Anthropological Archaeology, 18*, 137–167.

Clive, J. (1989). *Not by fact alone: Essays on the writing and reading of history*. New York: Knopf de Certeau.

Davidson, J. R. T. (1996). *Davidson Trauma scale*. North Tonawanda, NY: Multi-Health Systems, Inc.

Denzin, N. K., and Lincoln, Y. S. (1994). *Handbook of qualitative research*. Thousand Oaks, CA: Sage.

Edson, C. H. (1986). Our past and present: Historical inquiry into education. *Journal of Thought, 21*, 13–27.

Feldman, E. (1987). *Varieties of visual experience*. Thousand Oaks, CA: Sage.

Fleck, S. (1983). A holistic approach to family typology and the axes of DSM III. *Archives of General Psychiatry, 40*, 901–906.

Floud, R. (1980). *Introduction to qualitative methods for historians*. New York: Routledge, Chapman and Hall.

Figley, C. R. (1989). *Helping traumatized families*. San Francisco: Jossey-Bass.

Friedman, M. (2000). *Post-traumatic stress disorders: The latest assessment and treatment strategies*. Kansas City, MO: Compact Clinicals.

Fry, T. (1956). *Vision and design*. New York: Harcourt Brace Jovanovich.

Garber, A. (1968). *Christian iconography: A study of its origins*. Princeton, NJ: Prince-ton University Press.

Gardner, J. F. (1986). *Women in Roman law and society*. London: British Museum Press

Gilbert, R., & McCarter, W. (1988). *Living with art*. New York: Knopf.

Gladding, S. (1997). *Family therapy: history, theory and practice* (3rd ed.). Englewood Cliffs, NJ: Prentice Hall.

Glick, I., Clarkin, J., & Kessler, D. (1987). *Marital and family therapy*. New York: Harcourt Brace Jovanovich.

Goldenberg H., & Goldenberg, I. (1997). *Family therapy: An overview*. New York: Knopf.

Hall, J. (1994). *Illustrated dictionary of symbols in Eastern and Western Art*. New York: HarperCollins.

Hareven, T. K. (1978). Cycles, courses and cohorts: Reflections on theoretical and methodological approaches to the study of family development. *Journal of Human Development, 3*, 362–384.

Haskell, J. H. (1993). *The path to the history in the Dutch civilizations in the 17th century and other essays*. New York: F. Onger.

Hirsch, E. D. (1976). *The aims of interpretation*. Chicago: University of Chicago Press.

Holly, M. (1984). *Panofsky and the foundations of art history*. Ithaca, NY: Cornell University Press.

Huizinga, J. H. (1968). *History in the seventeenth century*. New Haven, CT: Yale University Press.

Johnston, F. (1969). *The Roman family: Marriage and family*. Illinois: Itasca, F. E. Peacock.

Klapisch-Zuber, C. (1985). *Tuscan families*. New Haven, CT: Yale University Press.

Lasch, C. (1977). *Haven in a heartless world*. New York: Basic Books.

Leedy, P. D. & Ormond, J. E. (2001). *Practical research: Planning and design* (7th ed.). Englewood Cliffs, NJ: Merrill, Prentice Hall.

Martinez, K. (1996). Art and historical research. Chicago: Chicago University Press.

Mathews, M. (1969). *Henry Ossmond Tanner, American artist.* Chicago: University of Chicago Press.

McGoldrick, M., Pearce, J. K., & Giordano, J. (1996). *Ethnicity and family therapy.* New York: Guilford Press.

Murray, A. (1983). *Germanic kinship structures: Studies in law and society in antiquity and Early Middle Ages.* New York: Springer.

Murstein, B. (1974). *Love, sex and marriage through the ages.* New York: Springer.

Nichols, M. P., & Schwartz, R. C. (2004). *Family therapy: Concepts and methods* (6th ed.). Boston: Allyn & Bacon.

Panofsky, E. (1962). *Studies in iconography.* New York: Harper and Row.

Sameh, W. (1964). *Daily life in ancient Egypt.* New York: McGraw Hill.

Silver, R. C. (1989). The effects of post-traumatic stress on adults experiencing trauma. *Journal of Neuropsychiatry and Clinical Neuroscience, 1,* 305–307

Silverman, T. (1997). *Ancient Egypt.* New York: Barron's Educational Series.

Spenser. A. J. (1982). *Death in ancient Egypt.* Hamondsworth, England and New York: Penguin Books.

Stokstad, M. (1995). *Art history.* Englewood Cliffs, NJ: Prentice Hall.

Trossman, H. (1986). Towards a psychoanalytical iconography. *Psychoanalytical Quarterly, 55*(1), 2.

White, J. (1991). *Dynamics of family development: A theoretical perspective.* New York: Guilford Press.

Zampelli, S. O. (2000). *From sabotage to success: Ways to overcome self-defeating behavior and reach your true potential.* Oakland, CA: New Harbinger Publications.

CHAPTER 2

The Development of Family Therapy and Family Art Therapy

JANICE HOSHINO*

INTRODUCTION

Family therapy and art therapy encompass a number of interesting parallels. Both professions emerged through the work of passionate, committed professionals who simultaneously but independently began to explore uncharted territories; networking provided the segue for these ideas to coalesce and be gradually introduced into mainstream psychotherapy. My professor James Framo used to recall how (budding family) therapists began to secretly seek each other out at psychological conferences to dialogue around their work with families—seeing an entire family in therapy was a radical departure from the prominent psychodynamic framework, and therefore was not acceptable in the earlier era of psychotherapy (personal communication, February 8, 1994). Although the process of development in family and art therapies was comparable, family therapy gained momentum and blossomed quickly. Art therapist Kwiatkowska (1978) noted that "art therapy is older than family therapy but has developed more slowly" (p. xii). However, from a systemic viewpoint, one could consider the development of both art and family therapy as serendipitous, as their roots were planted in a parallel manner.

This chapter is divided into three sections. First, the development of systems theory and family therapy provides the reader with the historical foundation of the profession of family therapy. Next, family art therapy is introduced

* I would like to express my deepest appreciation to Chua Seow Ling for her collaboration, assistance in research, humor, and energy with this chapter.

through the introduction of its pioneers and specific art therapy assessments they developed in research and clinical practice. Last, directives I have used both pedagogically and clinically are presented with art examples.

SYSTEMS THINKING AS A BUILDING BLOCK

For the first few decades of the early twentieth century, psychoanalysis was the stronghold of therapy. Following in the footsteps of Freud, therapists before the 1950s firmly believed that it was counterproductive and even dangerous to become involved with more than one member of the same family (Broderick & Schrader, 1991). However, the end of World War II ushered in changes in the society that presented new challenges, including family stress associated with hasty wartime marriages, baby boom pressures, and changing male-female roles as a result of new job and educational opportunities. This prompted clinicians and researchers to look beyond intrapsychic process and the individual to uncover the roots of psychological problems; this set the stage for the birth of family therapy.

Family therapy was, however, not a direct growth from mainstream psychology, but rather traces its roots to cybernetics and general systems theory. Norbert Wiener, a mathematician at the Massachusetts Institute of Technology was given the initiative to improve the technology of war in the early 1940s, began studying machines, comparing them with living organisms to understand and control complex systems (Becvar & Becvar, 2003). The result of the research undertaken by Wiener and his colleagues was the founding of *cybernetics*, the study of feedback mechanisms in self-regulating systems (David, 2004; Nichols & Schwartz, 2006). *Feedback* refers to the process in which the behavior of a system can be corrected and guided by information about its own performance. It contains information about the systems performance relative to its environment as well as the relationship among the system's parts. Feedback either prompts the system to restore the original state, known as *homeostasis*, or confirms and reinforces the performance of the system. In a home heating system, for example, feedback from the thermostat sets the furnace into action when the room temperature falls below a certain point, and signals the furnace to continue generating heat until the room has reached the desired temperature (Nichols & Schwartz, 2006).

Equally concerned with feedback loops and mechanisms are proponents of *general systems theory*. Though it has a lot in common with cybernetics conceptually, general systems theory was, in fact, proposed in the late 1920s by biologist Ludwig von Bertalanffy, who saw that any system, whether it be "physical like a television set, biological like a cocker spaniel, psychological like a personality, sociological like a labor union, or symbolic like a set of laws" (Davidson, cited in Nichols & Schwartz, 2006, p. 92), comprises smaller systems and at the same time is part of a larger system. A system is always more than the sum of its parts; the properties of the entire system arise not just from the characteristics of its constituent parts, but also from the interactions and relationships among the parts.

From general systems theory and cybernetics, the *systemic approach* or systems thinking has emerged as an overall concept, focusing on the relationship between elements rather than the attributes of the elements, as psychoanalysis has traditionally done. Though the terms are often used interchangeably, "cybernetics" is less commonly used in the United States than it is in Europe; rather, in the United States it was "systems theory," with which the family therapy movement became identified (Becvar & Becvar, 2003).

The systemic perspective profoundly impacted on the conceptualization of human problems and understanding of behavior. All human beings exist within systems such as family, community, culture, and society. Because elements (including subsystems) within a system are intricately linked to one another, one's action influences and is, in turn, influenced by the action of the other. Causality became a reciprocal concept instead of retaining its unidirectional, linear characteristic as scientists had previously conceived it. Because each element's action has an impact on other elements and on the system itself, "any complex person or agency that influences a complex interactive system thereby becomes a part of that system, and no part can ever control the whole" (Bateson, cited in Becvar & Becvar, 2003, p. 66).

Just as a system is an organized assemblage of parts forming a complex whole that is always greater than the sum of its parts, a family is more than a collection of individuals; it is a network of relationships. Similar to how feedback controls information-processing systems in cybernetics, families regulate interactions among its members and their behavior to ensure its stability, with some families becoming stuck in repetitive loops of unproductive behavior in the process (Nichols & Schwartz, 2006). Systems thinking therefore prompts clinicians to conceptualize human behavior within the social context, focusing not on the individual, but on the relationships the person has with the environment. Family therapy, which evolved from systems thinking, deviates from individual therapy by shifting its emphasis from the "why" to the "what" of human behavior, and from the past to the here-and-now. It should be mentioned that the past is not disregarded; indeed, family therapists often explore family of origin issues to understand the interplay of current dynamics and dysfunction. Nevertheless, family therapists are more concerned with what is presently happening within the family system than with why a problem developed or whether it has its roots in childhood (as psychoanalysts believe). The goal of family therapy is to understand the context, identify the patterns within the context that is sustaining the problem, and finally change the context so as to alleviate or eliminate the problem. The patterns that maintain the problem often include the family's attempted solutions and the family's communication about the problem (Becvar & Becvar, 2003).

Whereas individual therapy assumes that family influences are internalized and that intrapsychic dynamics are the dominant forces controlling a person's behavior, family therapy breaks away from the reductionistic and linear thinking to take on a holistic view by looking to the family context for answers, embracing the concepts of circular causality as determinants of behavior and reciprocity as the governing principle of relationships. This represents a *paradigm shift* that marks a conceptual leap from the personality characteristics to interpersonal transaction to the family as a basis for understanding individual functioning. The essence of family therapy is its view that "change calls for altering the process, not discovering the original culprit" (Goldenberg & Goldenberg, 2004, p. 16).

EARLY MODES OF WORKING WITH FAMILIES

Family therapy began "in a dozen places at once among independent-minded therapists and researchers in many parts of the country" (Broderick & Schrader, 1991, p. 21). Indeed, as one looks back on its history, one is astounded by the number of pioneers who inadvertently sowed the seeds for, stumbled onto, or otherwise discovered the field of family therapy.

Nathan Ackerman—Menninger Institute, Topeka

Though the field of psychotherapy hails Freud as its founding father, family therapy may debate who should rightfully claim that honor. Nevertheless, many consider Nathan Ackerman as family therapy's true founder, given his writings on family dynamics in the 1930s and clinical assessments of families in the late 1940s (Green & Framo, 1981). Throughout his career, he remained true to his psychoanalytic roots and focused on intrapsychic conflict as well as families' psychological impact on individuals. A chief psychiatrist at the Child Guidance Clinic at Menninger Institute, Topeka, in 1937, Ackerman believed that the outgrowth of family research in the area of schizophrenia in the 1950s and 1960s obscured family therapy's true origins "in the study of nonpsychotic disorders in children as related to the family environment" (Ackerman, cited in Becvar & Becvar, 2003, p. 22).

Ackerman noted the concept of circular causality in systems thinking, whereby intrapsychic conflict (such as that between feelings and desires) led to interpersonal conflict in the family and vice versa. To reverse symptomatic disturbances in the individual, the therapist aims to bring conflicts into the open through family interaction (Nichols & Schwartz, 2006). Ackerman's therapeutic approach involved a deep connection with the family where issues were deeply explored; these included the conflicts and fantasies buried in the individual's unconscious. The therapist functions as a dynamic catalyst who uses an open and provocative communication style, and is forthright and brutally honest in giving observations and interpretations.

Ackerman's free exchange of ideas with others included his organization of the first session on family diagnosis in 1955, where he, Don Jackson, Lyman Wynne, and Murray Bowen learned about each other's work and joined in a sense of common purpose (Nichols & Schwartz, 2006). He also cofounded *Family Process* with Jackson in 1962, establishing the first journal in the area of family therapy.

John Bell—Massachusetts

Perhaps the most underrated pioneer of family therapy, John Bell was, like Ackerman, one of the first to treat families. A psychologist at Clark University in Worcester, Massachusetts, Bell stumbled into family therapy by what some would call a "happy accident": He mistakenly believed that John Bowlby was treating families in his work with children and decided to experiment with this new method himself in 1951. Adopting the group therapy approach, Bell's primary role in family sessions was as a facilitator promoting an open discussion. Despite his early start, Bell did not publish his ideas until 1961. Also, unlike other founders of family therapy, he neither established an important clinical center nor produced well-known students (Nichols & Schwartz, 2006).

ERECTING THE THEORETICAL PILLARS: PIONEERS WHO STARTED WITH STUDIES IN SCHIZOPHRENIA

Though therapists such as Ackerman and Bell had begun to see families in their treatment of children by the 1950s, the true theoretical roots of the family movement was developed through studies in schizophrenia. Among the many who looked into family systems for a better understanding of the manifestation of the mental disorder was anthropologist and ethnologist Gregory Bateson. From him and his colleagues in Palo Alto, California, many theories and concepts were developed that provided the intellectual foundation of family therapy.

Gregory Bateson, Don Jackson, Jay Haley—Palo Alto

The Palo Alto group were trailblazers that examined *process* rather than *content* in understanding human behavior and mental illness (Guttman, 1991). Its founder, Bateson, a scientist in the classic mold, studied diverse subjects such as animal behavior, learning theory, ecology, and hospital psychiatry (Nichols & Schwartz, 2006). He recognized how the principles of cybernetics, with its emphasis on self-correcting feedback mechanisms and the interrelationships among the parts of a system, can be applicable to the human communication process. Adopting the holistic view of systems in cybernetics, Bateson worked on translating the practice of psychiatry into a theory of human communication (Becvar & Becvar, 2003). This theory purports that every message contains a *report* function which refers to the content of the statement and a *command* function which carries information about the relationship between the speaker and the recipient. For example, the statement "Go to bed" carries with it an overt message of the speaker's wishes as well as a covert message that conveys the speaker's authority. The implied command message is also referred to as *metacommunication*.

In 1952, Bateson received a grant to study the phenomenon of paradoxes in human communication, which led to the establishment of the seminal Palo Alto project. Bateson gathered an eclectic group of researchers, some of whom became significant figures in family therapy. They included Jay Haley, a communication specialist, and John Weakland, a chemical engineer and cultural anthropologist. In its first two years the Palo Alto group studied subjects of diverse interest, from otters at play to the social and psychological significance of popular movies (Nichols & Schwartz, 2006), all of which paid particular attention to the conflicts between different levels of communication.

Double-Bind Theory   In 1954, the group embarked on the study of schizo-phrenic communication (Becvar & Becvar, 2003). Joined by psychiatrist Don Jackson, the team focused on developing a communication model that might explain the origin and nature of schizophrenic behavior, particularly in the context of families. They examined pathological communication patterns within a family in relation to the development and maintenance of schizo-phrenic behavior in a family member. This effort culminated in the develop-ment of the landmark *double-bind theory* in 1956; Bateson and his colleagues defined this as a situation whereby a person is confronted with two contradic-tory messages on different levels from someone with whom this person has an intense relationship. The person, however, is unable to detect or comment on the inconsistency and thus finds it difficult to respond appropriately to, and impossible to escape from, the situation. An example cited by the team is the case of a mother who tells her child, "Go to bed, you're very tired and I want you to get your sleep." What lies beneath the overtly loving message can be the statement, "Get out of my sight because I'm sick of you." If the child responds to metacommunication and withdraws from the mother, she would inter-pret the withdrawal as a criticism that she is not a good mother and would either rebuke the child or bring herself closer to the child to prove him or her wrong. However, if the child denies the covert message and instead responds to the mother's loving overt statement by moving closer to her, the mother would be compelled to withdraw by her fear and helplessness. The child thus feels immobilized and confused, yet unable to escape from the situation. In other words, the child feels doomed to failure regardless of the response; he or she is said to be in a double-bind (Bateson, Jackson, Haley, & Weak-land, 1956; Goldenberg & Goldenberg, 2004). Bateson and his colleagues felt that the child would eventually learn to escape hurt and punishment by responding with equally incongruent messages, thereby losing the ability to understand the true meaning of communication, hence the manifestation of schizophrenic behavior. Currently, the double-bind theory of schizophrenia is largely disregarded as viable, due to biological influences. Nevertheless, this theory was monumental in ascribing to the mental disorder a process-oriented transactional dimension that points to the function of schizophrenia within human relationships, particularly in the family context.

Family Homeostasis   Besides the double-bind hypothesis, other important theories and concepts emerged from the Palo Alto group that served as building blocks of family therapy. Of noted importance are the contributions of Don Jackson, who joined the team when it started on its research into schizophrenia. Jackson rejected his psychoanalytic roots and instead focused his energy on interpersonal dynamics. Borrowing ideas from biology and systems theory, he developed descriptive constructs in understanding the family communication process. At the core of these constructs is *family homeostasis*, which is the state of stability and balance that families seek to maintain or, in times of stress, restore (Goldenberg & Goldenberg, 2004). Jackson felt that families, as units, tend to resist change. This view became a metaphorical mantra for family therapists during the inception of the field's development. It has since been suggested that an emphasis on family homeostasis underestimates the system's flexibility (Nichols & Schwartz, 2006). However, this concept explains what keeps families stuck in a problem and how an individual's symptoms preserve stability in families, for example, by bringing together parents in marital conflict and uniting them with the common goal of dealing with the symptoms.

Symmetrical and Complementary Relationships   Jackson defined two types of communication patterns within the family. In a *symmetrical* relationship, the behavior of one person mirrors that of the other, such as when two persons boast to each other, each intent on outdoing the other. This is, in essence, a one-upmanship dialogue. Consider, as an example, a married couple who strive to put each other down in front of their children ("Your father never cares for anyone but himself!" Or, "Your mother is always nagging, isn't she?") Each tries to win their children over by undermining the other's authority in the family. A symmetrical relationship can also be found between two individuals who continually try to please each other. A *complementary* relationship, on the other hand, is characterized by differences that allow the participants to fit together, such as when one person is assertive and the other submissive (Nichols & Schwartz, 2006). The wife may try to get closer to the husband by continually asking him to spend more time with her (thus playing a *pursuer* role), while the husband may perpetually shut himself out from her by spending more time outside the home (a *distancer* role).

Marital Quid Pro Quo   In his study of interactions among members within a family, Jackson observed that such exchanges follow certain patterns or rules. The marital dyad, in particular, carries a set of well-formulated rules in which each partner gives and receives something in return. Jackson coined this phenomenon *marital quid pro quo* (Goldenberg & Goldenberg, 2004). This "something for something" pattern may be obvious, such as when the husband takes out the garbage while the wife does the laundry, or much more subtle, as when a depressed person's maintenance of the symptom allows his or her partner to maintain a victim's role of having to be the caregiver.

Jackson's work produced significant concepts that became important theoretical underpinnings in family therapy. His view that human interactive sequences are driven by rules instead of personality traits or individual needs and drives was a profound departure from the psychoanalytic school of thought. In 1959, he founded the Mental Research Institute (MRI) in Palo Alto, which also became an intellectual powerhouse in family therapy. At MRI, Jackson expanded his research from schizophrenia to include delinquency, psychosomatic disorders, marital conflict, and other family issues. There, Jackson cofounded with Nathan Ackerman the first journal in family therapy, *Family Process*, in 1962; it continues to be an influential publication in the field.

Therapeutic Paradox in Strategic Family Therapy   The seeds of the communication model that were first sowed in Bateson's Palo Alto group in the 1950s grew to bear other fruits at MRI in the 1960s. Notably, Bateson's group was research oriented, whereas MRI's conviction was on clinical treatment of families. *Strategic therapy* emerged from the communication model and was developed by Jay Haley. Haley examined the double-bind theory and noted that "implicit in every interpersonal transaction is a struggle for control of the definition of the relationship" (Goldenberg & Goldenberg, 2004, p. 254). He felt that symptoms allowed the symptom bearer to deny any sense of control over those symptoms, yet could exert control over persons involved in a relationship with the symptom bearer. In other words, because symptoms are beyond one's control, the nonsymptomatic person maintains a relatively powerless position as he or she cannot institute change (Becvar & Becvar, 2003). This theoretical underpinning contributed the impetus for Haley's development of a *strategic family therapy*, although Haley's theory stemmed from Milton Erikson's strategic therapy (Haley, 1973).

Strategic therapy includes the use of directives and therapeutic paradox; change is induced through explicit or implicit *directives*, or tasks aimed at extinguishing ineffective interactional sequences (Goldenberg & Goldenberg, 2004). As Madanes (1981) notes, "the therapist's task is to design an intervention in the client's social situation" (p. 19). Directives that encourage clients to exaggerate a symptom may seem absurd and even countertherapeutic, but may, however, result in a *therapeutic paradox*: the client either performs the tasks and thus admits that the symptoms are not voluntary, or refuses to yield to the therapist's power and gives up the symptom (Nichols & Schwartz, 2006).

Two prominent family therapists who also had their early beginnings at MRI were Cloe Madanes and Virginia Satir. Like Haley, Madanes is noted for the development of strategic therapy, as well as her work with Salvador Minuchin in developing structural family therapy at the Philadelphia Child Guidance Clinic in the 1970s. In 1976, she and Haley left Philadelphia and founded the Family Therapy Institute in Washington, DC. Satir, on the other hand, is known for her experiential and humanistic approach to family therapy. Her focus on the emotional level of people added "a dimension of feeling that helped counterbalance what was otherwise a relatively cool and cerebral approach" (Nichols & Schwartz, 2006, p. 30). More on Satir is covered in Chapter 6.

Theodore Lidz—Yale

Other family therapy pioneers emerged from their interest in studying schizophrenia and family systems. One of them, Theodore Lidz, noted as early as the 1940s that patients with schizophrenia tended to come from families that were characterized by instability and strife (Broderick & Schrader, 1991). His research at Yale in 1951 involved a long-term comparative study of families of schizophrenic and nonschizophrenic persons, focusing on rigid family roles and faulty parental models of identification in the former group (Nichols & Schwartz, 2006). He refuted the prevalent view of maternal rejection by introducing the notion that fathers could play a destructive role in the development of schizophrenia. Specifically, Lidz theorized five patterns of pathological fathering: rigid and domineering, hostile, paranoid, aloof and distant, and passive and submissive.

Additionally, Lidz pointed out two patterns of chronic marital discord that distinguishes families of schizophrenic persons from the rest. One is *marital schism*, marked by open hostility between the parents as each vies for their children's affection and constantly undercuts the other's worth. Often in such families, the father is ostracized and becomes aloof and distant (Goldenberg & Goldenberg, 2004). The other pattern is *marital skew*, whereby one parent is overly dependent while the other is a dominant, even overbearing, personality. Both marital schism and marital skew highlight the lack of reciprocity in marital roles that underlies families of schizophrenic persons. Pathology is viewed from a relational focus and extends beyond the symptom bearer; therefore, family dysfunction is viewed as a matrix from which pathology may develop (Nichols & Schwartz, 2006).

Lyman Wynne—National Institute of Mental Health

Like Lidz and the Palo Alto group, Lyman Wynne conceived schizophrenia as a symptom within the family context, emphasizing communication and relationship patterns. Wynne felt that fragmented and ambiguous family communication influences how the schizophrenic person interprets events in confused, distorted ways, and increases social and interpersonal vulnerability (Goldenberg & Goldenberg, 2004).

Wynne, struck by the strangely unreal qualities of positive and negative emotions in the disturbed families, introduced the concepts of *pseudomutuality* and *pseudohostility*. *Pseudomutuality* is a façade of togetherness that masks conflict and blocks real intimacy between members of a family. It describes a family's "predominant absorption in fitting together at the expense of the differentiation of identities of the persons in the relation" (Wynne, Ryckoff, Day, & Hirsch, 1958, p. 207). Wynne suggests that, in families whose communication and individual perceptions are perpetually blurred by enmeshment, a person flooded with anxiety may act out in confusing and disruptive ways to achieve recognition of individual identity. However, the family may attempt to restore its homeostatic state of pseudomutual relations by labeling the person schizophrenic and excluding him or her from the family physically or psychologically. A mechanism by which families maintain pseudomutuality is the use of the *rubber fence*, which refers to the shifting boundaries around the family system. This maintains family togetherness and safety from the threatening environmental forces; however, the shifting family rules allow acceptable information flow as well as shut out undesirable influences.

Wynne later also introduced the concept of *pseudohostility* to describe families marked by a superficial split and constant bickering. The superficial alienation or conflict in these families masks its members' need for intimacy and affection as well as a deeper level of hostility among them. As in families with pseudomutuality, schizophrenia was seen to develop in pseudohostile families against a backdrop of distorted communication and impaired perception that prohibits rational thinking about the true nature of relationships (Becvar & Becvar, 2003).

Wynne is notably the only family researcher who continued his work with schizophrenic persons throughout his career. By 1978 he had studied over 600 families and formulated and offered strong supporting evidence for a theory of communication deviance that denoted the relationship between severe psychopathology and disorganized patterns of communication in the family (Becvar & Becvar, 2003; Nichols & Schwartz, 2006).

Ivan Boszormenyi-Nagy—Philadelphia

Ivan Boszormenyi-Nagy developed *contextual family therapy* that focused on ethical dimensions in his studies of families. A migrant from Hungary, he founded the Eastern Pennsylvania Psychiatric Institute (EPPI) in Philadelphia in 1957 as a research center for studying schizophrenia. After repeated failures to conclude a biochemical basis of the illness, Boszormenyi-Nagy focused on behavioral and psychological aspects; this eventually converted his interest in transgenerational issues within the family (Goldenberg & Goldenberg, 2004).

Boszormenyi-Nagy assessed that families are not independent entities free from their historical baggage. Every family carries with it a *family legacy*, or expectations handed down from past generations on the roles and behavior of its members. For example, the sons in one family may be expected to attend college like all the men in previous generations. With the legacy comes *entitlement*, when a son is given all the opportunities the family can afford to ensure academic success. The son is then ethically bound to fulfill his obligation and shape his life to accommodate his legacy. This also creates a "debt" towards his family. A *family ledger* defines the psychological make-up of every family that is essentially a multigenerational accounting system of who receives what from whom and who owes what to whom figuratively. According to Boszormenyi-Nagy, a parent who imparts his or her values to the child becomes the "creditor" in a dialogue of commitments, whereas the child becomes the "debtor." The debtor will "eventually have to settle his debt in the intergenerational feedback system by internalizing the expected commitments, by living up to the expectations, and eventually by transmitting them to his offspring" (Boszormenyi-Nagy & Spark, 1973, p. 47).

Thus, a person who has been beaten by his or her parents may end up beating his or her own children, an act which both lives a family legacy (of harsh disciplinarian ways) and a repayment of debt to the parents. From this perspective, the ledger may have been balanced when this debt is paid; however, the patterns are often perpetuated.

In examining cross-generational relationships, Boszormenyi-Nagy coined the term *parentification* to describe the process by which children are compelled to perform the role of a parent at the expense of their own developmental needs (Boszormenyi-Nagy & Spark, 1973). The oldest child in a single-parent family, for example, may be tasked with child-rearing responsibilities towards the younger siblings while the parent is at work; instead of engaging in age-appropriate activities such as play, he or she is "forced to grow up." At times, a breakdown in the marital relationship may drive one parent to look to one of the children as a substitute for the estranged or missing marital partner; the child becomes a confidante of the parent, serving to fulfill the parent's need for companionship and security, neglecting his or her own needs as a child.

At the heart of contextual therapy is *relational ethics*, which focuses on how members of a family strive to achieve balance and fairness so that their individual welfare is met. Between marital partners, for example, a balance between rights and responsibilities, merits and obligations is crucial for the survival of the relationship. Additionally, each partner needs to openly and honestly negotiate differences, especially when there are conflicting needs. However, such *reciprocity* or trustworthy give-and-take may not be present in all family relationships. The goal of contextual family therapy, then, is to rebalance the give-and-take and emotional ledgers of all family members and facilitate the development of a sense of fairness, trust, and accountability in their interactions with one another (Boszormenyi-Nagy & Spark, 1973).

BEYOND RESEARCH AND SCHIZOPHRENIA:
OTHER NOTABLE FIGURES

No discussion of the development of family therapy is ever complete without mentioning the names of Murray Bowen, Carl Whitaker, and Salvador Minuchin. Bowen, yet another psychiatrist specializing in schizophrenia, is celebrated for such influential ideas as differentiation of the self, the multigenerational transmission process, and emotional triangles. In contrast to Bowen's cerebral approach, Whitaker's witty, spontaneous, and no-holds-barred technique distinguishes him as an irreverent and creative therapist. Minuchin developed a comprehensive *structural model*, creating an unrestrained, provocative style in therapy sessions reminiscent of his teacher, Ackerman. The contributions and theories of these shapers of the family movement, along with those of Virginia Satir, will be covered in greater detail in subsequent chapters.

In addition to Whitaker, other experiential therapists worthy of mention are David Kantor, Fred Duhl, and Bunny Duhl, who cofounded the Boston Family Institute in 1969 and developed several expressive techniques. One such technique is *family sculpting*, in which one family member physically positions other members in a manner that symbolizes his or her perception of the power differentials as well as the degrees of intimacy among these members (Goldenberg & Goldenberg, 2004).

Like Bowen and Boszormenyi-Nagy, James Framo was influential in his ideas of transgenerational dynamics. Building on object relations theory, Framo saw hidden multigenerational forces as exerting a critical influence an adult's intimate relationships; people therefore choose mates who, they hope, will help them "cancel out, replicate, control, master, live though, or heal" unresolved conflicts arising from disturbing relationships in their childhood (Framo, 1992, p. 115). For example, a man who used to be ruthlessly criticized as a child by his mother may have developed an internal image, or *introject*, of women with whom he is to have a close relationship; as a result, even though he hates being put down he eventually marries a woman who fits the introject of his mother, whether because subconsciously he feels comfortable playing the role of a criticized child or because he hopes to undo his unhappy relationship with his mother. Framo is credited for the development of family of origin therapy, which involves getting together one's parents, siblings, and other members of the family of origin to work things out so that one may achieve resolution of the intrapsychic issues and move on to have satisfying intimate relationships.

FAMILY LIFE CYCLE

In addition to the major concepts highlighted thus far, to appreciate the theories of family therapy one also needs to be familiar with the notion of the *family life cycle*, first proposed by Betty Carter and Monica McGoldrick in

1980 and later refined through the years (Carter & McGoldrick, 1999). This framework outlines a sequence of developmental stages that families move through, just as individuals are conceived to move through a series of developmental stages. Six stages are proposed in family development, namely (a) leaving home: single young adults; (b) joining of families through marriage: the new couple; (c) families with young children; (d) families with adolescents; (e) launching children and moving on; and (f) families in later life. Each stage is characterized by a key developmental task and requires changes in the members or family system in order to successfully complete the task and progress to the next stage. For example, the second stage, the formation of a marital system, requires husband and wife to realign their relationships with their families of origin, extended families and friends. Without this, the key task of commitment to the new marital system cannot be accomplished. With the birth of their first child, the couple moves on to the third stage, when the marital system adjusts to make space for children and for the couple to take on parental roles.

A family evolves and moves through its developmental stages while under vertical and horizontal flows of stress from within and outside the family system. The *vertical stressors* stem from the family history and transactional patterns (including taboos, family attitudes, and labels) passed down through generations; the *horizontal stressors* comprise predictable developmental stresses (e.g., when the child reaches school-going age) and unpredictable events (e.g., untimely death, job loss) that may disrupt the life cycle processes (Carter & McGoldrick, 1999). Problems develop when the family is unable to cope with these stressors or make the necessary adjustments for a smooth transition into the next stage of the developmental cycle. As a useful organizing framework for understanding the family's conflicts and difficulties within its environment, the family life cycle model provides a context to the family system and focuses on family continuity. Just as systems thinking shifts the emphasis (and blame) away from the individual in traditional psychology by calling for attention to the family context, the family life cycle perspective depathologizes families by encouraging one to think about family problems as an outcome of an inability to circumnavigate its environmental and developmental challenges. This paradigm is instrumental in bringing to light the cultural context within which family development takes place.

FUNCTIONAL VERSUS DYSFUNCTIONAL FAMILIES

Carter and McGoldrick's (1999) view that family problems occur as a result of a failure to overcome environmental stressors or developmental challenges represents one of the many ways to construe family dysfunction (some of these views are explained in detail in subsequent chapters). These different theories may highlight different areas of focus within the family, but they are nevertheless united by some fundamental ideas that distinguish between functional and dysfunctional families.

All families are *open systems* in that, to various degrees, they interact with their environment and are able to regulate and maintain themselves by drawing in resources from the environment. Families differ in the extent to which they are open; the more open the family system, the more adaptable and accessible to change it is (Goldenberg & Goldenberg, 2004). What determines the level of openness is the nature of the *boundaries* that separate the family from its environment. *Firm boundaries* are permeable, allowing required information to enter the family system from the environment and vice versa. At the same time they are also durable, providing a reliable means for interpreting such information (David, 2004). *Diffuse boundaries*, however, are permeable but not durable, with no filter whatsoever to regulate what or who enters and exits the family system. *Closed boundaries* deny any form of exchange or interaction between the system and the environment. Another dimension along which to consider the nature of boundaries is whether they are rigid or flexible. *Rigid boundaries* do not change under all circumstances, whereas *flexible boundaries* respond to changing situations by making adjustments, that is, becoming more diffuse or more closed (David, 2004).

A healthy family is one that has firm and flexible boundaries, such as one in which parents appreciate the new ideas their children bring home as a source of enrichment (boundary permeability), discuss with their children issues about violence that they see on the television (boundary durability), and permit them to attend camps in summer (boundary flexibility; Nichols & Schwartz, 2006). By contrast, in a family with diffuse boundaries, the children may be free to associate with whomever they wish outside their home, and bring friends home anytime. Additionally, children in a closed family may expect to be at home all the time and not allowed much interaction with the external environment. Family therapists, especially structuralists, are mindful of boundaries around members and groups of members within the family and how they influence information flow between different groups. For further discussion, see Chapter 5.

To maintain homeostasis or stability, families rely on a set of rules to regulate the behavior of its members and their interactions. These rules range from explicit statements such as, "Don't eat in front of the television" to unstated agreements such as, "Never criticize one another." As Goldenberg and Goldenberg (2004) note, rules in well-functioning families help maintain order and stability while simultaneously allowing for changes in changing circumstances. Rules are essential to the organization of the family; however, they must be consistent and clearly communicated to everyone. Symptoms may emerge in a member of the family if the rules are too rigid to allow negotiation (e.g., when an adolescent is given the same restrictions as when he or she was a young child) or when rules are inconsistent, ambiguous, or unpredictable (such as in a disorganized or chaotic family).

Many therapists see family dysfunction as primarily a situation where the family is caught in a repeated use of the same failed solutions in a desperate attempt to restore homeostasis (e.g., Becvar & Becvar, 2003; Minuchin & Fishman, 1981). In other words, the inability to adapt and change its interaction patterns becomes a part of the problem by sustaining it. In the case of a family of the adolescent given rigid rules, the child may start acting out by not observing the curfew and arguing with the parents. The parents, anxious that their child's behavior should threaten the family stability, react by enforcing stricter rules, such as grounding the teenager for disobeying them. This fuels greater rebellion in the child, and soon both parents and child find themselves in a vicious cycle of escalating tension.

Another favorite measure of the well-being of families is the degree to which the needs of the family system are balanced by the needs of the individual members. We have seen in the discussion on pseudomutuality how a family's resolve to maintain a façade of harmony and togetherness may be detrimental to individual well-being (Wynne et al., 1958). As Goldenberg and Goldenberg (2004) eloquently put it,

> To the degree that a family is functional, it is able to retain sufficient regularity and balance to maintain a sense of adaptability and preserve a sense of order and sameness. At the same time, it must subtly promote change and growth within its members and the family as a whole. Well-functioning families are resilient and able to achieve change without forfeiting stability. (p. 80)

HISTORY OF FAMILY ART THERAPY

The development of family art therapy mirrors that of family therapy in that it took root and grew in several places simultaneously. However, unlike in family therapy, the founders of family art therapy largely did not bind themselves to extensive research work or formulate constructs and theories to explain the complex nature of family relationships and processes. Instead, their focus was mainly on developing assessments and developing clinical proficiency so families were effectively helped through art therapy; research provided a conduit to establish efficacy. Hanna Kwiatkowska's work at the National Institute of Mental Health paved the way for art therapy to be researched with specific populations, such as families. Several influential family art therapists emerged and have been recognized for their work in their assessment, research, and clinical work with couples and families. Several of these frontrunners are cited below.

Family art therapy gained recognition largely through research efforts like Kwiatkowska's, as well as case studies that illustrated how art influences the therapeutic process. From this perspective, no particular theoretical underpinning was necessary; art in and of itself was the theoretical lens through which family stories, dynamics, and structural characteristics came to life.

The use of art therapy with couples and families is, in my opinion, cost effective and time efficient—couples and families are often well-defended verbally, therefore are stuck in recursive patterns. Their stories and dialogue are often repetitive, well-orchestrated, and well-rehearsed rhetoric that sustains stagnation. How often have you heard from your clients, "I've talked until I'm blue in the face!!" Or, "No matter what I've tried, he just won't listen!" Or, "He'll never change!" Or, "We've been through this a thousand times!" Art therapy transcends verbal barriers and provides a fresh lens into the family system. Individuals cannot disregard the tangible qualities of art as readily as they might dismiss words, which may conveniently dissipate into thin air.

FAMILY ART THERAPY ASSESSMENTS

The following section provides the reader with an overview of art therapy assessments developed for couples and families. Some assessments were generated through research efforts whereas others were developed through clinical work with couples and families. Beyond presenting these assessments or clinical approaches, I felt it would greatly enrich the chapter to have the voices and reflections of those family art therapists actually cited below. Therefore, I contacted these individuals and posed the following three questions: *Would you provide the reader with an overview of your clinical work with families? Why do you feel art therapy is effective with couples and families? What theoretical approach do you find the most useful?* I am grateful for the contributions and reflections of those who graciously participated; their views are cited through "personal communication" below.

The final section introduces the reader to some directives I have used both in my pedagogical work in family systems as well as my clinical practice.

Hanna Kwiatkowska—Family Art Evaluation

Nathan Ackerman has sometimes been referred to as the grandfather of family therapy; likewise, Hanna Kwiatkowska was a frontrunner and could be considered the mother of family art therapy. Junge (1994) noted,

> Kwiatkowska, an artist and sculptor trained in her native Poland, fled during the Second World War to Brazil where she continued her successful artistic career. She spoke seven languages fluently and was educated in Switzerland, Austria, and Warsaw. She came to the United States and met Margaret Naumburg. (p. 68)

Kwiatkowska began her pioneering work at the National Institute of Mental Health (NIMH) where she began to investigate the use of art with families. Kwiatkowska (1978) credited, "Doctors Lyman C. Wynne and

Juliana Day Franz ... were an inspiration to my work. They gave me support through their trust in validity of my methods and, above all, through their invaluable collaboration" (p. xiii). Malchiodi (1998) noted, "Kwiatkowska ... introduced art therapy into family therapy sessions. She believed that specific drawing activities were helpful in identifying family members' roles and status and in providing a therapeutic experience of working together" (p. 36). She originally designed the assessment to be used with families with severely disturbed hospitalized adults or adolescent members of families in both inpatient and outpatient settings. Kwiatkowska (1978) felt:

> Family art therapy as the primary mode of treatment is certainly the most challenging and rewarding application of art techniques with families. However, it also demands a solid background in family therapy and extensive psychotherapeutic experience in addition to art therapy training. (p. 137)

Kwiatkowska's assessment specifically used 18-inch by 24-inch manila or white drawing paper, crayolas, and oil pastels. Families worked on an easel or taped the picture to the wall, which is preferable to working on a table. Her assessment consisted of two free or nondirected drawings and four directed drawings. Families were directed to complete all six directives in one setting, thereby discouraging the creation of elaborate drawings. After each procedure, participants usually remarked on each other's drawing. Participants were asked to title all drawings and label them with their names and the date. Kwiatkowska's (1978) assessment protocol and directives were designed to lead the family from "complete freedom in their choice of subject to more structured, increasingly stress producing procedures" (p. 86). The assessment follows:

1. *A free picture.* Each member is instructed to "draw a picture of whatever comes to mind."
2. *A picture of the family.* Each member is asked to "draw a picture of your family, each member of the family including yourself. ... We would also like you to draw the whole person." This directive is given to help provide insight and new information for the families.
3. *An abstract family portrait.* Kwiatkowska noted this directive was the most difficult to explain and recommended asking each member to draw an abstract family portrait and waited for questions.

After the third drawing, the art therapist introduces and demonstrates relaxing body and arm movements to help prepare the participants for the next three drawings.

4. *A picture started with the help of a scribble.* Following arm movements, the family is asked to "draw an individual scribble and find a symbol in it." Kwaitkowska encouraged the participants to turn their paper in different directions, add lines, or ignore them as well. She felt this directive gave accurate information on the participants' capacity for organized abstract thinking. Additionally, observing how individuals within the family system integrate may provide useful information.

5. *A joint family scribble.* This is a repeat of Directive 4. However, members are then asked to "choose one scribble to use as a basis of a joint picture after having decided together what they see in it." This directive allows direct observation of how a family can work together. By having the family work on a single sheet of paper, the therapist can observe the family's ability to tolerate closeness and the degree to which the family has a need for boundaries.

Following this directive, the family and therapist compare the individual and joint scribbles. This allows a window into the dynamics and communication of the family system. Kwaitkowska (1978) noted, "The joint picture may become more bizarre and disjointed than the individual ones; on the other hand, it may present more unity and integration" (p. 90).

6. *A free picture.* This second free drawing is felt to be potentially the most important picture, as it evaluates the family's tolerance for stress, identifies the degree to which the family remained stable over the course of the session or changed pre- to post-session (pp. 86–90).

A common question that my students often pose is, "How do you determine the line between assessment and therapy? Are they separate? How are they distinguishable? How does one know when an assessment is finished and therapy has begun?" And further, "Does research potentially have therapeutic benefits for the participants?"

What is currently pragmatic therapeutically in this age of managed care, evidence-based treatments, and short-term therapy, seems a significant departure from the era that funded research efforts to examine assessment techniques like Kwiatkowska's. Indeed, time constraints may not allow the luxury of such substantive assessments. In my weekly private practice, I find great value in many of the directives Kwiatkowska developed; however, to complete the entire assessment within one session seems daunting, if not impossible. Additionally, the therapeutic process must allow an opportunity for couples and families to describe their drawings, as well as consider the content and descriptions of the other family members. Systemic features such as alliances, boundaries, roles, closeness, and disengagement often are made visible through a concrete medium such as art; art therapy provides a venue whereby clients may actually *see* through the lenses of other family members for the first time. The opportunity to discuss and potentially redefine a more functional family system may therefore be overshadowed by an art therapist who zealously rushes through directives without giving the family pause to examine their significance and systemic connotation.

Robert Burns and S. Kaufman—Kinetic Family Drawings

Burns and Kaufman invented the Kinetic Family Drawing (KFD) technique in 1972 for children between five and ten years of age to understand two aspects of child development: self-concept and interpersonal relationships. The KFD is considered to be one of the most widely used family art assessments. Materials used in the KFD are 8 1/2-inch by 11-inch paper and pencils. The instructions for administering the KFD are, "Draw a picture of everyone in your family, including you, doing something. Try to draw whole people, not cartoons or stick people. Remember, make everyone do something—some kind of action. Initial and date your drawing."

The KFD was scored on several dimensions that included actions drawn by the client, the style of the drawing, that is, how figures were organized on the page, symbols included in the drawing, and the size of the figures and distance between them. In studying such drawings, the therapist can gather information about family dynamics as well as the child's adaptive and defensive functioning. Actions (movement or energy) reflected in the various figures drawn by the child will be measured. The style of drawings refers to the way figures are organized on the page and indicates emotional disturbance. Burns and Kaufman assessed the drawings of family members and self, with attention paid to aggression in drawings (that may or may not include weapons), and emotional content such as fear and anxiety (Arrington, 2001; Brooke, 2004).

Numerous research studies evolved from the use of the KFD, including those conducted with sexually, physically, and/or emotionally abused children, children of alcoholic families, as well as cross-cultural comparisons (Brooke, 2004). The KFD and a modification, the Kinetic Couple Drawing (KCD), are two of my favorite directives in my work with couples and families. Even the most simplistic of drawings yields rich information and promotes useful dialogue and new insights. Factors to consider are often inestimable, but attention should be paid to:

1. *Expression.* How are the facial expression and body language of the figures characterized?
2. *Closeness.* Do figures touch? Do they seem disengaged? Who seems aligned and synchronistic? Are there any figures who seem particularly distant or potentially scapegoated?
3. *Proximity of members to each other.* Who is placed next to whom? What are the members' positions in relation to each other? Interestingly, you may find parallels in the therapy room!

4. *Inclusion of members.* Are all the members included in the drawing? Exclusion, although often explained away by "I forgot" may reveal important information on the system. A mother once forgot to include herself in her KFD, upon which her two astute young children purported, "Mom you forgot to put yourself in!" Mom flushed and meekly remarked that she was in the house. However, this exclusion provided a window into the source of the family dynamics and dysfunction: Mom was indeed emotionally detached from her family. The artwork provided a window into the family system, which otherwise might have been denied easily by the mother.

5. *Figures' actions.* Are the family members actively involved or interacting with each other? Is their action passive, such as watching television, or active, such as hiking in a favorite spot? Is this a memory or a fantasy of their ideal system? This component of the directive provides an opportunity to observe the relationship of the couple or family.

6. *Environment.* What is included in the surroundings? Is the environment peaceful or threatening? The environment surrounding the couple or family may reveal important information about their psyche or the person's perception of it.

Kinetic couple and family drawings may reveal the health and resilience of the system in addition to the dysfunction and challenges. This directive is also useful to repeat from time to time, as growth and systemic shifts are often revealed with this directive.

Robert Burns—Family Centered Circle Drawings

Burns also developed the Family Centered Circle Drawing technique (FCCD) in 1990 to understand parent-self relationships for persons of all ages. Drawings were not scored; instead, guidelines for interpretation were presented. There are four types of FCCDs: (a) mother-centered; (b) father-centered; (c) self-centered; and (d) present self-centered. In this technique, the client is asked to draw symbols that represent items in the center and the perimeter of the circle (similar to mandalas of Jung). This drawing enables the art therapist to gain information about the client's family and relate it to the client's view of self and his or her inner parents. Positive and negative associations are made around the symbol systems that the client creates. The therapist might have an awareness of the client's visual communication potential and also a broader interpretive context that is not heavily dependent on verbal skills (Brooke, 2004).

Judy Rubin—Family Portraits and Murals

Judy Rubin has conducted family art therapy since 1963 in inpatient, partial hospitalization, outpatient, and community settings. Rubin has worked with a large variety of groupings (Rubin, 1984): couples, parent-child dyads, siblings, grandparent-child dyads, the nuclear family, the extended family, and groups of parents (mothers, fathers, both), mother-child groups, and multifamily groups (personal communication, May 11, 2006). Rubin feels her theoretical approach with families includes influences by all established family therapy approaches, as well as psychoanalytic theory, attachment theory, and interpersonal dynamics (personal communication, May 11, 2006).

Rubin's vast clinical experience influenced her development of many possible tasks and directives. Regarding her family work, Rubin noted:

> Engaging in creative tasks—especially those that require family members to work together and those which invite them to represent the family—provides a rich storehouse of information in a natural kind of atmosphere. I've used both unstructured and structured approaches in family art evaluation and therapy, depending on the goals of the session. (personal communication, May 11, 2006)

Three specific tasks Rubin developed were used with families when a child or adolescent was being treated. These were:

1. *Scribble drawing*. Rubin found this introductory directive nonthreatening and extremely valuable as a potential diagnostic tool. She observed that young children who had not developed the capacity to project an image onto a scribble could draw whatever they liked. Rubin limited the media choices and found informal conversations could occur with this directive.
2. *Family portraits*. Rubin utilized both realistic and abstract family portraits with both two- and three-dimensional media. She felt broader media choice could alleviate some of the stress this directive intrinsically produces. She provided the family with plenty of space, that is, easels and tables.
3. *Family murals*. With a large sheet of paper taped to the wall, a large drawing space is created for the therapist to observe family interactions. Rubin suggested having the family "first decide together what they will do and then work on the paper" (p. 130). In addition to the projective possibilities, this directive encourages joint decision making and collaborative process. She felt this could be a very effective diagnostic tool for the therapist.
4. *Free drawings*. The directive, "Draw whatever you want" was given if the other directives were completed. She allowed liberal use of media in this drawing.

Harriet Wadeson—Joint Pictures Without Talking and Self-Portraits Given to Spouses

Harriet Wadeson began her art therapy training and career at the National Institute of Mental Health (NIMH), a part of the National Institutes of Health

(NIH), at its Clinical Center in Bethesda, Maryland. She apprenticed under Hanna Kwiatkowska, who was working with Lyman Wynne. Wadeson notes that most studies were investigating the nature/nurture question, particularly in regards to schizophrenia and included twin studies as well as work with whole families. After a brief time, Wadeson branched out from Hanna's direction and worked with William Bunney, MD, a psychiatrist who focused on affective disorders for eight years. She later returned to research investigations on schizophrenia, headed by Will Carpenter. Wadeson notes, "During my 14 years at NIH, I was very much influenced by all the research of the units on which I worked" (personal communication, May 19, 2006).

Wadeson (1980) developed an assessment for couples while she worked with Roy Fitzgerald, who was studying the marital dynamics of couples in which one spouse was hospitalized at NIMH for manic-depressive illness. The directives were as follows:

1. *Joint picture without talking*: The couple is instructed to "develop one well integrated picture together without verbal communication" (p. 285). Wadeson felt this task allowed the couple to work in close proximity, as they share one piece of paper. "Not allowing verbal communication heightens the power of the non-verbal interactions" (p. 290).

2. *Abstract of the marital relationship*: The couple is asked to "draw an abstract picture of their marital relationship simultaneously but not separately" (p. 290). Wadeson modified Kwiatkowska's abstract family portrait to create this similar directive, which explores the individual's capacity for abstract thinking and elicits strong affect.

3. *Self-portrait given to spouse*: Each spouse is requested to draw a realistic, full-length self-portrait on a full sheet of vertical paper. Next, they are requested to symbolically give themselves (their self-portraits) to one another and are given the opportunity to do anything they want to their partner's self-portrait. Wadeson notes, "The joint picture making and the exchange of self-portraits prompted some very expressive and telling responses, often eliciting strong emotions from both members of the couple" (personal communication, May 19, 2006).

The results of this study revealed a strong concordance among the couples along several parameters, highlighting a common dynamic pattern among all the "manic" couples (Wadeson & Fitzgerald, 1971; Wadeson, 1980). Wadeson remarked that she "applied these techniques to other couple populations both at NIH and in my private practice and published descriptions of them as well—see Wadeson, 1972a, 1972b, 1973, 1980 (personal communication, May 19, 2006).

Clinically, Wadeson often worked with a male cotherapist with couples, couple groups, family groups, and multiple group families (Wadeson, 1976,

1980). She found, "This process was especially useful in addressing the issues of 'fluid families,' in which there were changing constituencies of families, often making family boundaries and roles unclear" (personal communication, May 19, 2006).

Wadeson's career path shifted in 1978 to academia where she began to write and publish on art therapy and family art therapy (Wadeson, 1980, 2000). When asked how she found art therapy to be effective, she stated:

1. Images often convey more than words, especially for those with difficulty articulating. For example, at NIH, a couple was referred to me because the psychiatrist and social worker could get nowhere with them after 10 sessions ... the hospitalized husband, who was severely depressed and withdrawn, refused to speak. They asked me to try art therapy as a last resort. When asked to draw an abstract picture of their marital relationship, the nonverbal husband drew a tight circular enclosure and indicated that was how he felt in his marriage. From this one session alone, the therapists were able to continue work with the couple, and from this one expression, the husband began to voice how he felt in relation to his wife.

2. Particularly in joint picture making, the couple or family often has fun together, a rare occurrence for many of the people with whom I have worked.

3. The action-oriented nature of some of the exercises, such as the exchange of self-portraits and joint scribble making, mobilizes both creative and physical energy with often dramatic results that bring about new communication and insights.

4. In work with several generations of family members, the art activity often levels the playing field so that children are communicating in a familiar mode, whereas in verbal communication alone, parents are often more articulate than their young children.

5. When exploring family or couple dynamics, an expression of a spatial matrix, as in a picture, is often more appropriate than a verbal description that is sequential in nature, as the family pattern is experienced all at once in any given moment.

6. In working with the family or couple, the transformative nature of clay can be very effective in dramatizing how the family is experienced by each individual and then in the transformation of their clay pieces to show how they would like it to be. Such communication is often more complete and more comprehensible to other family members than are words alone.

7. The catharsis possible in creating art together can galvanize couples and families to see each other more clearly and to work

together more effectively toward solutions to their problems. (Personal communication, May 19, 2006)

I echo Wadeson's thoughts and acknowledge these are excellent directives that often reveal numerous systemic factors, including boundaries, the capacity for the couple/family to share, nonverbal communication patterns, and hierarchical factors. Another interesting component of this assessment is to observe the couple/family's ability to "play." So often individuals are caught in unconscious interplay and dialogue that are repetitive, unproductive, and fixed; art can transcend these verbal blocks and enable the family to recognize these communication patterns. The art therapist can cultivate the family to develop more appropriate patterns.

Helen Landgarten—Verbal and Nonverbal Team Art Tasks

Helen Landgarten began her art therapy career in 1967 at the Thalians Outpatient Clinic, Los Angeles, California, a clinic that was a major resource for family therapy while the field was developing. Landgarten noted, "Dr. Saul Brown, Chief of Staff, took a risk and hired me as an art therapist (although such a title was as yet unknown)" (personal communication, May 16, 2006). Landgarten recalls:

My Chief of Staff found my innovative approach to be amazingly successful. In the initial session as the entire family drew pictures together, the family system and the roles each member played was immediately revealed. By observing the way the drawings were created I could understand the family dynamics.... Art therapy is effective with couples and families because it is an "in the moment" experience. It is simple and non-threatening for clients. The protocol is expeditious and brings remarkable results. The clues that are gathered during the evaluation stage act as a "floor plan" upon which the treatment is built. The work revolves around the family dynamics and the way positive changes can be made. (personal communication, May 16, 2006)

Landgarten's work led to the development of the assessment, as outlined below. For this assessment, she used colored markers, colored paper, glue, and 12-inch by 18-inch white or manila paper. Although this task is presented as a game-like process, the process allows the art to be a window into the family's artistic communication and behavior. The assessment involves the following three directives:

1. *The nonverbal team art task.* This process has the family divide themselves into two teams; each team then works on a single piece of paper. Each person on both teams is asked to select a color marker that is different from the others and to use it throughout the session. The family members are told not to speak, signal each other, or write notes to each other while working on the art. When they feel they have finished they are asked to stop. After all tasks are completed, the family is permitted to talk in order to title their artwork.

2. *The nonverbal family art task.* This process is a replication of the first, except the entire family works together on a single piece of paper. Upon completion they may speak again in order to title their drawing.

3. *The verbal family art task.* This task allows flexibility in verbal communication and media choice; each person is asked to use one colored marker, one color of plasticine, or paper.

These directives allow alliances between family members to be revealed. Additionally, the use of a different color for each person provides visual evidence regarding each member's contribution. Landgarten (1987) created "points of observation," which provided a framework for therapists to observe and record the therapeutic process, as outlined above. These 17 points are identified with the following questions:

1. Who initiated the picture and what was the process that led to this person making the first mark on the page?
2. In what order did the rest of the members participate?
3. Which member's suggestions were utilized and which were ignored?
4. What was the level of involvement on the part of each person?
5. Which participants remained in their own space versus those who crossed over?
6. Did anyone "wipe out" another member by superimposing their own image on top of someone else?
7. What type of symbolic contact was made and who made these overtures?
8. Did the members take turns, work in teams, or work simultaneously?
9. If there was a shift in approach, what precipitated the change?
10. Where are the geographical locations of each person's contributions (central, end, corner, all over)?
11. How much space did each person occupy?
12. What was the symbolic content of each person's contribution?
13. Which members functioned independently?
14. Who acted as initiators?
15. Who were followers or reactors?
16. Were emotional responses made?
17. Was the family's working style cooperative, individualistic, or discordant? (p. 15)

Landgarten feels fortunate to have worked with a broad spectrum of individuals, couples, and families at every stage of development. Regarding theoretical approaches, Landgarten pondered,

> In spite of the latest family theory (fad-like, a new one thrown into the hopper every few years) I find the oldest ones to be most effective. If I had to associate myself with a single theory it would be structural family therapy.... I believe the therapists' style is reflective of their personality. The directness appealed to me and I found that it caused clients to gain confidence and trust in me early on. (personal communcation, May 16, 2006)

Maxine Junge—Family Art Therapy

Maxine Borowsky Junge apprenticed under Helen Landgarten in art therapy, and began her "official" art therapy work in 1974 when Landgarten invited Junge to teach in the Immaculate Heart College's art therapy master's program (Kaplan, 2007). Junge recognized that:

> there was neither the global village then, nor emphasis on diversity and multiculturalism. The current world has become too complicated for individual thinking and conceptualizing. The obvious paradigm shift needed in art therapy, not exactly new, is toward *a systems approach.* (Junge, as cited in Kaplan)

Junge (as cited in Kaplan, 2007, p. 41) further characterized systems thinking as natural to any painter.

> A painting is a system in which all parts must work together to make a whole. To change one thing is to change the whole. For example, to change a bit of color is to change the whole painting and the rest must be adjusted to fit the change …

Junge first encountered family therapy through observing a talented therapist, Joan Schain. Her decision to return to school to learn family therapy eventually led to her apprenticeship with Landgarten at Thalians Outpatient Clinic, Los Angeles, California. Junge acknowledged, "I always say that Helen was trying to save the world from me because, with no knowledge, I was trying, badly, to use art in therapy … sitting in her therapy sessions, at her elbow, I learned the art of art therapy from a master" (Junge & Wadeson, 2006, p. 342). She has been a systems-oriented therapist since 1971 and has published on family art therapy (Junge, 1985). She currently provides consultation for family art therapy (personal communication, May 1, 2006).

Landgarten's work inspired Junge to develop a "modified" family art therapy assessment, which she unequivocally always uses. She conducts one verbal session with the family and introduces the art assessment in the second session. She considers herself to be a systems thinker using a structural approach, although she feels that art can be integrated with any theory or used to further whatever goals. Last, she believes humor can be very important (personal communication, May 1, 2006). Her modified one-hour session follows.

First, *warm up each family member*. The therapist directs each member to first make his or her initials big on an 8 1/2-inch by 11-inch paper, then decorate them in any way the member wants. Next, each family member is directed to hold his or her drawing up so others can see. Others can ask questions if they like. The process takes about 10 minutes.

Second, *family drawing (big paper, on wall, 18 inches by 24 inches or more)*. The family is instructed to create a drawing together in whatever way they like. The therapist remains unobtrusive during the creation. However, the family is to observe three rules when working: (a) They must choose one color marking pen and use it throughout the drawing; (b) all members must take turns; and (c) talking is not allowed. When the family has completed the drawing, they are directed to discuss among themselves a title for it. The family art therapist and family members then discuss the process. The time frame for art making is roughly 10 to 20 minutes. Time permitting, a third drawing may be given, although this is not likely, due to time constraints (personal communication, May 1, 2006).

Shirley Riley—Integrative Family Art Therapy

Shirley Riley offered a rich dimension to the family art therapy profession, as she was perhaps one of the most expansive family art therapists in terms of her approach and theoretical base. Malchiodi (Riley & Malchiodi, 1994) described Riley as "integrative" because her philosophy encompassed a variety of family therapy theories that she utilized to meet the needs of the client and second, Riley's integration of process and product set parameters for the family system and enhanced interventions. Malchiodi (Riley & Malchiodi, 1994) further noted:

> Her major strengths are the application of art therapy to family work and her ability to integrate and synthesize family therapy theories in work with clients. In this postmodern era of single parenthood, blended families, and reinvented family roles, as well as economic distress and societal violence, Riley's approaches to clinical intervention with families are in the forefront of the necessary evolution of the practice of family art therapy. (p. 8)

Indeed, Riley's publications spanned a broad theoretical base. Included in her family art therapy approaches were structural, strategic, social constructivist, family of origin, and postmodern approaches. Because of these extensive theoretical approaches, one might ponder if this influenced Riley to not create or ostensibly adhere to one particular art therapy assessment. Riley (2003) observed:

In most families a myth persists that everyone is in agreement about "how they understand the problem" and, moreover, what to do about it. However, it is not likely for the family to have an agreement or consensus concerning problem solving. Art expression can address multiple perspectives, helping the family to see how each other defines the problem and it's solution.... Multiple images of the same problem can be expressed and all can be witnessed by the family and therapist. (p. 89)

Cathy Malchiodi, who worked closely with Riley for years, contributed some thoughts on Riley's career. Malchiodi noted:

One interesting thing about Shirley that few people know is that Shirley studied improvisation for more than 20 years ... she had this skill in terms of drama—to be able to work in various situations or events, which positively influenced her skills as a family art therapist. (personal communication, May 11, 2006)

She further stated Shirley often said she would have been an actress, had she had the voice, as she loved acting so much (personal communication, May 11, 2006).

As one examines Riley's work in its entirety, it is noteworthy to consider the breadth of both her theoretical approach and her use of art media, which included drawing, painting, collage, paper construction, Plasticine, and clay. Because Riley worked with a broad range of clients and in various settings, she developed an impressive array of art directives to meet the needs of the clients. Riley (Riley & Malchiodi, 2003) noted the need for a "philosophy that allowed the clients to model their own treatment, illustrate their own invented truth and find, with the support of the art therapist, a more acceptable reality to embrace their lives" (p. 36).

Doris Arrington (1984)—Family Landscapes

Doris Arrington has been an art therapist for 35 years and has been teaching at Notre Dame de Namur University, Belmont, California, for 29 years. Over the past six years, Doris has expanded her teaching to countries such as China, Poland, and the Ukraine (personal communication, April 27, 2006). Although she cites the contributions of Gottman and attachment theory, she is currently energized when she considers the blending of family systems in neuroscience. Doris states:

I am so excited that neuroscience and art therapy are merging. Now we are beginning to scientifically understand (through neuroscience research) that implicit memory is absorbed in the right hemisphere through the senses. That includes seeing, hearing, tasting, touching and feeling or theoretically, attachment. Like other senses of hearing, and seeing, feelings and attachment are developed in a certain time frame. Couples, learning to live with each other need to look back to how they metaphorically interpreted the environment in their initial homes. Metaphor and art, graphic narrative, help the right hemisphere remember and pass that information along to verbal narrative in the left hemisphere. More information is passed non-verbally than through words. (personal communication, April 27, 2006)

Arrington developed a directive of family landscapes that enabled family members to explore boundary issues and compassion between family members. Though any clean paper would suffice for this task, Arrington favored rice paper or soft papers such as newsprint or tissue papers, as they mimic the look of a map. With the papers, colored pencils, watercolors, brushes, and black pens are used. The assessment follows:

1. The client is asked to think of a specific time between 3 and 12 years of age, considering the psychological space that he or she grew up in. Arrington might ask, "How did it feel emotionally? Crowded? Quiet? Cramped? Comfortable?"
2. The client is asked to draw a symbolic landscape, seascape, or desertscape that represents the psychological space as defined in the first step. Each family member is to be included in the landscape, with consideration given to emotional closeness and distance. Arrington (2001) notes, "this always elicits intense emotions within a family system as symbols are expressed and coalitions are identified" (p. 197).
3. The client is asked to place a legend on the landscape that identifies each member of the family.
4. The therapist elicits the client to consider any significant changes during the ages of 3 to 12 years of age. Events such as death, divorce, remarriage, foster placement provide consideration for the emotional climate at this time. The client is asked to draw a different landscape that depicts this period and create a legend for it. If there are numerous events, the client may create several landscapes to depict the various emotional climates.
5. Last, the client is asked to draw, with the same intensity, a landscape from the viewpoint of the person that was the furthermost away from him or her.

Arrington (2001) notes:

This reframe of space between family members often begins an empathetic process not previously experienced. Encourage the client to draw the view from the symbol of each family member in the family landscape and discuss what he or she experienced. (p. 197)

Arrington utilizes this assessment to enable clients to explore their feelings around the family space, defense mechanisms, and insight into proximity and distance in the family system.

OTHER DIRECTIVES TO CONSIDER IN CLINICAL WORK AND ACADEMIC TRAINING

Comprehension and appreciation of family systems theory is desirable for all art therapists, regardless of what population one may work with or from which framework one may practice. All individuals were created from some family system, and family of origin issues often emerge in therapy, even if the client is seeking individual therapy for an unrelated crisis or event. Understanding family systems serves to enlighten and inform the person, whether one is a graduate student embarking on his or her education, or a client seeking therapy. Recognizing the value of the basic tenets of family systems theory also enables one to consider how one functions within other systems as well, such as school, work, community.

Exploring one's family system through art often has a different impact than engaging in a verbal dialogue. My approach to teaching family systems theory includes numerous directives created to engage the students more fully in appreciating their family system and its influence. The following directives were completed by graduate students enrolled in a family of origin and art therapy class at Antioch University Seattle.

Creative Genogram

Bowen's approach with families was to guide family members towards differentiation through the exploration of multigenerational patterns. Bowen views himself not so much as a therapist, but a "coach" who actively engaged his clients into in-depth exploration of family of origin. Beyond the usual assignment of creating a genogram, I also ask my students to complete a "creative genogram." (Figure 2.1). The student's creative spirit and wit with this directive always inspire and provide for rich dialogue.

Family Tree Creation

Many people describe their families in relation to their "family tree." I thought it would be enriching for students examining their families of origin to do a creative piece around their family tree. This directive is given as homework, whereby the student is asked to create his or her family tree visually. Figure 2.2 shows an example of such a creative piece. The student, who was an adopted child along with her brother, portrayed herself as branching out of one side of the box to meet her birth family. The fragmented branch on the other side symbolizes her brother, who has no desire to contact his birth family. Every branch of the tree represents an aunt, an uncle, or a cousin—

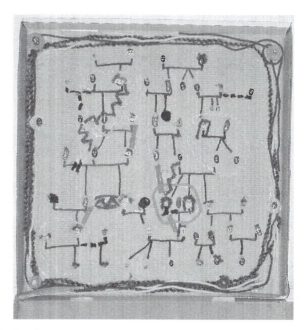

Figure 2.1   Creative genogram.

Figure 2.2   Family tree.

members of her family. On every leaf is a family member's name. The fruits, depicted with glass beads, are people who have passed on; they now nurture the family. A fallen leaf denotes a member who has been disowned by the family, while a broken branch at the base of the tree symbolizes a person from whom the student experienced abuse as a child and would like to have broken off from the family.

Family Roles

Many lively discussions have occurred in my family of origin and art therapy class around the roles that people are given and sometimes maintain in their family system. The rigidity that sometimes accompanies family roles merits consideration for change; and change may evoke apprehension and fear.

For this activity, students are asked to recall their childhood (around 6 years of age), then make a puppet to represent a fear they had then. The puppets are used to create a dialogue around their family roles and fears, in an effort to examine how this may impact their clinical development (see Figure 2.3).

Childhood Family Masks

Class discussions around one's family of origin inevitably lead to the "image" the family presents to the outside world as opposed to the family system that is privy only to its family members. Family masks can provide a powerful tool to examine the family image, boundaries, and the juxtaposition between the private and outer worlds. The mask in Figure 2.4 depicts one's examination of one's cultural identity and privilege.

Figure 2.3 Family roles puppets.

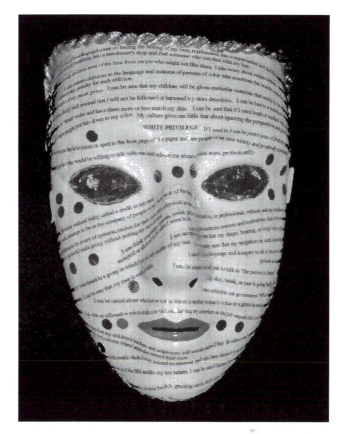

Figure 2.4   Childhood family mask.

Family of Origin Analysis

Assignments such as the ones described above are included in a comprehensive analysis of one's family of origin. Beyond an extensive paper that details the family system, dynamics, roles, structure, etc., students create an art piece that describes visually their systemic lens of their family of origin.

Figure 2.5 is a creation inspired by a favorite game of the student's family, Monopoly™. Unlike the original game, the markers are clay figures of the family of origin and the properties are intergenerational theories. Whenever a player lands on a theory, he or she has a choice whether to purchase a therapeutic session or move on; a purchase in this game is indicated by a therapeutic chair. Life Events cards may advance the player to the nearest theorist for consideration of therapeutic insight; unfortunate Life Events, however, send the player to jail. The winner is the one with the most therapy sessions and is declared "differentiated."

Figure 2.5 Family of origin analysis creative piece.

Figure 2.6 shows a deceptively simple piece that embodies the approach to life in the student's family of origin, which is reflected in a poem that hung over the kitchen stove, "Life is hard—Yard by Yard\Inch by Inch—it's a cinch!" The family embraced life inch by inch, focusing on the positive aspects and using humor to "make light" of every serious situation. Many things were often glossed over with a smile; the family was able to handle the "inch" but not the "yard" of life.

Unfinished Business Creative Piece

Dissention among family members may result in cut-off, adversarial relationships, and a fixed, unyielding stance toward the individual with whom he or she is in conflict. Often, both sides remain stubbornly paralyzed. Providing a method whereby one can dissect the situation in a new framework may indeed reduce defensiveness and provide new insights into why and how this

Figure 2.6   Family of origin analysis creative piece.

relationship evolved to this place. Below are two creations that visually portray their unfinished business.

Figure 2.7 is the artwork of a student who dealt with her mother's drinking problem with empathy and forgiveness. She describes having achieved closure through the creation of this piece, understanding that "her mother coped the only way she knew how—through drinking and isolation." She envisions a message in a wine bottle thrown into the depths of the ocean, gone forever, putting to rest her negative feelings towards her mother's alcoholism and the havoc it created in her family.

In Figure 2.8, the student described, "the large bird represents the dominant family member. The least dominant is represented by the nest. The two lower birds are not the same as the large flashy one, and mysteriously a flower emerges from the single egg left in the nest. How could these very different subjects form a 'family'? That was the point."

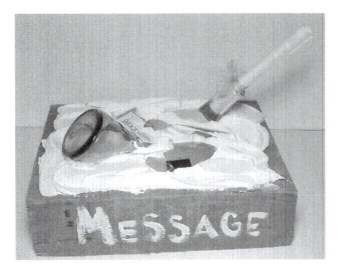

Figure 2.7   Unfinished business creative piece.

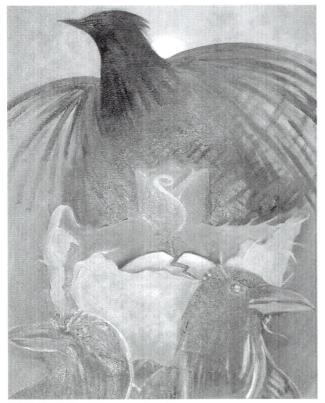

Figure 2.8   Unfinished business creative piece.

Related Readings Directives

Family dynamics often are more easily understood by examining families through nonacademic readings or books. Often, I choose readings that are rich in the interplay of family and cultural components. Figure 2.9 shows a creative response to the book, *Like Water for Chocolate* (Esquivel, 1992). The mixed media piece, entitled, "Enmeshed in dysfunction; time can be stagnant," represents the family relationships among the characters of the book.

CONCLUSION

The juxtaposition of art and creative process in relation to the underpinnings of systems theory may seem contrary; art is expansive, while cybernetics is reductionistic. However, the marriage of the two provides a framework that is infinitely useful for diverse clients in various settings, who may not respond as prolifically to verbal therapy alone. This chapter provided an overview of the pioneers who shaped, nurtured, and launched new ideology and theory. The collective wealth from these pioneers will undoubtedly contribute towards the changing social and diverse landscape in the twenty-first century.

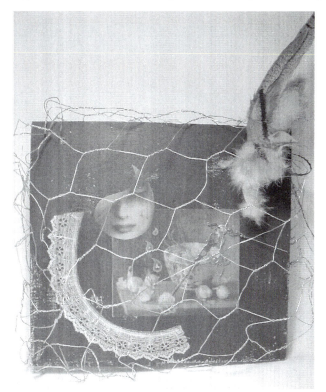

Figure 2.9 Related readings creative piece.

REFERENCES

Arrington, D. B. (2001). *Home is where the art is*. Springfield, IL: Charles C. Thomas.

Bateson, G., Jackson, D. D., Haley, J., & Weakland, J. H. (1956). Toward a theory of schizophrenia. *Behavioral Science, 1,* 251–264.

Becvar, D. S., & Becvar, R. J. (2003). *Family therapy: A systemic integration* (5th ed.). Boston: Allyn & Bacon.

Boszormenyi-Nagy, I., & Spark, G. M. (1973). *Invisible loyalties: Reciprocity in intergenerational family therapy*. New York: Harper & Row.

Broderick, C. B., & Schrader, S. S. (1991). The history of professional marriage and family therapy. In A. S. Gurman & D. P. Kniskern (Eds.), *Handbook of family therapy* (Vol. II, pp. 3–40). New York: Brunner/Mazel.

Brooke, S. L. (2004). *Tools of the trade: A therapist's guide to art therapy assessments* (2nd ed.). Springfield, IL: Charles C. Thomas.

Burns, R. C. (1990). *A guide to family-centered circle drawings*. New York: Brunner/Mazel.

Burns, R. C., & Kaufman, S. H. (1972). *Kinetic family drawings (K-F-D): An introduction to understanding children through kinetic drawings*. New York: Brunner/Mazel.

Carter, B., & McGoldrick, M. (1999). Overview: The expanded family life cycle. In B. Carter & M. McGoldrick (Eds.), *The expanded family life cycle: Individual, family, and social perspectives* (3rd ed., pp. 1–26). Boston: Allyn & Bacon.

David, P. (2004). *A systems guide to human communication*. Seattle, WA: Cascade Press.

Esquivel, L. (1992). *Like water for chocolate*. New York: Anchor Books.

Framo, J. L. (1992). *Family-of-origin therapy: An intergenerational approach*. New York: Brunner/Mazel.

Goldenberg, I., & Goldenberg, H. (2004). *Family therapy: An overview* (6th ed.). Pacific Grove, CA: Brooks/Cole.

Green, R. J., & Framo, J. L. (Eds.). (1981). *Family therapy: Major contributions*. Madison, WI: International Universities Press.

Guttman, H. A. (1991). Systems theory, cybernetics, and epistemology. In A. S. Gurman & D. P. Kniskern (Eds.), *Handbook of family therapy* (Vol. II, pp. 41–62). New York: Brunner/Mazel.

Haley, J. (1973). *Uncommon therapy: The psychiatric techniques of Milton H. Erikson*. New York: Norton.

Junge, M. B. (1985). "The book about daddy dying": A preventive art therapy technique to help families deal with the death of a family member. *Art Therapy*, 4–18.

Junge, M. B. (1994). *A history of art therapy in the United States*. Mundelein, IL: The American Art Therapy Association, Inc.

Junge, M. B., & Wadeson, H. (Eds.) (2006). *Architects of art therapy: Memoirs and lifestories*. Springfield, IL: Charles C. Thomas.

Kaplan, F. (Ed.). (2006. *Art therapy and social action* London: Jessica Kingsley Publishers

Kwiatkowska, H. Y. (1978). *Family therapy and evaluation through art*. Springfield, IL: Charles C. Thomas.

Landgarten, H. B. (1981). *Clinical art therapy: A comprehensive guide*. New York: Brunner/Mazel.

Landgarten, H. B. (1993). *Magazine photo collage*. New York: Brunner-Mazel.

Madanes, C. (1981). *Strategic family therapy*. San Francisco: Jossey-Bass.

Malchiodi, C. A. (1998). *The Art therapy sourcebook*. Los Angeles: Lowell House.

Minuchin, S., & Fishman, H. C. (1981). *Family therapy techniques*. Cambridge, MA: Harvard University Press.

Nichols, M. P., & Schwartz, R. C. (2006). *Family therapy: Concepts and methods* (7th ed.). Boston: Allyn & Bacon.

Riley, S., & Malchiodi, C. A. (1994). *Integrative approaches to family art therapy.* Chicago, IL: Magnolia Street.

Riley, S., & Malchiodi, C. A., (2003). Solution-focused and narrative approaches. In C. A. Malchiodi (Ed.), *Handbook of art therapy.* New York: Guilford Press.

Wadeson, H. (1972a, February). Conjoint marital art therapy techniques. *Psychiatry,* 89–98.

Wadeson, H. (1973). Art therapy techniques used in conjoint marital therapy. *American Journal of Art Therapy, 12*(3), 147–164.

Wadeson, H. (1976). The fluid family in multi-family art therapy. *American Journal of Art Therapy, 15*(4), 115–118.

Wadeson, H. (1980). *Art psychotherapy.* New York: John Wiley & Sons.

Wadeson, H. (2000). *Art therapy practice: Innovative approaches with diverse populations.* New York: John Wiley & Sons.

Wadeson, H., & Fitzgerald, R. (1971). Marital relationship in manic-depressive illness: Conjoint psychiatric art evaluations. *Journal of Nervous and Mental Disease, 153*(3), 180–196.

Wynne, L. C., Ryckoff, I. M., Day, J., & Hirsch, S. I. (1958). Pseudo-mutuality in the family relations of schizophrenics. *Psychiatry, 21,* 205–220.

CHAPTER 3

Object Relations and Attachment Theory

Creativity of Mother and Child in the Single Parent Family

SHARYL THODE PARASHAK

Come at the world creatively,
create the world;
it is only what you create that has meaning for you

D. Winnicott (1968)

INTRODUCTION

The image of a mother and her child holds strong significance for each of us. We are reminded of the American Impressionist Mary Cassatt and her paintings of mother and infant in everyday life. A nurturing, comforting softness, and warmth radiate from the canvas. We can feel the attentive caring of the mother, see the loving look on her face, and experience her gentle touch. Memories of the person that we felt closest to may come to our mind. More than likely, this is the person who took primary responsibility for us, this is mother. We learned about care and nurturing through mother. The foundation of object relations and attachment is based on the first understanding and expectations of the world that we developed in this partnership. The partnership is the source for all subsequent relationships in life.

As a new being in the world, the infant finds the other person looking down at her to be the one who can be counted on to be there through hunger, pain, joy, and fear. The infant comes to know that the mother will be here today, and she will be there tomorrow, and the infant begins to feel confident that she will appear and make everything "good enough." However, what happens when there isn't a person who can be depended upon to care for the infant? What happens if that person caring for the infant is unavailable emotionally or physically or is impaired by alcohol, drugs, or mental illness? What if the mother is so young herself that she is not yet emotionally ready to care for an infant? A realistic look at the challenge of motherhood can alter the fantasy depicted by Mary Cassatt. Motherhood today presents a complex picture of positive and "less than optimal" circumstances that can challenge even the most skilled mother. External realities, such as single parenting, economic challenges, family issues, and social pressures influence the mother-infant partnership. Internal contributions of both the mother and child may be genetic, physiological, and psychological; each brings much to the relationship. The nature of the developing attachment and resulting object relations between mother and child can predict the child's future pattern of relationships. Shared creative experiences enhance the attachment experienced between mother and child.

ATTACHMENT

Throughout life, we find ourselves attached to people, places, and things. The nature of an individual's attachment is formed early with an important person. John Bowlby (1982) defines attachment as "proximity promoting behaviour" (p. 374), that are as important as feeding, clothing, and shelter. The purpose of the behaviors is to sustain physical and psychological closeness to significant persons throughout life. There may be more than one attachment for the child, but usually there is a primary attachment. That person most often is the mother or another important person who is the "mothering object," someone who is near and available. When the infant is born, this special person feeds, holds, and, when necessary, comforts the infant. The infant comes to know this person as the center of his or her life and responds to the care with a progressive confidence. The definition of confidence is "a feeling or consciousness of one's powers or of reliance on one's circumstances (*Merriam-Webster's Collegiate Dictionary*, 1994. p. 241). The infant's consciousness of his or her power is the driving force to explore and learn in a more social context. If the infant does not sense his or her own power, then challenges may occur when moving outside of the "mother-infant constellation."

Beverly James (1994), in her research of attachment in children, states, "an attachment is a reciprocal, enduring, emotional, and physical affiliation between a child and a caregiver" (p. 2). The affiliation between child and primary caregiver begins prior to birth and continues throughout childhood.

However, the time between birth and age three remains important for the reciprocal pattern of interaction to develop and be suitably reinforced so the child feels secure enough to go beyond the protection of the mother. The child is then free to explore what else there is in his or her world.

The primary attachment is stimulating, with mutual sharing; delight in the other accompanies sensory arousal that provides the baseline for attachment. The mission of the primary attachment person is threefold, and each mission bears its own message (James, 1994, p. 68):

> A secure attachment means that mother is a protector, provider and guide; as protector, she relays the message: "Everything will be OK. I'll take care of you, set limits, and keep you safe." As provider, she lets the infant know: "I'm the source of food, love, shelter, excitement, soothing, and play. As guide, she creates an environment that lets the infant know: "This is who you are and who I am. This is how the world works. (p. 2)

Psychologist Daniel Stern states, "human beings are seen not as passive recipients of their environment but as active shapers, using their perceptions to 'construct' their view of the world" (cited in Worden, 1999, p. 9). Stern speculated about the infant's inner subjective experience with the world and how the sense of self emerges through interpersonal interactions. Active shaping of the infant's world starts at birth and continues as an ongoing developmental process during the first 3 years of life. Attachment issues continue throughout life via secure attachment outcomes such as heightened self-esteem, engaged and cooperative relationships with caregivers and peers, greater impulse control, emotional stability, and age-appropriate autonomy. "Attachment security is more than just the absence of insecurity; it is more than not being caught in the fear of rejection or abandonment" (Whiffen, 2003, p. 393). The securely attached child is confident that the important person in the child's life will be emotionally available and ready for engagement.

"Mother–infant interaction" is a field of knowledge developmentalists use to explain the growing relationship between mother and child. Seeing and being seen is the background of the formation of the self. Looking, smiling, touching, and sensitivity to the infant's cues are the elements that give shape to the relationship with the outer world.

Looking

> When I look, I am seen, so I exist.
> I can now afford to look and see.
> I now look creatively and what I apperceive I also perceive.
> In fact, I take care not to see what is not there to be seen
> (unless I am tired).

(Winnicott, 1971, p. 114)

Eye contact or gaze, which provides focus and an early form of communication, is an event that gives the infant a sense of self. As the infant and mother gaze at each other, they see their own reflection in the other's face. "In individual emotional development the precursor of the mirror is the mother's face" (Winnicott, 1971, p. 112). For the infant, this is not yet a differentiated experience. Differentiation comes with progressive development and repeated intimate exchanges between mother and child. The reflection from the mother gives the child his or her conscious and knowing self, shaped by reciprocity of action and image. Looking and touching are the two thresholds through which the infant discovers the world.

However, looking has two sides. There are situations when the mother may be looking at but not looking after the infant, through a distanced, unempathic gaze. "Distance seems to be of the essence; the look seems to keep the other person at a distance, out of contact, far from any possibility of touch or closeness" (Wright, 1991, p. 35). This contradicts the idea of gaze perceived as loving and mirroring for the child. The mother may also react to her child in such a way that is difficult for both to understand. Responses may be a result of unconscious reactions to past events, particularly when the child reaches the age of early trauma for the parent. "Attachment injuries are powerful and enduring wounds that can profoundly influence the course of the [mother-infant] relationship and interfere with the process of repair" (Whiffen, 2003, p. 390).

Touching

Harry Harlow (1958) discovered the significance of gentle touch in experiments with monkeys. Psychologist Harlow explored the nature of attachment, feeding, and physical contact. He found that physical comfort of the monkeys took priority over proximity to food. The monkeys spent the majority of their time clinging to a covered wire surrogate that provided softness and warmth rather than just food. Harlow's research involving primitive psychological needs has contributed much to the literature about each human's early search for comfort.

The connection between mother and infant is formed and continually reinforced through sensorial contact, which includes gazing, smelling, tasting, hearing, touching, rocking, feeding, playing, and vocalizing (James, 1994, p. 3). Physical containment of the infant when in distress is also an important component of touch in attachment and aligns with Winnicott's holding environment. Touch derives from letting the infant feel the warmth of the mother's skin. The infant senses that mother is good and holds her goodness inside. Mother's goodness is maintained internally when she is near and when she is away. It is necessary for the child to achieve this important developmental skill before he or she can successfully join a preschool or spend significant time away from mother. Robbins (1994) reminds us that the bond in therapy is much like the early mother-infant relationship in that "it contains all the trusting qualities of an early mother-child relationship where the basic mode of communication is one of a soft touch or perhaps a sweet sound" (p. 32).

Mother's softness and warmth creates a place of comfort for the infant that is a tactile/sensory experience and initially not so much perceived objectively as "this is mother." The integration of visual images and tactile bodily experiences is something that is learned, "it has to be discovered that the breast that is seen is the same as the full, warm softness *felt* in the mouth and the warm, smooth surface that meets the fingers…" (Wright, 1991, p. 57).

Smiling

"What, in purely behavioral terms, on the level of the smile, is mutual reinforcement, [and] in experiential terms, on the level of communication, is mutual affirmation" (Wright, 1991, p. 12). Mutual affirmation exhibited through smile and resulting "positive affect-setting," structures the environment for an exchange of joy and confident expectation of the relationship.

Figure 3.1   "Me smiling, I'm happy."

Below is an example of a positive affective response to "How are you feeling today?" The following drawing by a 4-year-old boy (Figure 3.1) may be the result of a positive affective environment in which the boy's healthy sense of self was allowed to develop.

The infant recognizes that the mother is available and will not let the child become emotionally overwhelmed. A child who is overwhelmed may not explore and feels less confidence in his or her ability to interact with new objects. The mother's emotional availability and capacity for empathic responses to the child's needs are essential. Needs fulfillment leads to a sense of feeling safe and protected and makes exploration beyond the proximity of mother possible. Confident expectation promotes a climate that validates the child and creates a place where he or she feels unrestricted and available for new experiences (James, 1994, p. 3). Parental encouragement validates experience through exploration of the child and facilitates separation and individuation, a concept researched by Margaret Mahler (1979). When new environments and situations occur, however, the mother may revert to old established patterns from the early relationship with her own mother. The mother's emotional or physical availability may be restrained or absent, presenting a less-than-optimal environment for attachment. "Unavailability at moments of need conveys the message that neediness and vulnerability are shameful and embarrassing emotions, which should not be articulated or acted upon, a message that also is likely to foster avoidance of closeness in its recipient" (Whiffen, 2003, p. 390).

Sensitivity to the Infant's Cues

With the sensitive attunement of mother to the baby's cues, a mutual pattern of interaction builds which allows the baby some mastery over the environment. Mother–infant interaction is the foundation for later strengths in ego development, such as sense of self, anticipation of joy, and beginning mastery of the infant's own body.

> A good enough environmental provision in the earliest phase enables the infant to begin to exist, to have experience, to build a personal ego, to ride instincts, and to meet with all the difficulties inherent in life. All of this feels real to the infant who becomes able to have a self. (Winnicott, 1971, p. 304)

Optimal development occurs when the mother is emotionally available to her child in an empathic manner. In contrast, mother-infant interaction can also be intrusive and impinge upon the growing freedom and individuation of the child. Mahler and colleagues (Mahler, Pine, & Bergman, 1975) made an interesting point associated with the less-than-optimal environment. They described how children who seemed overpowered by the mother in the earlier symbiotic phase tended to keep their distance from her once they had the opportunity to do so. They also observed children who seemed to have had

too little close and satisfactory handling in the earlier subphase of individuation. These children seemed reluctant to part from their mothers and found
emotional and physical distance to be something that was threatening and
thus, avoided. An effective balance between closeness and distance is a negotiated skill between the mother and infant and one that is never static.

Self Emerges Through Meaning

Experiences with mother and other people and things begin to take shape
after further development of perceptual skills. A set of representations based
on feelings, memories, and consequently, assigned affects emerge based on
shared experiences in the infant's environment. Repeated actions reinforce
meaning. New perceptions take on new meanings and eventually, feelings
become attached to certain events. The result is a new understanding of
the world and people. This circular response paradigm originated with the
mother. She created the first sense of comfort and caring. Most "other" experiences are based on the initial pattern of reciprocity that grew within the
mother-infant partnership (James, 1994, p. 67).

A child's sense of self emerges in the attachment relationship. Ideally, the
child learns he or she is competent, worthy, interesting, and able to communicate needs as well as influence other people. The mother "gives permission"
to the baby to look outside of the mother-infant dyad for added experiences.
However, the mother continues to mediate and control the experiences outside
of the dyad by imposing limits. Limits placed on the infant's activities are communicated and imposed in a thousand ways. The infant is still free to look, but
may act only within assigned restrictions, which helps to control impulses.

An infant who is encouraged to explore the outer world of other objects
will engage and disengage within the environment to suit his or her attention
and energy needs. This action gives infants the first opportunity to regulate attention and pursue experiences shared with the mother. Regulation
of attention means that the infant is initially experimenting with control of
emotions, which contributes to ego strength and signifies a certain level of
developmental skill and adaptation. The mother first creates the physical and
emotional "holding" and then allows the child to move, play, and interact with
other objects. The infant maintains the internal confidence that mother is still
there when needed, will provide the necessary comfort and then "let go" once
again. Securely attached children tolerate separations with less distress allowing more time to explore the environment.

The sensitive "dance" of emotional attunement and availability is not intrinsic in each human being, but a part of a known and often unconscious pattern of
interaction. Mothers from troubled backgrounds can be good mothers, but conscious efforts towards new sensitive approaches to their child may be in order.
Outside services and interventions for mothers and their children may serve to
heighten awareness, reveal strengths, and offer other models of mothering.

The child's need for secure early attachments was not always recognized. John Bowlby (1988) was an early pioneer of attachment theory. Bowlby believed that attachment theory has the potential to make enormous contributions to the understanding and treatment of emotional distress. He was a man of vision, and it has taken us a long time to fulfill his prediction. More than 30 years after the publication of his three volumes on attachment and after Mary Ainsworth's seminal work on mother-infant attachment, we are just beginning to apply attachment theory to the understanding and treatment of clinical problems (Whiffen, 2003, p. 389).

John Bowlby established the basic view from which we may determine the meaning of our relationships. He believed that the child built up an internalized nurturing prototype that gave him or her the capacity for self-help and letting others help. Bowlby was significant in raising the awareness that adults also need reliable and caring relationships in order to maintain psychological health, as do children.

Mary Ainsworth (Ainsworth, Blehar, Waters, & Wall, 1978) developed experiments using mother and child dyads in the "Strange Situation," an experiment in which mother and child were separated and then reunited. Ainsworth assessed the child for quality of attachment, determined by responses from the separation. This assessment is still used today. Mary Mains, who continued the work of Ainsworth, was interested in the personal narrative in therapy. Main's research that combined narrative ideas and attachment theory created transformative possibilities using personal stories that contributed to the study of resilience (Holmes, 1996). Resiliency refers to a "marked ability to recover from or adjust easily to misfortune or chronic life stress—that is, adaptation despite challenging or threatening circumstances" (Osofsky, Hann, & Peebles, 1993, p. 112). Resiliency contributes to ego development and is connected to the quality of object relations. It is one of many innate biological factors in the individual child. Resiliency is a protective factor that acts as a buffer against emotional trauma.

Separation–Individuation

Margaret Mahler (1979) recognized the steps necessary to move beyond the mother-infant dyad towards greater individual independence when differentiating from mother. Settlage (1992, cited in Kramer & Akhtar, 1994) stated:

> Differentiation involves a sorting out of oneself from the mother in the early process of separation, and the initiation of the process of becoming a unique individual human being. This process is conceived to include further separation–individuation within the later childhood, adolescent, and adult stages of development. (p. 22)

The child is moving emotionally and physically away from the mother–infant constellation when he or she is able to hold the concept of mother internally. The child now feels safe enough to continue briefly without her.

Object Relations

Object relations theory is closely associated with attachment. It emphasizes important human relationships, particularly those earliest in life, which are a prototype of patterns for interacting with others. Robbins (1987) speaks of the foundation of object relations, the "'object' in object theory refers to the who and what in which a person's libidinal energy is invested" (p. 66). Object relations theory focuses on the capacity for intimate connections with others that begins in the mother-infant dyad and then ripples out to other people and things. Other object investment becomes essential for the child's potential growth. Fairbairn (1954, cited in Framo, 1982) proposes that the need for a satisfactory object relationshop represents an essential life good.

"The internal object relations function as a kind of template that determines one's feelings, beliefs, expectations, fears, wishes, and emotions with respect to important interpersonal relationships" (Horner, 1991, p. 8). Representations of the self and those around the child develop very early through reciprocity during the first three years of life. "Objects" supply knowledge to the child, which he or she assimilates into his or her developing relational structure. The infant then recognizes his or her competency and ability to form and maintain close relationships in the world beyond mother. Flaskas (2002) also discusses the psychoanalytic concept of therapist as both subject and object and extends this thinking to the "therapeutic relationship in systemic therapy ... that the same to-and-fro movement happened in the therapist's use of self" (p. 183).

Both of these conceptual frameworks helped to humanize psychoanalytic theory by speaking of the importance of what happens between mother and child. Positive experiences build a positive sense of self. Occasional failures in the relationships may serve to strengthen the child's ability to seek out and maintain connections. Failures serve the ego as long as they are infrequent and not intense. Overwhelming the vulnerable young child may break the connection with the object. The mother can learn a great deal from attempts towards reparation, because a change in the mother's approach may lead to a new level of sensitivity to the child and, consequently, strengthen the attachment. This is one important outcome of mother-infant therapy.

THE IMPORTANCE OF ATTACHMENT THEORY IN TREATMENT

Studies (Barnard, Morisset, & Spieker, 1993) have shown that "primary prevention" may avoid developmental problems attributed to environmental conditions such as poverty, lack of education, and social and personal resources. Primary prevention requires structuring the environment to change the overall conditions that may be damaging to the individual(s). The idea is to make changes when a possibility of injury, disease, or abuse may occur before it actually happens. This is an advanced step in injury control and harm reduction. There may be emotional consequences for the child who is temporarily sent to alternative care, particularly during significant separation-individuation periods of 18 months to over 3 years. Below is the artwork of a child placed in therapeutic preschool whose mother was working hard to have her children returned after social services placed the children in foster care because of neglect (Figure 3.2). The young boy was language impaired, but was able to eloquently express his longing for his mother (encapsulated in the inner circle; his younger infant brother is seen at the bottom with "fingers and toes"). The family successfully reunited after 6 months in therapy.

Many mother-infant programs provide an interactive environment conducive to active engagement with the child. Studies confirm that mothers who had a positive past tend to engage their own infants on a greater variety of levels than mothers with a disturbed past (Bowlby, 1988). Psychoeducational modalities, such as direct teaching, demonstration, and information on positive parenting can help mothers identify detrimental parenting practices. Therapists can teach parenting skills through modeling and direct instruction during joint therapy sessions (Fraiberg, 1980). In the therapy process itself, there is a significant interchange within the world created by the mother-

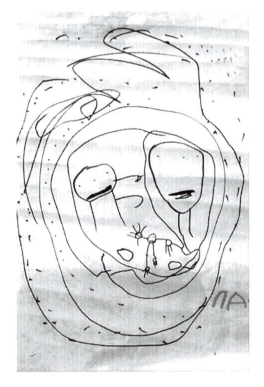

Figure 3.2 Young preschool boy, infant brother, and mother.

infant and therapist. A strengthened relationship takes place through alliance, therapeutic frame, and other circumstances of the therapy. This, in turn, allows trust to grow and offers the opportunity for change. The mother and infant attachment styles are observed in early parenting programs. Further assessment may indicate that assistance is necessary in order for a secure attachment to be established.

CONTEMPORARY FAMILY THERAPY

Family Systems Theory

Family systems theory is a departure from more traditional methods of therapy in that it takes the perspective of the overall family structure and acknowledges that each family member has an impact on the others. A change in one family member will require a change in others within the family context. Mark Worden (1999), who writes about family therapy, believes that attachment is a relational process. Worden and other family therapy theorists take into account the social milieu in which close relationships develop. Family therapists have recently renewed their look at classic attachment theories, which help to examine patterns of relating among family members. Winnicott (1971) advocates important ideas about early relationships that have contributed to family therapy. There was a shift with Winnicott's work in the understanding of the human being that went from a "one to a two person psychology" and offered a foundation for object relations. This explains why we examine the mother-infant dyad and try to understand the growth and responses of mother and child within this system. A systemic look begins with the mother-infant interaction and attachment outcomes and closely aligns with contemporary family therapy systems model.

A new interest in the intersubjective and interpersonal perspectives has emerged in Western therapy concepts (Flaskas, 2002). James Framo (1982) believed that "characteristics of individuals are peculiar to their context or system and can best be explained by analyzing the system, not just the individual" (p. 7). "Attachment theory offers the therapist an understanding of couple and family systems. Attachment theory is an integrative perspective. It is a systemic theory that focuses on behavior in context and patterns of communication" (Whiffen, 2003, p. 9).

Flaskas (2002) maintains that theorists should "allow the space for theory diversity in enriching family therapy knowledge and practice," and she now looks for "resonance with systemic themes...." in psychoanalytic concepts (p. 175). Postmodern theorists have moved to a more circular understanding of the mother-infant dyad in the context of a relational system. The circular context regards each person's behavior within the system and that "everyone's behavior impacts everyone else" (Worden, 1999, p. 6). Likewise, Holmes (1996) maintains that the therapist is part of the system when working with the family and, therefore, does not "intervene" or act upon the family system, but functions within it as another object.

The therapist may act as "assistant autobiographer" (Rycroft, 1985, cited in Holmes, 1996, p. 18) in helping the mother (infant) become more aware of the authentic mother-infant relationship of the present, not the defensive or recapitulated relationship from the mother's past. "Current attachment research is beginning to link the capacity to develop coherent narratives about attachment experience with the possibility of transforming attachment patterns" (Flaskas, 2002, p. 175). Change in the nature of attachments occurs by listening to and working with the narrative created by the mother. The mother's narrative may be a prediction of the story she is now creating with her own child. However, sometimes those with troubled pasts do not have adequate words to express their story because of their developmental level or the use of repression as a defense. The therapy itself need not rely on words; the expressive therapies are particularly suited for those who cannot find their narratives exclusively through verbal expression.

Social Influences

Social constructionists think about knowledge that gives meaning through constructed social interaction, such as in the family system. Construction of the family "truth" emerges through its members, who form meaning about things that guide their perceptions of the world. A "narrative" or personal story develops of each life and the family system as a whole.

Attachment conceptualized in family therapy takes into account not only internal qualities of the mother and child, but also processes that materialize externally in relationships outside of the dyad. Beyond the family constellation, a larger system influences the mother and infant as well as other family members. Lev Vygotsky (1896–1934), believed that humans live in a dynamic environment and theorized that competencies grow from interactions between skilled and less skilled members, such as in a family. The more skilled individuals help guide the less skilled. A sociocultural view takes into account the growth of the child through repeated influences of the structure in which the child lives (Berger, 2003). The mother-infant dyad is a part of a larger system that involves sociocultural, biological, and developmental influences.

ADOLESCENT MOTHERS

Adolescent pregnancy has become a major social problem in the United States and has increased within certain communities during the past decade. Young Black women under the age of 15 are particularly at risk (Osofsky et al., 1993). Risks include short- and long-term psychological, economic, and social factors. These risk factors affect both the infant and the mother and, consequently, future generations of children.

Adolescent pregnancy and motherhood creates potential problems for the mother and child. "… researchers find differences in the quality of parenting given by teenage mothers as compared to adult mothers" (Teen Parent Child Care Quality Improvement Project, Florida Partnership for School Readiness, 2001). There are adolescents who have the skills to parent adequately. However, studies have shown that many adolescent girls are not physically and emotional ready to be wholly responsible for a small infant. What makes this so? Psychoanalyst Peter Blos believed "adolescent individuation is the reflection of those structural changes that accompany the emotional disengagement from internalized infantile objects" (cited in Akhtar & Parens, 1991, p. 202). Additionally, "teenage mothers … are likely not only to lack knowledge, but to be poor and less well educated, to have lower self-esteem, to have more conflicted relationships in their own family of origin, or lack the stable support of a husband, and to place other competing needs above those of the child" (Bromwich, 1997, p. 63). Shirley Riley (1993) writes of the hurdles of the adolescent phase of development, "[the adolescent's] exposure to sex, violence, drugs, and temptations of every sort, as well as to domineering and aggressive peer group pressures, are all compressed in a time warp that allows for little if any integration or resolution of adolescent tasks" (p. 3).

Individuation and separation issues are working concurrently with the adolescent mother and her infant, both needing to attach and then separate in order to individuate. This can be a confusing order of development with parallel separation–individuation processes. Peter Blos (1967) recognizes that the adolescent goes through a natural "second individuation" much like that of the 18-month-old child. He states that "without a successful disengagement from infantile internalized objects, the finding of new, namely, extrafamilial love objects in the outside world either is precluded, hindered, or remains restricted to simple replication and substitution" (p. 164). This means that a truncated or unsuccessfully negotiated individuation from early objects, due to early motherhood, keeps the adolescent mother in a kind of "limbo" of separation issues.

One of the definitions of the adolescent development is the search for identity, which often includes isolation from those from which she is trying to individuate. This may interfere with allowing the space for the infant to search for self—when the mother's journey is far from complete. When this includes distancing from the ever-demanding infant, further development of the child may be derailed. Regression, at least occasionally, is normal for an adolescent. At this time, she is also managing the intense and often fluctuating regression of her child, particularly around the age of 18 months, a time identified as the rapprochement crisis (Mahler et al., 1975). Rapprochement is a phase where mood swings, ambivalence, and tantrums emerge after a relatively calm earlier phase of development. Rapprochement denotes that the child is aware of advanced developmental skills, but is also aware of the relative lack of control over the environment. The adolescent mother experiences a similar feeling of lack of control. The outcome may be a volatile mix between mother and child. Raising a child can be a challenge when the mother is the recipient of over-whelming responses from her child. This is particularly difficult when the ado-lescent mother is engulfed in her own rapprochement phase. The adolescent's early emotional connections with her mother may have formulated a pattern of future disturbed relationships embedded in the rapprochement phase.

Adolescent mothers have a high rate of depression, which may endanger the infant's success towards communication. Depressed mothers tend to be less "tuned in" to their infants, reducing the child's ability to exert any influ-ence on the mother. Mothers who talk to their children facilitate language acquisition in the child. Attachment therapy, which encourages active engage-ment of the mother and infant, may increase the likelihood of movement beyond the depressive stance to a more active interpersonal engagement. Improved resiliency may also be an outcome of therapeutic intervention with the mother and infant.

Primary and early intervention programs for adolescent mothers have proven to be effective. Social support of teen mothers is associated with maternal competence and gratification in the maternal role (Mercer, Hackley, & Bostrum, 1984). Studies have shown that primary prevention attempts to avoid developmental problems attributed to certain environmental situations such as poverty, as well as lack of education and social and personal resources for the single parent family of mother and infant. Artwork surrounding the theme of family relationships and taking care of one's self evoked an intense artistic response from a young woman who was struggling with her child and her memories of her own childhood (Figure 3.3).

Figure 3.3 A young woman struggles with her child and memories of her own childhood.

ATTACHMENT THEORY AND ART THERAPY

Many programs described in the literature provide educational and creative opportunities for parents to work with their young children. Lucille Proulx describes programs in Montreal, Canada, which included individual therapy, parent-child interaction, art therapy, and play therapy. Within mother-infant group therapy, art, play, movement, and music provided a foundation of communication and interaction (Proulx, 2003).

Jacquelyn Gillespie (1994) discusses object relations and the use of art therapy with mothers and children. "Art therapy partakes to an unusually great extent of the kinds of affective interactions that were part of that early mother-and-child experience" (p. 4). She reminds us that to remain effective, the art therapist should feel at ease with the "potential space" when the mother and child make art. The art therapist is not making the art with the mother and child, but is sharing the experience. This dynamic is much like the mother who watches carefully as her child explores, ready to provide nurturing or guidance if necessary, but allows the child to search independently, to learn about things on his or her own.

Elizabeth Muir (1992) (cited in Proulx, 2003, p. 25) aligned psychoanalytic approaches to a mother-infant program that trained the mother to respond only upon the child's active exploration. This would heighten the sensitivity of the mother to the actions of her child, enabling further investigation and manipulation of her surroundings.

Nicole Roy (1999, cited in Proulx, 2003, p. 25) describes her work using art therapy with high-risk pregnant mothers who had identified their adult attachment problems. Ellen Nelson-Gee (1994) adopted an expressive therapy approach within a therapeutic nursery school in which she modeled consistency. She discusses her role as therapist and that her patient "must learn that she can trust me to be consistent in my demands so that she may learn to be consistent in her reactions to these demands" (p. 303). Reliable interventions helped this young girl learn about herself.

Judy Rubin (1978) conducted joint mother-child group art sessions at intermittent intervals and found the groups offered assessment and therapeutic advantages. Rubin discovered that a shared creative experience for the mother and her child might help them find a new form of communication.

Beverly James (1994) wrote about a program that furnished services for an adolescent mother and child. She recognized the importance of providing for the mother's unmet needs within the program, while trying to increase sensitivity to her infant's actions and communication. "When working with single adolescent mothers, I attempt to balance the needs of mother and child to facilitate the building of their relationship" (p. 116). When the unmet needs were addressed, the mothers became more accessible to their infants, and the relationship between mother and child strengthened. James (1994) was sensitive to the necessity of a secure base for the mother so she could feel free to express herself. The mother can acknowledge past experiences, and with guidance and encouragement, focus on her relationship with her infant. So, in a sense, unmet needs were addressed twofold within the mother/infant group.

CREATIVITY OF MOTHERS AND INFANTS

Play and Art

"There is no such thing as a baby.... If you show me a baby you certainly show me also someone caring for the baby ..." is Winnicott's famous remark (cited in Holmes, 1996, pp. 2–3). It reminds us that the baby does not exist or develop alone, but only within a mother-infant partnership. Winnicott determined the importance of the playful and creative relationship that develops between mother and child. He referred to the intermediate area where playing takes place as "potential space" (p. 196). Within this space is a capacity for creativity. In this space the child engages in a "significant interchange with the world," a shared procedure in which enrichment alternates with making sense of the world of objects.

Winnicott believed that "the intermediate ... is the area that is allowed to the infant between primary creativity and objective perception based on reality testing" (Winnicott, cited in Holmes, 1996, p. 319). There is a significant interchange in the world created by the client and therapist, through alliance, therapeutic frame, and other conditions of the therapy. This, in turn, allows trust to grow. Winnicott believed that the roots of an individual's creativity are through the mother-infant relationship. Winnicott stated: "To be creative a person must exist and have a feeling of existing, not in conscious awareness, but as a basic place to operate from.... Creativity, then, is the retention throughout life of something that belongs properly to infant experience: the ability to create the world" (Winnicott, 1986, pp. 39–40). Play, in John Bowlby's terms, is only possible when an infant is free of threats to its attachment; this echoes Winnicott, who states that play can only occur in situations of trust that allow relaxed exploration of the environment. Play itself helps to sustain the illusion of the mother's presence because it "celebrates, and in a sense recreates the original creative interchange with the world that the mother had first made possible" (Wright, 1991, p. 77). Plach, a music therapist (1996) states:

> ... certain types of mental health problems can inhibit the individual's willingness or ability to engage in age-appropriate play activities. For example, symptomology in the individual experiencing major depression might include low levels of energy and motivation, rigidity in physical appearance and thought process, and an inability to see or experience situations as pleasurable. To help combat these symptoms in a group setting, the leader can introduce a series of play therapy activities in session. (p. 59)

While in play, a sensitive and attuned mother responds to the infant's gestures for connection and allows her to disconnect when needed. Disconnection can be healthy because it permits further development of the infant's sense of self. This primary level of communication is mostly unconscious. Emerging feeling states between mother and child help the child define the sense of "self." The concept of "self" refers to the combination of "ego and internal objects in a unique, dynamic relation that comprises the character and gives a sense of personal identity that endures and remains relatively constant over time" (Scharff & Scharff, 1992, p. 7).

Mother-infant therapy helps facilitate the intermediate, playful area between mother and child through provision of art, music, and movement activities. These allow the mother to experience, with her baby, the richness of the activities and media. "Very young children need to explore the material world by handling things physically. Exploration of many media is therefore valuable at this age" (Kramer, 1971, p. 22). Programs that include infants do not so much involve art making of the child as a separate study because of the age of the participants. Therapists can focus, however, on the attachment of the mother and child and the possibility of strengthening the ties through shared creative experiences. The mother can be more "in-tuned" to her child through means of shared action. Spontaneous art expressions need to be adapted in most activities because of the limits of the child's cognitive and developmental capabilities. Nevertheless, very young children and their mothers can achieve satisfaction from engaging in playful media exploration. Rubin (1999) discusses the parameters of art therapy and states, "art and play are closely related, since playfulness is part of any creative process, and there is considerable artistry in good play therapy" (p. 69).

Creating initially involves feeling something and then seeing what it might be (Wright, 1991, p. 55). The mother initiates the feeling part with the child during play established between mother and child. Sensations first appear and then perceptions, which later connect to feeling states that evolved between mother and child during activities and everyday life. Feeling states are readily fashioned with joy and occasional subtle frustration while interacting, and both feelings are essential to build a positive mastery over the environment. Visual images become meaningful through trial and error exploration and perceptions of what certain things mean. The integration of visual images and tactile bodily experiences is something that must be learned. "Like everything else in our world, it must be laboriously built up through experimentation and exploration, a collating of visual and tactile experience over time" (Wright, 1991, p. 57).

Joint mother–infant experiences enable both to move from being in a disorganized and uncreative state to creating crude and primitive artwork, and finally to channel and express their inner worlds effectively. A key factor in the healing process is the need and ability to discharge and then channel difficult feelings into artistic expression. Continued use of this sharing of potential space in art and therapy fosters the growing relationship between mother and child. Personal writing, media explorations, and the mother's own artistic expression gives concrete examples, allowing the mother an opportunity to return to the piece and modify with a new awareness. Therapists may also observe a strengthened attachment between mother and child. However, the relationship is not static in that mother or child may change sensitivity and therefore, the pattern of relationship in order to create new meanings.

Attachment, Expression, and the Mother–Infant Creative Growth Program

A therapeutic creative arts approach to mother–infant interaction was developed for the Southern Illinois University at Edwardsville Art Therapy Counseling Program through a Head Start associated with the university. The goal of the program was to help adolescent mothers who attended a nearby high school find special ways to connect with their infants by engaging in creative activities. The mothers also created art of their own.

The purpose of the Mother–Infant Creative Growth Program was to provide a series of play, drama, art, and other activities that were sensory-motor based and encouraged mother-infant interaction. Mother–infant interaction sets the stage for enhancement of many developmental milestones, which include attachment, object relations, and communication. The program was developed and initiated during the 1998–1999 school year. The targeted population was selected from a teen parent program at a nearby high school. Services in this program supplied a laboratory-learning environment for first-year graduate students' fieldwork in the art therapy program. The art therapy curriculum emphasized a strong theoretical foundation in attachment theory and object relations. Fieldwork offered students the opportunity to put theory into practice by serving as cotherapists in the group.

The overall goals of the program were:

1. To enhance the development of children from birth to three years of age, within the context of their families and communities, in the areas of physical social, emotional, and intellectual development and to build a foundation of security, self confidence, and strength that enables them to achieve future successful social relationships and continued learning and development. (Head Start Mission Statement, 1998)
2. To provide a group environment for identification, development, and enhancement of the mother-infant relationship through sequentially and developmentally appropriate activities, which included preart, art, play and drama.
3. To complete a creative journal that documents the growing relationship of mother and child through activities and images that are created by the teen mother with her child.

4. To accomplish creative activities outside of the center and group which promote further development of parenting skills, continuity of care, and enhancement of the mother-infant relationship.

STRUCTURE OF THE PROGRAM

Mothers who participated in this program were attendees in an in-school program that allowed them to attend high school while they spent time with their infants during the school day. The mothers participated in educational programs about their baby's growth and attended other classes with their baby. Adolescent mothers and their infants were chosen for the program based on the mother's interest and availability after school. The program was limited to mothers and their children because the in-school program allowed only mothers and children. All of the children ranged in age from three months to one and one-half years. Signed consent forms explained that photographs would be taken of the mother and her baby for the mother's journal, but that confidentiality would be maintained. The mothers and children attended group for one and one-half hours for five consecutive weeks. Head Start provided transportation of the mothers and children to a designated facility.

During an initial interview, mothers identified the expectations and wishes that they had for their infants. Mothers answered initial questions such as "3 things I really like about my baby" and "3 things I would like to do with my baby in this group." This information was used to develop certain activities for the group. An informal assessment during the interview offered insight into the interactions between mother and child. Documented responses from the interview were placed in the mother-infant journal that was provided for each mother. The mothers were encouraged to think about the relationship with their child as a special form of partnership.

Stations for each creative activity were set up around a large room. Two of the stations had a mat used for playing with toys or movement to music. A large full mirror and a "boom box" were placed on one mat and toys and containers were placed on the other mat. The other two stations had tables for making art. One art station offered a variety of simple art media for the children with mother's help and the other station was the mother's mural.

Description of the Media or Activities at Activity Stations

Toys   Careful attention was given to choosing stimulating, age-appropriate toys. Soft toys that could be used by mothers to throw, roll, and play grasping games were purchased. Nonchoking toys for the children had pieces that could be placed in and out of containers. All toys were washable. An array of toys positioned around the activity mats allowed for better access for the children. The mothers and children went to the stations of their choice.

Media Purchasing media presented a challenge. Graspable, nontoxic, and washable media were carefully chosen. Media included paints in containers with sponge tops, large brushes with short, thick handles, colorful clay, and nontoxic glues that were easy to apply with the mother's help. Washable markers with broad tips and paper large enough to withstand wide, swinging scribbles added to the likelihood of free expression for both mother and child. Tables for the program were flat with washable tops. Mothers often had the children on their laps when helping them with the media, sometimes resulting in shared creative efforts (Figure 3.4).

Mothers were also encouraged to work on the floor mat with their children in order to allow maximum movement. Children explored the media while mothers were given information regarding developmental limitations and strengths. Mothers were strongly encouraged to dress their children (and themselves) for messy fun.

Music and Movement Music was played during the group session. Although not music therapy per se, music was used in "the accomplishment of therapeutic aims. Specifically, music as it applies to group therapy can be defined as the use of music or music activities as a stimulus for promoting new behaviors in and exploring predetermined individual or group goals in a group setting" (Plach, 1996, p. 3). Juliette Alvin, in her book entitled *Music Therapy* states:

Figure 3.4 Mother and child clay sculpture.

Even in its most simple forms, music is evocative of sensations, moods, and emotions. It can reflect the feeling of the moment or change it by its presence. It can also increase the actual mood and bring it to a climax or dispel it. (Alvin, 1975, p. 60)

When listening to music, the mothers often wanted their favorite style of music—hip hop and rap, even when more "child friendly" music was available. The children's ability to move and respond to the music was limited by the mothers' excited responses to their own choices. Initially, most of the mothers withdrew attention from the child during this music and movement activity and seemed engrossed in their own pleasure. Reengagement was occasionally necessary. Mothers were encouraged to respond to their favorite music in safe and gentle ways with their children. Additional choices of music were offered with examples of how to move, soothe, and sing to their babies. The mothers seemed to redirect their attention to how they could move with either kind of music, creating a playful atmosphere. Attention and sensitivity to baby's emotional and physical responses to the music were pointed out and encouraged.

The Journals   The use of the journal emerged as an important feature of the mother-child activities each week. Three-ring notebooks served as a journal for the mother to record ideas and indicate thoughts about her infant, which incorporated activities, free expression, and "fill-in-the-blank" type of responses. Entries included the infant's first experimentation with media, suggested writing subjects, and what types of activities were suitable for the child's physical, cognitive, and emotional level. Below is an example of one journal activity.

Make a print of your baby's hands on the provided page with paint. Carefully place your baby's hand into the paint. Try to get an even amount of paint on the hand. You may want to use a paper towel to pick up the excess paint. Carefully place your baby's hand on the page. Repeat this with the other hand. Clean off your baby's hands with the provided towels and water. Show the prints to your baby and say "what a good job you did." Any left over paint will come off after another bath. After you have printed the hands, fill in the words. This hand print page will go into your folder to share with your baby. (Parashak, 1998, p. 5)

The mothers wrote about positive and creative things they hoped their children would do with their hands. In the future, the mother could use the journal to discuss the hopes she had for her child.

The journal included additional related activities that mothers and children could complete together at home. Journals had a transitional function for the mothers, concretely representing their love for their infants, holding creative expression of art and writing, and then taken home for further use.

Inserted blank pages persuaded additional creative activity. Each of the printed activities was simple and emphasized the use of readily available media and objects for play. For example, as a termination activity, mothers were provided with a precut form of a hand puppet from felt. Mothers added on eyes, mouth, and other facial features. The accompanying activity sheet explained:

> Take the puppet and play with your baby. Pretend to talk with your baby with the puppet on your hand. Use a different voice as you make the puppet talk with your baby. Try to get your baby to smile and play with you. Since we are saying goodbye as a group today, use your puppet to say goodbye with your baby. (Parashak, 1998, p. 7).

A simple approach to the playful interaction reduced the mothers' apprehension and increased their participation.

Mothers were encouraged to think about creating an environment that was safe for their children. Additionally, attention to their children's bodies and protective maneuvers were taught through the movement process. For example, when the child moved about on the activity mat, the mother was encouraged to move down to the child's level and examine the placement of the toys. Did the play area seem safe for the child? Were the toys graspable? What could the mother do if the child did not show interest in the objects placed on the mat? The mothers examined possible options.

Mother's Mural   The following is an example of the mother's art experience:

> We are making a "MOM MURAL." This mural will have pictures and words about what it means to be a MOM. Add pictures and words of your own to the mural. You may draw your own pictures and words or use the magazine pictures and words. Talk to your baby when you work on the mural. Point to pictures and say "Look at the face of this Mom," "This Mom is smiling!" or "Say hello to the baby; good work!" Smile and talk to your baby when you do this—the baby will believe that this is a game. Repeat. (Parashak, 1998, p. 4)

The spontaneous "mother's mural" became an established activity in the weekly group.

Food   A component of this program was to provide healthy snacks for the mother and child. Because the program occurred after school, most of the mothers were hungry by the time they arrived to group. Mothers of the very young infants brought their own baby food, thus eliminating any problems about what to feed the youngest children. Other snacks offered were bananas, fruit juice, and crackers. Sustenance for both mother and child provided a metaphor of the nurturing mother and mother/therapist.

Photos   Therapists took photographs of each mother and child pair. The mothers responded to the photos with excitement and seemed to value the images taken. Photographs placed in the journal served as a beginning point for other creative activities in the group and at home.

CLINICAL VIGNETTES

Many outside issues emerged in group. The babies' fathers were often a topic of conversation. It was discovered that one baby's father was dating another mother within the group and tension quickly emerged. This potentially harmful drama quickly went beneath the surface and was avoided by both parties throughout the rest of the group. The baby's mother seemed to distance herself emotionally from the group, but was later encouraged to participate at a comfortable level. Efforts on the therapist's part to address the situation were avoided. This was one drawback in the group; the group's culture was well established before the mothers even arrived at the program. Group dynamics around this issue could have been harmful to the overall goals of the program. However, the mothers turned their attention to the activities of the program and the interactions with their babies, rather than dwell on the conflict within the group. Defenses such as sublimation enabled the mothers to use the art, as with the mother's mural, to channel more unacceptable feelings that arose within the group.

The mothers often had unreasonable expectations of their children's developmental abilities in the area of creative expression. The mothers were knowledgeable about when their children would get their first tooth, take their first steps, and when to receive certain shots. However, the mothers had little knowledge of realistic expectations of their children in areas of media use, representational skills, and the joy of "playing and making a mess." Mothers had to be taught how to set up a creative environment for their children and to allow exploration to occur without too much impingement on their part. Mothers were given information about playing creatively with their children at home.

Intervention during the creative activities was occasionally necessary in order to keep the mother focused and therefore the child. If a struggling mother did not have an interest in the materials, it was difficult for her to engage with her infant. The therapist offered redirection and whenever possible, fresh approaches to her infant. Therapist, mother, and child often played at each one of the stations. The therapist and graduate student co-therapist modeled getting down on the floor mat and playfully interacting with the children.

Activities were child focused, but it became evident that the mothers had a hunger for artistic expression and wanted to use the materials with and without their children. They explained that they did not have a chance to take art at school because of their other responsibilities.

The mother's mural became very popular with the group members (Figure 3.5). Images from magazines and drawings were collected and glued down on a large piece of butcher paper. The chosen pictures included both "loving and caring" pictures representing their idealized maternal feelings and those that represented the more challenging maternal moments. New photos and drawings appeared weekly. When looking over their work, the mothers were encouraged to discuss some of their ambivalent feelings. The adolescents resonated with each other when discussing shared concerns, such as behavior problems, isolation from friends, and their occasional lack of patience. All members of the group, including the therapist, were empathic to the challenges of motherhood and offered additional support and encouragement.

After Group

Mothers were encouraged to interact creatively with their children when away from the group. Information was offered about how to set up a "kid's art cor-

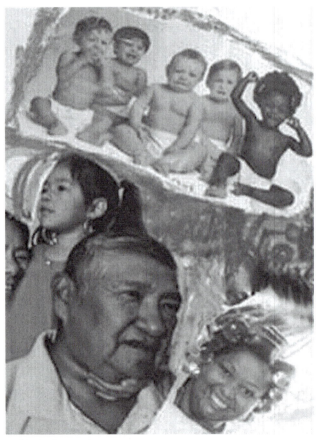

Figure 3.5   Mother's mural.

ner" in their homes, mostly around the kitchen table. Mothers were encouraged to place inexpensive, age-appropriate media in a box or cabinet, safely allowing the children access when they were a little older. Mothers discussed where they could create a gallery of their children's artistic work and how they could make an inexpensive portfolio for art creations. All activities could be adapted for the home environment.

DISCUSSION

The purpose of the Mother–Infant Creative Growth Program was to provide a series of play, dramatic, pre-art, and art activities, to encourage mother–infant interaction from birth to 3 years of age. Pre-art materials are defined as those that are sensory based and appeal to individuals operating on earlier developmental levels such as the sensorimotor stage of development. This is also a crucial consideration for other populations, such as individuals with developmental delays or autism. Susan Aach-Feldman and Carol Kunkle Miller (1987) advocate assessment of the developmental level of the child using the following techniques: (a) nondirective work with traditional and pre-art media, (b) structured work with traditional art media, and (c) structured work with pre-art media (p. 255). Media that offer a better chance of success will reduce anxiety of the mother and consequently, the child.

Play and art stations were set up so that availability of toys, music, and media were incorporated into the interventions. Structured activities promoted the creative "potential space" between mother and infant, but unique approaches were always encouraged. Positive interactions were attempted and immediately reinforced when observed by the art therapist. Mothers received suggestions for supplemental activities to do at home with their children. However, the mother and child's personal way of approaching creativity was strongly emphasized.

> If [the art therapist] trusts the power of imagery and the healing forces within her client, she will allow her groups to flow naturally and organically. She will trust herself to be sensitive to their emergence so that she can foster their exploration and encourage the growth potential of the art therapy group and its individual members. (Wadeson, 1980, p. 158)

Structured activities provided a foundation for many developmental milestones, which included attachment, object relations, communication, and language acquisition in the child. Mutual engagement, mirroring, close body contact, soothing music, and joyful play encouraged mothers to engage with their children in a pleasurable manner. There was an observed increase of positive attachment behaviors among several children in the group through additional exploration of the environment.

Transference and countertransference issues are particularly sensitive when working with mothers and infants. The mothers bring into the therapy old feelings about their own mothers that have a powerful influence. The influence ripples out to their children and to the therapist. Countertransference responses of the therapist can be both an avenue for wisdom and a minefield of potential trouble. Art therapists should thoughtfully evaluate their own emotional reactions and notions about the mother and child. It is essential that the therapist not try to become "the better mother" or one who will rescue the child. Processing transference and countertransference responses ought to be included in weekly supervision meetings between therapist and assistant.

The Mother–Infant Creative Growth Program provided beginning fieldwork experience for graduate art therapy students. Many students had not experienced working with another individual as closely as the mothers and their infants. The students learned about the special relationship, challenges, and needs of the mother–infant dyad. Questions emerged with the students' new awareness. The following is the poignant reflection written in a group process note of one of the assisting graduate students:

> The art project for this group was creating hand and foot prints. The moms were to paint the kid's hands and feet and print them onto paper, which would later be inserted into their notebooks. They were then asked to write things that they would like their children to do with their hands and feet in the future. When [the therapist] asked the moms to come up with some ideas for this, I noticed that they had a hard time seeing past the near future with their children ... I found myself feeling sort of sad [and] wondered what the [mothers] planned for their own futures.

FUTURE WORK AND SUGGESTIONS

"Infants and toddlers learn by experiencing the environment through their senses (seeing, hearing, tasting, smelling, and feelings), by physically moving around, and through social interaction" (NAEYC, 1989, p. 5). Sensory approaches in programs written for young children should include activities and equipment for a wide range of development interest and abilities. Adults in the programs should also be prepared to adapt any activity for special needs of the children. A strong education in child development is essential for a therapist who wants to work with the mother–infant dyad.

Programs that attempt to strengthen the parental bond should include the father if possible. Teen fathers infrequently attend therapy programs with their infants. However, surveys suggest that many teen fathers want to be more involved in their children's lives" (Phares, 1999, p. 84). Proulx (2003) discusses a group of fathers and their three-year-old offspring. "Through father-child dyad art therapy, play and discussions, fathers learned about the needs of their toddlers and became more sensitive to them" (p. 25). Research has also confirmed that the mother–infant therapy can be effective if the mother communicates to the father what she has learned and together they implement new parenting patterns (Phares, 1999).

Videotaping would be helpful for mother–infant groups in that it allows a visual review of the session. Mothers, armed with new information regarding infant development, could make determinations for themselves and their babies. Mothers may want to revise the goals that they established earlier in the group based on what they view on the tapes. When videotaping a group, it would be important for the therapist to inform clients before the group and figure ways to incorporate the camera so that it does not act as an intrusion in the treatment alliance. However, taping the mother–infant can stand as a testimony of the deeper engagement of the partnership of mother and child through effective interventions.

REFERENCES

Aach-Feldman, S., & Kunkle-Miller, C. (1987). A developmental approach to art therapy. In J. Rubin (Ed.), *Approaches to art therapy, theory and technique* (pp. 251–274) New York: Brunner/Mazel.

Ainsworth, M. D. S., Blehar, M. C., Waters, E., & Wall, S. (1978). *Patterns of attachment: A psychological study of the strange situation.* Hillsdale, NJ: Lawrence Erlbaum.

Akhtar, S., & Parens, H. (1991). *Beyond the symbiotic orbit: Advances in separation-individuation theory* (pp. 189–208). Hillsdale, NJ: The Analytic Press.

Alvin, J. (1975). *Music therapy.* New York: Basic Books.

Barnard, K., Morisset, C., & Spieker, S. (1993). Preventive interventions: Enhancing parent-infant relationships. In C. H. Zeanah Jr. (Ed.), *Handbook of infant mental health* (pp. 386–401). New York: Guilford Press.

Berger, K. (2003). *The developing person through childhood and adolescence* (6th ed.) (pp. 48–51). New York: Worth Publishers.

Blos, P. (1967). The second individuation process of adolescence. *Psychoanalytic Study of the Child, 22,* 162–186.

Bowlby, J. (1982). *Attachment* (Vol. 1, 2nd ed.) (pp. 371–374). New York: Basic Books.

Bowlby, J. (1988). *A secure base: Parent child attachment and healthy human development* (pp. 1–19). New York: Basic Books.

Bromwich, R. (1997). *Working with families and their infants at risk* (pp. 50–70). Austin, TX: Pro-EPublishers.

Flaskas, C. (2002). *Family therapy: Beyond postmodernism, practice challenges theory* (pp. 1–10). New York: Brunner Routledge.

Fraiberg, S. (1980). *Clinical studies in infant mental health.* New York: Basic Books.

Framo, J. (1982). *Explorations in marital and family therapy.* New York: Springer.

Gillespie, J. (1994). *The projective use of mother-and-child drawings: A manual for clinicians* (pp. 1–26). New York: Brunner/Mazel.

Harlow, H. (1958). The nature of love. *American Scientist, 54,* 244–272.

Holmes, J. (1996). *Attachment, intimacy, autonomy: Using attachment theory in adult psychotherapy* (pp. 3–33). Northvale, NJ: Jason Aronson.

Horner, A. (1991). *Psychoanalytic object relations.* Northvale, NJ: Jason Aronson.

James, B. (1994). *Handbook for treatment of attachment: Trauma problems in children* (pp. 2–67). New York: Lexington Books.

Kramer, E. (1971). *Art as therapy with children* (2nd ed.) (pp. 1–24). Chicago: Magnolia Street Publishers.

Kramer, S., & Akhtar, S. (1994). *Mahler and Kohut: Perspectives on development, psychopathology and technique* (pp. 22–64). Northvale, NJ: Jason Aronson.

Mahler, M. (1979). *Separation individuation: The selected papers of Margaret S. Mahler* (Vol. 2) (pp. 119–165). New York: Jason Aronson.

Mahler, M., Pine, F., & Bergman, A. (1975). *The psychological birth of the human infant* (pp. 39–109). New York: Basic Books.

Mercer, R. T., Hackley, K. C., & Bostrum, A. (1984). Social support of teenage mothers. *Birth Defects, 29,* 245–290.

Merriam-Webster's collegiate dictionary (1994) (10th ed.) (p. 241). Springfield, MA: Merriam-Webster.

NAEYC (National Association for the Education of Young Children). (1989). Developmentally appropriate practice in early childhood programs serving children from birth through age 8 (ed. Sue Bredekamp) (pp. 5–6). Washington, DC: NAEYC.

Nelson-Gee, E. (1994). Play, art and photography in a therapeutic nursery school. In A. Robbins (Ed.), *A multi-modal approach to creative art therapy* (pp. 275–303). London: Jessica. Kingsley C. Publishers.

Osofsky, J., Hann, D., & Peebles, C. (1993). Adolescent parenthood: Risks and opportunities for mothers and infants. In C. H. Zeanah, Jr. (Ed.), *Handbook of infant mental health* (pp. 106–119). New York: Guilford Press.

Parashak, S. (1998). Mother-Infant Creative Growth Program. Unpublished manuscript (pp. 1–17). Phares, V. (1999). *Poppa psychology: Fathers in present-day families* (pp. 1–95). Westport, CT: Praeger Publishers.

Plach, T. (1996). *The creative use of music in group therapy* (pp. 3–10). Springfield, IL: Charles C. Thomas.

Proulx, L. (2003). *Strengthening emotional ties through parent-child dyad art therapy* (pp. 20–33). London: Jessica Kingsley.

Riley, S. (1993). Rethinking outpatient adolescent art therapy treatment. In E. Virshup (Ed.), *California art therapy trends* (pp. 1–15). Chicago: Magnolia Street Publishers.

Robbins, A. (1987). An object relations approach to art therapy. In J. Rubin (Ed.), *Approaches to art therapy* (pp. 63–74). New York: Brunner/Mazel.

Robbins, A. (1994). *A multi-modal approach to creative art therapy* (2nd ed.) (pp. 30–36). London: Jessica Kingsley Publishers.

Rubin, J. (1978). *Child art therapy: Understanding and helping children grow through art* (pp. 151–161). New York: Van Nostrand Reinhold.

Rubin, J. (1999). What is art therapy? In *Art therapy: An introduction* (pp. 61–84). Philadelphia: Brunner/Mazel.

Scharff, J., & Scharff, D. (1992). *Scharff notes: A primer of object relations therapy* (pp. 3–10). Northvale, NJ: Jason Aronson.

Teen Parent Child Care Quality Improvement Project, Florida Partnership for School Readiness. (2001). Florida State University Center for Prevention and Early Intervention Policy [Online]. Retrieved April 15, 2005, from http://www.cpeip.fsu.edu/project

Wadeson, H. (1980). *The dynamics of art psychotherapy* (pp. 141–167). New York: John Wiley.

Whiffen, V. (2003). What attachment theory can offer marital and family therapy. In S. Johnson & V. Whiffen (Eds.), *Attachment processes in couple and family therapy* (p. 393). New York: Guilford Press.

Winnicott, D. (1958a). Anxiety associated with insecurity. In *Collected Papers: Through paediatrics to psycho-analysis* (pp. 97–100). New York: Basic Books.

Winnicott, D. (1958b). Transitional objects and transitional phenomena. In *Collected papers: Through paediatrics to psycho-analysis* (pp. 229–242). New York: Basic Books.

Winnicott, D. (1968). Communication between infant and mother and mother and infant, compared and contrasted. In What is Psychoanalysis? Review of Psycho-Analysis 16:89–100.

Winnicott, D. (1971). Mirror-role of mother and family in child development. In P. Lomas (Ed.), *The predicament of the family* (p. 114). New York: Routledge.

Winnicott, D. (1986). Living creatively. In R. Winnicott, R. Shepherd, & M. Davis (Eds.), *Home is where we start from* (pp. 39–40). New York: W. W. Norton.

Worden, M. (1999). *Family therapy basics* (pp. 6–9). Pacific Grove, CA: Brooks/Cole Publishing.

Wright, K. (1991). *Vision and separation between mother and baby* (pp. 12–57). Northvale, NJ: Jason Aronson.

CHAPTER 4

Bowen Family Systems Theory (BFST) and Family Art Therapy

CHRISTINE KERR

INTRODUCTION

During my doctoral studies, I was introduced to the family therapy theory of Dr. Murray Bowen by my professor, Dr. Marc Pilisuk, at the Saybrook Graduate Institute in San Francisco, California. As I began to research Bowen's family therapy constructs, I was profoundly moved by the comprehensive quality of his theory. Bowen's emphasis on *family of origin exploration, differentiation of self, family projective process, and the multigenerational transmission process* proved to be central in my training as a therapist. The reverberating echo that appeared in all of Bowen's writings was that nothing in a family happens in isolation.

Bowen (1972) was the first family therapist to publicly discuss the use of his own family of origin in his work (Anonymous, 1972). This public examination of both his nuclear and intergenerational families became a pivotal point in his own professional career. In his public presentation, Bowen discussed his own family environment, noting that he was often handicapped with his family's unfinished business. According to Bowen (1972), his family's emotional cutoff as well as fusion appeared to increase his family's emotional reactivity from one generation to the next. The rationale for openly speaking about his personal family history was Bowen's (1976, 1978) conviction that the therapist and/or client could not be free from early family experiences by denying their significance or ignoring them. He argued that early childhood could repeat in the present, perhaps with different characters or perhaps in different contexts. His goal for his clients was to increase their level of differentiation.

As a family therapist, Bowen was committed to understanding his own blind spots in order to increase his objectivity when working with clients.

Bowen (1972) stressed, in this *family of origin* presentation, the need for the therapist to remain objectified, as family exploration was certain to "stir up the pot" of old resentments and unfinished business. According to Nichols and Schwartz (2004), "the resolution of emotional reactivity in Bowen's family was as significant for his work as Freud's self-analysis was for psychoanalysis" (p. 54).

The insights gleaned from Bowen's own therapeutic journey gave credence to my beginning awareness that although we may leave our families of origin physically, we rarely leave them emotionally. As a seasoned art therapist, planning to engage in family art therapy, I was cognizant that my therapeutic competence would be rooted, not only in clinical psychology, family therapy concepts, and the technical aspects of the visual arts, but also in my willingness to address personal blind spots that had been forged in my own family of origin. Therapeutic blind spots relate directly to most therapists' self-concept and their ability to successful meet their clients affectively and developmentally. As Jourard (1976) aptly notes, "a therapist cannot himself lead a person to a freer existence than he himself has attained" (p. 40).

This chapter introduces the professional accomplishments of Bowen's eminent career. From a pedagogic perspective, key terms of Bowen's theory will be elaborated and explored. In the later portion of this chapter, other family therapy authors who have contributed to Bowen's theory will briefly be discussed, such as Framo (1992), and McGoldrick and Gerson (1985). In the final section of this chapter, family of origin work will be introduced as a teaching tool for future family art therapists. This final portion of the chapter will highlight a graduate art therapy student's verbal and artistic journey as he explores his own family of origin.

OVERVIEW OF DR. MURRAY BOWEN'S CAREER

Murray Bowen (1972, 1976, 1978) was a dominant force in the family therapy movement. Traditionally, the evolution of family therapy has not formally been associated with psychoanalytical theory or practice. However, Murray Bowen's family theory (1972, 1976, 1978) is more closely associated with psychoanalysis than other schools of family therapy. The influence of psychoanalysis and its emphasis on abreaction of repressed material, gaining insight, and the goal of achieving an individuated self, appears to have shaped Bowen's theoretical orientation. But, in the shaping of Bowen's theory there appears to be an evolution of psychoanalysis from Bowen's epistemological perspective. Bowen states:

> Back in the 1940s, I believed that Freudian theory would not be able to move towards science without evolution, which would connect living matter with the universe, the sun, the earth and all living

things ... When it was necessary to develop a term to describe my theory and the therapy, I chose Family Systems Theory and Therapy, to imply it was a combination of the family, as seen through the lens of some Freud, plus evolution, integrated by natural systems theory. (Kerr & Bowen, 1988, p. 383)

From a psychodynamic perspective, Bowen (1972, 1976) emphasized the historical and causal factors that relieve symptomatology for individuals within their nuclear and intergenerational families. However, Bowen moved beyond the dominance of psychoanalysis in understanding severe psychopathology, when he conducted research at both the Menninger Clinic and the National Institute of Mental Health.

Late in 1940, Bowen began to develop a comprehensive approach to understanding family dynamics when he was a psychiatrist at the Menninger Clinic (Kerr & Bowen, 1988; Nichols & Schwartz, 2004). Bowen became intrigued with the "exquisite emotional sensitivity" between schizophrenic patients and their mothers (Nichols & Schwartz, 2004, p. 76). Thoroughly trained in psychoanalytic principles, Bowen (1972) began to notice that this unique mother-child dyad displayed alternating cycles of closeness and distance. This dyad was intensely "sensitive to shifts in emotional tension between mother or child" (Nichols & Schwartz, 2004, p. 142). Instead of viewing this emotional reactivity as the result of a psychoanalytical symbiotic attachment, Bowen (1972) hypothesized that this relationship was a manifestation of an "exaggeration of a natural process, a more intense version of the tendency to react emotionally to one another that exists in all relationships" (Nichols & Schwartz, 2006, p. 77). Second, Bowen observed that in the schizophrenic family, alternating patterns of closeness and withdrawal resulted in an *anxious attachment* between family members. This emotional phenomenon deregulated self-control as well as increased cognitive dissonance for both the mother-child dyad and the overall nuclear family. Consequently, Bowen began hospitalizing entire families that contained a schizophrenic member. "He observed that these troubled families were prisoners of the way that they behaved together. The hallmark of these emotionally stuck-together, or fused relationships was a lack of personal autonomy" (Nichols & Schwartz, 2004, p. 77).

The National Institute of Health project ended in 1959, and Bowen began working with clients and families at Georgetown University. At this time, the field of family therapy was evolving rapidly, and new treatments for couples, families, and individuals became varied and as diverse as each theorist's perspective on what constituted a functional or dysfunctional family (Kerr & Bowen, 1988).

FAMILY OF ORIGIN EXPLORATION

The Bowenian School of Family Therapy and Theory has become one of the most influential approaches based on *family of origin exploration* (Bowen, 1972, 1978). The historical precedents for this exploration reflect the psychoanalytical philosophy of freeing the individual from the entanglements of the past that are restricting the individual's life in the present. Although Virginia Stair's (1971) family of origin work and personal growth interventions predate Murray Bowen (1972), Bowen was the first family therapist to develop a complete theory about intergenerational emotional reactivity and how this may affect the physical, social, and emotional functioning of the nuclear family. According to McGoldrick & Gerson (1985), "Families repeat themselves. What happens in one generation will often repeat itself in the next, i.e., the same issues tend to be played out from one generation to generation, though the actual behavior may take a variety of forms" (p. 5).

What is *family of origin work?* Family of origin work is defined as a person's attempt to examine and change the patterns of interaction that occur in his or her family. The client is asked to examine the structural, relational, and functional psychodynamics of his or her family. As this exploratory process begins, the overall process can be viewed from both a *horizontal perspective* by examining one's own immediate family, as well as from *a vertical perspective* that examines the family intergenerationally (McGoldrick & Gerson, 1985; Nichols & Schwartz, 2004).

Family of Origin Work and Emotional Triangles

As the client analyzes his or her immediate nuclear family from a structural perspective, the client is asked to review the current functional degree of affective interplay among family members. This analysis often measures the number and degree of perceived anxieties within one's own family members. According to Bowen (1978), Kerr and Bowen (1988), and McGoldrick and Gerson (1985), this structural analysis allows the client the ability to measure "the flow of anxiety emanating from current stressors in his/her family as it moves through time, coping with inevitable changes" (McGoldrick & Gerson, 1985, p. 6). Bowen (1976) notes that anxiety can easily develop within family relationships as the family moves through developmental life stages and encounters stressful situations. In times of stress, family members may often recruit other family members to reduce anxiety and gain stability within a specific dyad. This is Bowen's (1976) concept of *triangulation*. When two people are in conflict, one person attempts to draw in a third person to stabilize the system (McGoldrick & Gerson, 1985, p. 7). Triangles occur because it is usually difficult for any two people in a relationship to focus just on themselves and maintain a one-to-one relationship. Although triangulation may superficially lessen the emotional tension between two people, the underlying conflict is not addressed. In most families triangles increase rather than reduce problems between two people.

Again from a structural perspective, the client explores the degree of closeness and or distance among family members from previous generations. Closeness or distance among family members is a result of the way that families manage anxiety and emotional reactivity. ("At one extreme are family members who are very distant from or in conflict with each other. They have emotionally cut-off from their family of origin. "Often these individuals display limited resources in emotional responsiveness and consequently, experience fusion in marriage; where they typically project all their needs on to each other") (Nichols & Schwartz, 2004, p. 79). At the other end of the spectrum are those families that are fused and overdependent on each other. Families that are fused have a limited repertoire of emotional relatedness due to their "stuck-togetherness." The family's emotional boundaries are rigid and closed. Fused families have great difficulty adapting to life-cycle developmental changes. Bowen (1978) noted that the greater the emotional reactivity, intergenerationally, the greater the degree of dysfunctional *fusion* and or *emotional cut-off* among family members. The greater the emotional cut-off, the greater the lack of differentiation there will be in the nuclear family.

Fogarty (1976a) expanded on Bowen's theory of *closeness* and *distance* and spoke about the phenomenon of the *distancer-pursuer* in marital functioning. Pursuers are those types of individuals who require emotional intimacy. Distancers often feel suffocated when intimacy is actively sought from another. Fogarty (1976a) argues that people are usually attracted to others who have the same need for closeness or distance; most people inevitably manage to find a comfort zone.

However, when the comfort zone becomes unbalanced, families often express their anxieties through reversal of roles or greater alignment with either being a pursuer or distancer. Inevitably, this creates stress on the relationship and the individual's ability to maintain emotional equilibrium. Although some individuals are capable of reversal of these types of roles, there is usually a pervasive family blueprint defining these specified roles from one generation to the next.

A functional analysis of the family of origin explores the various roles of each family member as parents, siblings, grandparents, and extended family. The client then examines the equality of emotional relatedness of each family member. These levels are identified as the client attempts to investigate and measure reciprocal patterns of relating and functioning that are thought to have been transmitted historically down through the generations. Bowen (1976, 1978) hypothesized that this inventory allows the client the opportunity to evaluate the degree of the family's overall *intergenerational projective process*. The multigenerational projective process is thought to transmit anxieties, themes, myths, rules, and emotionally charged issues from one generation to the next. The impact of this emotional transmission inevitably equates to the client's degree of personal differentiation.

Differentiation of Self

The concept of *differentiation of self* is the cornerstone of Bowenian family theory and therapy. Bowen considered this process to be one of the basic tasks that must be completed to achieve adulthood and to establish intimate and satisfying relationships. The concept of differentiation of self describes two distinct but intrarelated processes. One process describes something that occurs within an individual and the second process describes the way people function together in a relationship. Differentiation of self as an internal process refers to the capacity of the individual to be aware of differences between their intellectual and emotionally determined functioning (Bowen, 1972, 1978; Nichols & Schwartz, 2004). The individual should be able to make a choice about the degree to which each type of functioning governs his or her behavior.

Differentiation of self also describes the way that people function together in relationships. In this sense, it refers to the variation between people in terms of their ability to maintain emotional autonomy within a relationship system. Within this construct, Bowen (1972, 1978) hypothesized the relevance of a psychological separation of intellect and emotions between family members and the independence of self from family members. The greater the individual's differentiation of self, the better able the individual is to respond objectively to the family and to keep from being drawn into dysfunctional patterns with other family members. The highly differentiated individual does not demonstrate a high degree of fusion (overinvolvement with others) nor does the individual cut-off from others to minimize anxiety. The differentiated individual has the ability to take an "I position" and to think, feel, and act independently, regardless of pressure from others.

It is important to note that Bowen (1976) believed that every individual has some degree of unresolved emotional attachment to his or her family of origin. Often the level of individuation is determined by the child's relationship with his or her immediate family, as well as with members of other generations. Consequently, how an individual develops emotionally within a family is intrinsically based on a multigenerational process (Bowen, 1976).

In a functional family, individual family members differentiate from one another emotionally. The degree of differentiation is passed down from generation to generation. Based on this assumption, Bowen (1972) argues that families are tied in thinking, feeling, and behavior to transactional sequences of family functioning. In dysfunctional families, these transactional sequences spring from symptomatic thoughts and actions from previous generations. Those individuals with the strongest affective connections (or fusion) are the most vulnerable to emotional stress from their family of origin. The degree to which an individual develops a separate sense of self, independent from the family, is directly correlated with the individual's ability to resist being over-whelmed by emotional reactivity (Kerr, 2000b).

The Family Projective Process and Multigenerational Transmission

The family projective process and multigenerational transmission describes the influence of prior generations on the emotional development of offspring. Bowen (1978) and Kerr and Bowen (1988) argue that the levels of differen-tiation of the parents in a nuclear family are projected onto their offspring. Emotional fusion of the parents creates instability and conflict, where the par-ent often triangulates a selected child. This emotional fusion predisposes this child to unhealthy attachments. As noted by Nichols and Schwartz (2006), "this attachment is different than caring concern; it's anxious, enmeshed con-cern" (p. 80). The more the child becomes enmeshed with the parent, the less the child is able to function in an independent fashion.

Multigenerational transmission describes the process where the child most involved in the family's emotional life moves towards a lower level of differentiation, while the child least involved moves towards a higher level of differentiation. Often parents or extended family who are overly involved in family tradition, myths, and rules project their own concerns onto their offspring. When children cannot think autonomously or they feel emotionally constrained, they often are compelled to either conform to or rebel against family traditions (Nichols & Schwartz, 2004).

JAMES FRAMO: FAMILY OF ORIGIN WITH COUPLES

Many of Bowen's ideas have been incorporated into the work of James Framo (1979, 1992). The core of Framo's theoretical approach is the relationship between early childhood intrapsychic conflicts and their expression in cur-rent adult transactional interaction. Framo's (1992) intergenerational approach is best defined as emanating from the object relations theory of Fairbairn (1952). Framo (1992) contends that the need for satisfying relationships with some object (i.e., another person) is a fundamental motive for life. From an object relations standpoint, the individual unconsciously introjects memories of loss or unfulfillment from early object loss during childhood into adult relationships. This process of introjection affects the ability of the individual to achieve adult intimacy.

Framo (1992) argues that treatment is based on helping couples to become aware of these unconscious and unresolved object losses from their family of origin. By therapeutically investigating the client/couples family of origin, the couple is able to uncover interlocking pathologies from their past. Often these pathologies contribute to the ability of the individuals in the client/couple to build satisfying relationships with their respective spouses, immediate fam-ily, and offspring.

Framo's Therapeutic Interventions in Couple's Treatment

Framo developed a three-phase treatment approach that provides couples with a therapeutic process to deal with family of origin conflicts. Specifically, this three-phase program includes (a) therapy with the couple, (b) couples group therapy, and (c) family of origin therapy. Couples in treatment are required to write an intergenerational family biography.

The goal in the initial phase of treatment is to help the couple reestablish a more empathetic and positive communication style. Assisting the couple in increasing their individual capacity for empathy towards each other may increase spousal trust. It is the skills of the family therapist that also aid in empathy training with the couple in treatment. It is the goal of the family therapist to assist both the husband and wife to understand each other as separate individuals as well as partners. In the initial sessions, the therapist asks relevant questions to diagnostically seek information about (a) the problem(s) with the marriage, (b) previous therapy and results, (c) prior marriages, (d) each spouse's family of origin, (e) commitment to sustaining the marriage, and (f) the level of each spouse's motivation for change (Framo, 1992).

In couple's group therapy, the couple is encouraged to develop new and, hopefully, more adaptive communication skills. The family therapist highlights negotiation training. As in any therapeutic group treatment, the experience of listening verbally, participating, and processing group information can be a powerful experience. Group counseling may increase interpersonal output, where group members provide feedback to each other. Group counseling also allows the individual to gain relief through verbalizing frustrations. Group counseling creates a sense of universality where each member of the group may learn that he or she is not alone. Importantly, couple's group counseling allows each member the opportunity to engage in family reenactment. This is often an unconscious process where individual group members relive their families of origin in the context of the group process (Framo, 1992; Yalom, 1980).

In the third phase of treatment, Framo (1992) encourages the couple to make contact with their respective families of origin. Each spouse is asked to contact their families of origin, which often includes parents and siblings. Sessions are held with the family therapist, the individual spouse, and the couple's respective family members. Framo (1992) believed that having the other spouse present in these sessions would distract from the overall purpose of correcting the perceived problems in the individual spouse's intergenerational conflicts. The goal of this final phase of treatment is to have an "emotional corrective experience" (Framo, 1992, p. 62). These meetings often allow the spouses to get to know their parents as real people. The individual spouses have the unique opportunity to share important thoughts and feelings with their respective families. Often the spouse is given the opportunity to express forgiveness or to tell their individual parents that they were loved.

The individual clients may increase differentiation (Bowen, 1972) from their families of origin, which may lead to enhanced relationships with members of their families of origin, as well as within their current family. Framo (1992) feels the importance of these curative outcomes cannot be overstated.

Framo and Family Art Therapy

How does the family art therapist work within this model? During the early phases of treatment, the family art therapist may request, "conflict drawings" to augment the information gathering process. Family of origin conflict drawings (Kerr, 2000b) made by the couple in treatment may be a powerful statement of perceived intergenerational stress. These drawings may be used later in treatment to aid in the couple's exploration of their own family of origins.

According to Kwiatkowska (1962) an individual may often use a drawing to reveal certain underlying reports of family problems. For many clients it is easier to relate to marital problems through the art process, which may provide a personal vehicle for the visual statement to become a focus for discussion, analysis, and self-evaluation.

This couple was referred for treatment because of the husband's depression as well as his withdrawal from his wife and social peer group. At the initial session, the husband reported that he had begun to think of divorce and often felt helpless and hopeless. During this first session, the wife reported that her husband was "weak," indecisive, and "caved in to his mother." In this initial session, the husband was asked to draw the "perceived conflict" he was experiencing with his young wife. The client was also asked to think about the influence that his immediate family of origin might have on the presenting marital problems. In Figure 4.1, the husband quickly rendered this depiction of his reaction to his marital situation. He stated, "She's like my mother." His comments during the session noted his overdependence on his wife in many

Figure 4.1   Husband and visual depiction of his marital situation.

aspects of their relationship. He talked about being enmeshed with his wife and overly dependent on her financially. His responsibilities as a spouse were often superceded and compromised by his overcontrolling wife. "She won't let me do anything." He began speaking about a list of household responsibilities where he had failed to meet his wife's expectations. Last, the young man spoke about his wife's emotional dependence on her mother. When asked if the woman on the far right-hand side of the picture was his wife or his own mother, he hesitated and stated, "I really don't know."

The drawing (Figure 4.1) depicts the husband's anger towards his wife. There are visual indicators of entrapment. The heightened color usage and the windows being heavily blackened may suggest this. The perspective that is indicated in this drawing further suggests that his relationship is unbalanced; the couch is tilted and the wall hanging is drawn at a tilted angle (Hammer, 1958; Oster & Gould, 1987). The profile of this man's face denotes anger and frustration. The face being colored blue may suggest that he is internalizing his rage.

In following sessions, the husband was able to reflect back on this drawing. The family's stories unfolded. The husband spoke about the intense anxiety he had experienced as a child living with his mother. He spoke about his need to seek her approval and his mother's critical nature. The degree of emotional rejection he had experienced as a child appeared to overwhelm him. Over time, he was able to gain insight into how his current relationship with his wife in some ways mirrored his relationship with his mother. Conversely and perhaps more importantly, he was also able to realize that the therapeutic consequence of this unresolved conflict with early childhood attachments had impacted his current relationship with his wife.

MCGOLDRICK AND GERSON'S GENOGRAM

McGoldrick (1982) and McGoldrick and Gerson (1985) integrate Bowen's theory with various action-oriented techniques. They encourage families to use genograms for their own personal growth work. The family genogram looks at the intergenerational as well as current family constellation in a visual format. McGoldrick and Gerson (1985) ask trainees to look for parallel processes across client families and their own family.

From a transgenerational view of family therapy theory (Bowen, 1978), family therapists and family art therapists often use a genogram in the early assessment phases of family treatment. These diagrams allow the clinician the opportunity to map the family structure and to update the family picture as treatment evolves. In this task, which is easily translated to an adaptable art task, the family creates a genogram. Within family art therapy individual family members are requested to draw a circle. Each family member is then asked to place him or herself somewhere within the circle. Second, each family member is asked to draw a representation of all family members. These figures are placed on the paper either inside the circle or outside the circumference of the circle. Sometimes, clients will draw family members on the edges of the paper; even on the back of the paper.

Of particular interest in this type of family drawing are the patterns of relational distance that are depicted in the drawing. At one extreme, family circle drawings depict family members who are drawn very distant from each other. These types of drawings often occur when a family is in crisis. At the other extreme, are those drawings where there is little or no space between drawn figures. According to Bowen (1978), Carter and McGoldrick (1980), and Carter, McGoldrick, and Orfanidis (1976), when there is minimal distance among family members, this is defined as an emotional fusion. Often, emotional fusion is found in those families that are poorly differentiated. Symptomatically, these types of families are vulnerable to dysfunction. Notably, this dysfunction occurs when the level of stress or anxiety exceeds the system's capacity to deal with it (Bowen, 1978).

Family art therapists must be vigilant and selective in the use of the information gleaned from family art productions. As in any of the helping professions, the art therapist must determine the timing for sharing or using the exposed information. It is imperative that the family art therapist understands the twofold potential of the art experience. Family emotions are often intensified by the directness of the art experience.

Second, the art product produced within family art therapy treatment provides concrete evidence not only to the art therapist, but also to the family about their current level of functioning. It is necessary for the family art therapist to slowly develop a therapeutic alliance with the family. The family art therapist must be particularly aware of his or her empathic responses and the pitfalls of bias or personal projection.

Figure 4.2 shows a family genogram that was completed by a young woman, age 22, during the middle phase of family therapy with her family of

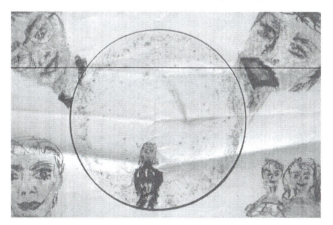

Figure 4.2   Family genogram

origin. By engaging in this circle–genogram, this young woman was allowed the opportunity to safely problem solve and weigh alternatives related to her feelings about leaving her home and seeking employment in a distant location. The youngest daughter of three, this young woman had experienced significant anxiety about leaving home. Though she had completed college, she had chosen to attend a college where she could still live at home. Developmentally she had experienced significant difficulty in attempting to move into a more independent adult lifestyle. Her attempts at differentiating from the family had been unsuccessful due to her parents unwillingness to accept her need to move away from the family.

In Figure 4.2 the young woman places her father, mother, siblings, and grandparents on the outside of the circle. Her self-image is depicted on the lower edge of the circle. From a relational perspective she appears small in comparison to how she views other members of her family. She stated during the family session, "they all talk at me … they are trying to invade the circle." The depiction of her mother in the upper right-hand side of the drawing suggests the daughter's statement that they "all are talking *at me.*" The mother image is attached to the boundaries of the daughter's circle. The daughter has drawn her mother's face with pronounced facial features. The mother's mouth is depicted in a garish manner, rigidly reinforced with a black marker. The other female figure, in the upper left-hand quadrant was the daughter's depiction of her maternal grandmother. Though this image is less garish, the daughter clearly views her grandmother as also being enmeshed with her. The daughter has drawn her grandmother also attached to the outer boundaries of her circle. Both the depiction of the mother's mouth and the grandmother's mouth have similar graphic emphasis. As noted by Hammer (1958) and Oster and Gould (1987), the emphasis on the mouth may suggest verbal aggressiveness. Bodwin and Bruck (1960) have noted that when drawn by adolescents it may suggest poor self-concept.

This drawing was pivotal in subsequent family therapy sessions. Noting the difficulty that this particular family was having with coping with the family life cycle change, this drawing served as a concrete example of episodic family difficulties. Also, this drawing was a clear indication of the lack of intergenerational differentiation among the female members of the family. As the family was able to process their *emotional stuck togetherness* as well as their anxious *attachment* as the offspring of the family moved away from the established family circle, the daughter was able to gain some insight into her own need for adult differentiation. Ultimately, she was able to successfully move away from the family without residual emotional consequences.

FAMILY OF ORIGIN WORK AS A TEACHING TOOL
FOR FAMILY ART THERAPY TRAINEES

Overview

To facilitate a greater awareness of the student's interpersonal and behavioral patterns, Hart (1982) argues for traditional family therapy training models that help students learn to separate feelings from thinking and to maintain a therapeutic stance of nonreactivity with future client/families. To meet this curriculum objective, traditional family therapy programs have often supported the exploration of "the person" of the therapist within training. In developing the "person" of the therapist, a growing body of research has indicated that "family of origin" (FOO) exploration as a curriculum and training tool may be particularly useful. Family of origin curriculum work is defined as personal growth exercises, where the trainee examines the patterns of interactions that occurred in his or her family. This family of origin model is based on the student's development of a family genogram of his or her family and the student interviewing his or her family over three generations. A family genogram is a curriculum tool where the student draws a family tree that records information about family members and their relationships over the last three generations (McGoldrick & Gerson, 1985). This visual record may not only assist the student in exploring family of origin issues, but also may aid the student in making beginning hypotheses about his or her family from multiple perspectives. Because the information on a visual art genogram is best understood systematically, the genogram additionally offers the student an overall visual gestalt of complex family patterns. Information gleaned from these interviews is brought into the class for supervision. The goal in this exploration is to increase the student's awareness of emotional blind spots. Recent literature in educational outcome and assessment of family therapy training programs has supported the inclusion of this technique (Aponte & Winter, 1987; Braverman, 1994; Duhl & Duhl, 1981; Kerr & Bowen, 1988; McGoldrick, 1982).

Family art therapy training also needs to address the importance of the family art therapist's self-concept as it relates to the therapeutic alliance with future client families. In the training of the family art therapist a family of origin curriculum training model was designed as a teaching tool (Kerr, 2000a). This teaching model was incorporated into the overall course content of family art therapy study at Long Island University C. W. Post Campus (Fontes, 1998; Getz & Prontinsky, 1994; Kane, 1996; McDaniel & Landau-Stanton, 1991).

Family of origin exploration is considered an optimal teaching tool to help the trainees examine the emotional and behavioral patterns of interactions occurring in the family in which the trainee was raised. When this examination is completed, it is argued that the trainee has a greater understanding of potential biases and blind spots. Trainee bias may impact negatively on the therapeutic alliance with future clients/families (Kerr & Bowen, 1988;

McDaniel & Landau-Stanton, 1991). Family therapy trainers have asserted that the overall family training process is enhanced when the family therapy trainee has examined and reconciled his or her own personal biases through a systematic examination of his or her own intergenerational family patterns (Aponte & Winter, 1987).

The Family of Origin Training Model

Within the classroom, personal growth development refers to training models that emphasize techniques that may increase the trainee's capabilities in forming and sustaining a therapeutic alliance with future clients/families by increasing the student's awareness of his or her self-concept. Aponte and Winter (1987), Kerr and Bowen (1988), LaMonica and Karshmer (1978), and McGoldrick (1982) argue that this training model should consist of teaching interventions that address the student's overall current interpersonal behavioral patterns. These personal growth experiences should therefore emphasize educational initiatives in the areas of (a) differentiation of self from the trainee's family of origin, (b) countertransference, and (c) the primary conditions for empathy, such as respect, warmth, genuineness, and self-disclosure. All of these areas may be quintessential in helping the trainee to better understand his or her self-concept interpersonally, intrapsychically, and affectively.

Bowenian Family of Origin and Personal Growth Training Model

The concept of "differentiation of self" from one's family of origin is the cornerstone of Bowenian family theory. Bowen (1976) considered this process to be one of the basic tasks that must be successfully completed to achieve adulthood and to establish a functional, intimate relationship with others. The growth that Bowen (1976) refers to is the individual's internal acceptance that he or she has developed an identity with values and perspectives that differ from those learned in early childhood, independently and regardless of pressure from others.

Family of origin work for the family therapy trainee supports the assumption that an integral part of the therapist's development must be to explore family of origin characteristics. The family therapy trainee should explore the impact these variables may have on current levels of differentiation by engaging in activities designed to increase the level of differentiation for the therapist (Kerr & Bowen, 1988; Schnarch, 1991; Titelman, 1987).

Countertransference Training and the Personal Growth Training Model

From an historical frame of reference, family of origin work may touch on the psychoanalytic concept of countertransference. Though based on a theoretical construct that focuses on the individual in analysis, countertransference and psychoanalytic theory support the analysis of transference for the trainee. Freud (1912) stated, "the psychoanalyst should undergo a psychoanalytical purification and become aware of those complexes of his own which would be apt to interfere with his grasp of what the patient tells him" (p. 16). Thompson (1950) defines countertransference as reaction patterns taken from the past and applied indiscriminately to present situations. Wilson (1981) states that countertransference has traditionally been understood to mean the therapist's inclination to transfer unconscious concerns onto the relationship with the client. In this sense, this process serves to fulfill the therapist's own needs and interferes with his or her ability to attend to the client or family's needs. Bean (1992) has defined countertransference as the therapist's living response to the totality of the client's emotional state at any moment. Training programs have an obligation to address issues of intrapsychic countertransference and interpersonal sensitivity for the developing therapist (Corey, Corey, & Callanan, 1998). This may assist the student in becoming a more useful therapeutic instrument (Kerr & Bowen, 1988).

Affective Sensitivity Training and the Personal Growth Training Model

One goal in the training of a family art therapist is to increase the quality of the student's level of interpersonal relating. Often this type of training focuses on the development of a student's understanding of the role of empathy in the helping professions. LaMonica and Karshmer (1978) have defined empathy as an understanding of the private world of the helper in terms of his or her feelings, attitudes, wants, and goals.

Empathy is a complex phenomenon that is frequently embedded in other processes. LaMonica and Karshmer (1978) note that empathy extends to: (a) the therapist's nonverbal behavior, (b) the ability to perceive the client's feelings, (c) active listening skills, (d) unconditional regard for the client, and (e) a therapeutic stance of openness and flexibility on the part of the therapist towards client/families. Bennett (1995) argues that empathy is an interpersonal process. Consequently, the multidimensional condition of empathy often results in an increase in the trainee's capacity for respect, warmth, genuineness, self-disclosure, and flexibility with clients (Carkhuff, 1969).

Outline of the Family of Origin Model Course Curriculum

Within the family art therapy course, the student interviews family members to critically review the current relational patterns among his or her immediate family constellation. The student is asked to interview one or more members of his or her own family of origin. They are asked to take notes on the interview and write a personal family history and profile of the information they have gleaned from the interview. The personal family history profile is approximately 10 to 15 pages. This requires that the student's writing be highly compressed. The goal of this assignment is to have the family art therapy student begin to look at his or her family in a new way, using the lens of major family systems concepts and particularly the concepts of Murray Bowen (1972). These interviews should focus on the following family themes (Saybrook Graduate School and Research Center, 1997).

Historical Continuities and Changes within the Student's Family of Origin
The student is asked to construct a family genogram over four generations. In
the interviewing process of the student's family, the student is asked to question his or her family on areas such as ethnic history, as well as key historical
and mythological themes from his or her grandparents or the student's parents. The student is asked to question his family of origin on what were the
themes, tasks, roles, struggles, and myths that make up his family of origin.

Structure and Dynamics of the Student's Family of Origin   The student
is asked to recall his or her own perceptions about the structure of his or her
family. What were the rules regarding power, authority, closeness, individuality, decision making, relating to outsiders, sexuality, etc.? How were personal
boundaries defined within the family of origin? What were the major triangles and family coalitions?

Different Realities   Within most families, it is sometimes striking how family members see things differently. Often different family members have different recollections or interpretations.

Family Evolution   A family moves through time and often experiences crisis. Individuals grow, change, and adapt in response to these events. The
student is asked to record through interviews, how his or her family of origin
has adapted over time and often in response to key developmental changes.
How has the family coped with crisis? Was the family able to grow and adapt
or perhaps did they resist change? How did the family differentiate and evolve
over the generations? What themes or struggles were passed on to the student,
and if relevant what themes and issues does the student suspect he or she is
passing along to his or her children?

Differentiation of Self and Sense of Self   The student is asked to explore a
sense of personal identity from his or her family of origin. How has this identity been carried over to the student's current family structure? What is the
student's network of intimate relationships? How did the student develop his
or her personal career choice? In what ways has the student's family history
made it difficult to develop a sense of self, and in what ways is the student still
enmeshed within what Bowen (1972) calls undifferentiated ego mass?

Family Art Therapy Assignment   In the final portion of this assignment,
the student is asked to make a three-dimensional visual art representation
of the summation of his or her findings. The use of a three-dimensional art
assignment easily lends itself to family therapy systems theory, as it enhances
the dimensionality of the artist's endeavor. In addition to the art assignments,
the art therapy student engages in class discussions, written notation, and in-
group and peer supervision.

Figure 4.3   Student family of origin exploration (©).

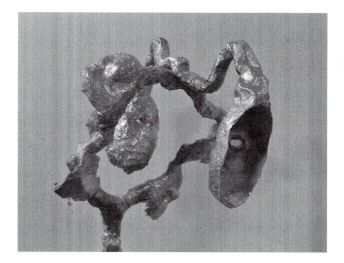

Figure 4.4   Student family of origin exploration: right-angle view.

Figure 4.5   Student family of origin exploration: three-dimensional view.

Figure 4.6   Student family of origin exploration: full view.

A Graduate Student's Response to the Family of Origin Exploration   In a family art therapy class, a graduate art therapy student began his family of origin exploration early in a fall semester. This portion of the chapter highlights the student's direct narratives from his family of origin assignment and his final art piece. Sam was an exceptional student. At the beginning of class in September, all students were encouraged to begin the process of interviewing their family members. Students were advised to develop interview questions, using the rubric that had been presented in the class syllabus. As noted in Bowen's (1972) personal family of origin exploration, there is often considerable time required for personal reflection, as the individual approaches and asks family members to cooperate in this process. To begin the family of origin process requires significant sensitivity in *how* to approach family members who are emotionally distant. As Sam writes:

> For the purposes of this study, I interviewed myself and four other family members including my nuclear family (mother Alice, father Mark, and brother Jack) and my father's sister Barbara. I initially had only interviewed three members of my family, but I decided only a week ago to involve Sue as well. I guess that I find my father's side of the family to be more mysterious and steeped in family struggles. I just never understood what went wrong in my father's family system and I yearned to understand a little better. I added my mother because I also realize that her input would be extremely valuable in regards to the overall picture that is my nuclear family system.

Family and Ethnic Heritage   Understanding a family's ethnic history is an intrinsic portion of the family of origin process. Ethnic and cultural history is often directly linked to the multigenerational transmission process. The multigenerational transmission process describes the influence of prior generations on the emotional development of offspring. Bowen (1978) and Kerr & Bowen (1988) argue that the levels of differentiation of the parents in a nuclear family are projected onto their offspring. Emotional fusions of the parents create instability and conflict, where the parent often triangulates a selected child. Sam begins to speak about his cultural heritage. He states:

> Let's start from the top. My brother and I know so little about where we come from that it is positively saddening. My brother only knew that he is Jewish-American. I at least knew that my grandparents originally came from Russia and Poland. The most startling piece of information came from mother. My maternal grandfather, Nathan, escaped to America after witnessing the murder of his parents when he was about 10 years old because of the wave of pogroms that swept through Russia in the early 1900s. He came to America to live with his much older sister in Brooklyn where he was to spend the rest of his life.

My maternal grandmother, Jean, moved to this country at about the age of 15 with her entire family from what was then part of Poland but is now Russia. Her family consisted of her mother, father, twin brothers, and one sister. They settled in Brooklyn where my grandmother was to spend most of her life until she relocated to Oceanside so that she could live closer to her daughters (my mother and her sister Phyllis). She is still alive and looks great for a woman in her mid-nineties! Nathan passed away close to 10 years ago, when I was an undergraduate in college. I have very fond memories of a kind, quiet man who was delighted by every little thing that his grandson (being me) did. I'm actually getting teary-eyed just thinking about him, but in a good way.

Themes, Loyalties, and Struggles   When an individual defines the themes, loyalties, and struggles within their family of origin, they often become aware that they experience difficulties in verbalizing their recollections. This was the case in Sam's written notation of this portion of the exercise.

My brother and I drew a blank with this question. All I could think of was that my grandparents were alive during the time of the Holocaust and even though they were not directly influenced by this atrocity, they must have felt scared by the very nature of such an event occurring during their lifetime. I wonder now that if this could be why my Jewish heritage has been so watered down. I was brought up with little to no emphasis on religion in my life, leaving me rather jaded and ambivalent about my own spiritual nature as it relates to Judaism. This is particularly relevant now that I am about to bring a child into the world. How will I raise my son or daughter?

The Art Process

The more I learned about my family, the less I realized I had ever known. I find it very upsetting that I've never cared enough to find out where I came from. I'm a fairly inquisitive individual and I guess that I'm more upset at myself than anybody else. But then I gathered information from my parents who, in turn, knew almost as little about their parents as I did, and that made it even worse.

The art became an outer reflection of an inner conundrum. Who am I? Where do I come from? What has made me the person I am today? If this class has taught me one thing more than anything else it's that I am who I am as a result of my family system. This process has been interesting, yet gut-wrenching to me. I feel empty, devoid of a rich family history, but oddly closer to understanding that I am. The analogy of the mirror is symbolic of this deep kind of introspection that I went through over the course of this semester. The faces around the edge of the mirror are representative of the four members of my nuclear family and how the face I see in the mirror (however distorted it may be at times) is a result of the dynamics of my family system. The red and blue eyes are symbolic of my distortion of reality over the course of my life. How long have I been looking at the world as if it were a 3-D movie instead of reality? The piece asks as many questions as it answers, but I feel that I'm finally on the right track.

Where I'm at Today

So how did all this affect the way I've turned out? I feel that my family system exists in a primarily environmentally sensitive paradigm. We've got our issues but we feel normal to me. There is a strong support system between us and we are open about our feelings to one another. My parents are extremely supportive and proud of my accomplishments. I have been able to open my rigid boundaries to my parents more and more (but not *too* much) as I came into my own. I think I needed to figure out who I was better before I could allow my parents into my world. I hope that I satisfactorily explained myself through this paper. I do feel that I know myself better as a result of writing it.

As I'm on the verge of being a father myself, this paper and class put a lot of things into perspective for me. I feel that I'm ready for this next step now, which is probably why I've been calm and collected so far, let's see how I am in May and June though! I understand the significance of subsystems, triangles, and boundaries and I'm going to try to keep everything aligned to the best of my ability. All I know is that if therapy ever becomes necessary, I'm dragging the whole family with me!

CONCLUSION

One's family of origin has a powerful influence. None of us grows and comes of age in a vacuum. Consequently, the impact and influence of where we came from is not restricted to childhood recollections. "Even if you put an ocean between you and your family of origin, or you never return home again, you will continue to re-enact the dynamics of your original family in any new family you establish" (Richardson, 1997, p. 1).

The works of Murray Bowen (1972, 1976), James Framo (1992), and McGoldrick and Gerson (1985) have all contributed important insights into the psychodynamic concepts of the family *and the ties that bind* (Richardson, 1997). Through adaptable art interventions, the family art therapist can augment this important process by allowing client/families to internally as well as externally visualize and document this journey. Second, the importance of family of origin work for the family art therapy trainee cannot be understated.

We strive as family art therapists to help our clients, intuitively knowing that we can only take them as far as we were willing to go ourselves.

REFERENCES

Anonymous. (1972). Toward the differentiation of self in one's own family. In J. Framo (Ed.), *Family interaction* (pp. 125–126). New York: Springer.

Aponte, H. J., & Winter, J. E. (1987). The person and the practice of the therapist: Treatment and training. *Journal of Psychotherapy and the Family, 3*(1), 85–111.

Bean, M. (1992). The poetry of counter transference. *Arts in Psychotherapy, 19*(5), 347–358.

Bennett, J. (1995). Methodological notes on empathy: Further considerations. *Advances in Nursing Science, 18*(1), 36–50.

Bodwin, R. F., & Bruck, M. (1960). The adaptation and validation of the Draw-A-Person test as a measure of self-concept. *Journal of Clinical Psychology, 16*, 427–429.

Bowen, M. C. (1972). Becoming a family therapist. In A. Ferber, M. Mendelson, & A. Napier (Eds.), *The book of family therapy* (pp. 61–64). New York: Science Hour.

Bowen, M. C. (1976). Principles and techniques of multiple family therapy. In M. P. H. Guerin, Jr. (Ed.), *Family therapy: Theory and practice* (pp. 388–404). New York: Gardner Press.

Bowen, M. C. (1978). *Family therapy in clinical practice.* New York: Jason Aronson.

Braverman, S. (1994). Family of origin as a training resource for family therapists. In C. E. Mursen (Ed.), *Family of origin applications in clinical supervision* (pp. 210–226). New York: Hawthorne Press.

Carkhuff, R. (1969). *Helping and human relations: A primer for lay and professional helpers. Vol. I. Selection and training.* New York: Holt, Rinehart, and Winston.

Carter, E. A., & McGoldrick, M. (1980). *The family life cycle: A framework for family therapy.* New York: Gardner Press.

Carter, E. A., McGoldrick, M., & Orfanidis, M. (1976). Family therapy with one person and the therapist's own family. In P. J. Guerin (Ed.), *Family therapy* (pp. 29–34). New York: Gardner Press.

Corey, G., Corey, M. S., & Callanan, P. (1998). *Issues and ethics in the helping professions.* Pacific Grove, CA: Brooks/Cole Publishing Company.

Duhl, B. S., & Duhl, E. J. (1981). Integrative family therapy. In A. S. Gurman & D. P. Knisknern (Eds.), *Handbook of family therapy* (pp. 176–187). New York: Brunner/Mazel.

Fairbairn, R. D. (1952). Theoretical and experimental aspects of psychoanalysis. *British Journal of Medical Psychology, 25*, 122–127.

Fogarty, T. F. (1976a). Systems concepts and dimensions of self. In *Family Therapy: Theory and Practice* (pp. 162–170). P. J. Guerin, Ed. New York: Gardner Press.

Fontes, L. (1998). Self issues for family therapy educators. *Journal of Marital and Family Therapy, 24*(3), 305–320.

Framo, J. L. (1979). Family theory and therapy. *American Psychologist, 34*(10), 990–992.

Framo, J. L. (1992). *Family of origin therapy: An intergenerational approach.* Philadelphia: Brunner/Mazel.

Freud, S. (1912). *The dynamics of transference* (Vol. 12). London: Hogarth Press and the Institute for Psychoanalysis. (Standard edition 1963)

Getz, H., & Prontinsky, H. (1994). Training marriage and family counselors: A family of origin approach. *Counselor Education and Supervision, 33*, 183–190.

Hammer, E. F. (1958). *The clinical application of projective drawings.* Springfield, IL: Charles C. Thomas.

Hart, G. H. (1982). *The process of clinical supervision.* Baltimore, MD: University Park Press.

Jourard, S. (1976). Changing personal worlds: A humanistic perspective. In A. Wandersman, P. J. Popper, & D. F. Ricks (Eds.), *Humanism and behaviorism: Dialogue and growth* (pp. 35–53). New York: Pergamon.

Kane, C. (1996). An experimental approach to family of origin work with marital and family therapy trainees. *Journal of Marital and Family Therapy, 22*(4), 481–487.

Kerr, C. (2000a). Kerr Counter-transference Awareness Scale: Unpublished measurement scale. Long Island University at C. W. Post, Brookville, New York.

Kerr, C. (2000b). *Family conflict drawings.* Long Island University at C. W. Post, Brookville, New York. (publication, Encarte, Luxembourg).

Kerr, M., & Bowen, M. (1988). *Family evaluation: An approach based on Bowen theory.* New York: Norton and Co.

Kwiatkowska, H. Y. (1962). Family art therapy: Experiments with a new technique. *Bulletin of Art Therapy 1*(93), 3–15.

LaMonica, E. L., & Karshmer, J. F. (1978). Empathy: Educating nurses in professional practice. *Journal of Nursing Education, 17*, 20–24.

McDaniel, S., & Landau-Stanton, J. (1991). Family of origin work and family skills training. *Family Process, 30*(4), 459–471.

McGoldrick, M. (1982). Through the looking glass: Supervision of a trainee's trigger family. In J. Byng-Hall & R. Wiffen (Eds.), *Family therapy supervision* (pp. 64–74). London: Academic Press.

McGoldrick, M., & Gerson, R. (1985). *Genograms in family assessment.* New York: W. W. Norton.

Nichols, M. P., & Schwartz, R. C. (2004). *Family therapy: Concepts and methods* (6th ed.). New York: Gardner Press.

Oster, G. D., & Gould, P. (1987). *Using drawings in assessment and therapy: A guide for mental health professionals.* New York: Brunner/Mazel.

Richardson, R. (1997). *Family ties that bind.* Vancouver, BC: International Self-Counsel Press.

Satir, V. (1971). The family as a treatment unit. In J. Haley (Ed.) *Changing families* (pp. 196–205). New York: Grumer & Stratton.

Saybrook Graduate School and Research Center. (1998). *Family therapy module.* San Francisco, CA: Saybrook.

Schnarch, D. M. (1991). *Constructing the sexual crucible.* New York: W. W. Norton.

Thompson, C. (1950). *Psychoanalysis: Evolution and development.* New York: Hermitage House.

Titelman, P. (1987). The therapist's own family. In P. Titelman (Ed.), *The therapist's own family: Toward the differentiation of self* (pp. 3–41). Northvale, NJ: Jason Aronson.

Wadeson, H. (1980). *Art psychotherapy.* New York: John Wiley & Sons.

Wilson, S. (1981). *Field instruction: Techniques for supervisors.* London: Macmillan.

Yalom, I. (1980). *Existential psychotherapy.* New York: Basic Books.

CHAPTER 5

Structural Family Art Therapy

JANICE HOSHINO*

INTRODUCTION

While I was in my doctoral training, we were discussing family dynamics and therapeutic interventions. An exacerbated student asked our professor how she is able to really *see* the family dynamics, be able to remain neutral, and not get "sucked into" the family dynamics. The professor stated that she likened her families to a puzzle, and it was her job to figure out the puzzle pieces. I remember thinking art therapy may provide an effective segue into the family puzzle. I have long felt that verbal therapy alone is limiting—those who hold the least power within the family system may not have a voice in the therapeutic setting; art balances the power differential inherent in families and provides all family member with a nonverbal "voice" through the art process. Therefore, art therapy is useful when clients do not have the language skills (e.g., young children), when the emotions are filled with so much tension it prohibits access through verbal means, or when family rules forbid discussion of feelings and conflicts. Likewise, Manicom & Boronska (2003) noted the art process provides an alternative channel for communication that might otherwise not be accessed, as the image allows for unconscious feelings or unknown family stories to surface

Riley (1994) noted that art therapy products created by families in treatment are valuable as assessment tools, fresh modes of communication, and levers of change. Family art therapists who practice from a structural framework may find this approach expansive and successful with a breadth of

* I would like to express my heartfelt appreciation to Chua Seow Ling for her collaboration, assistance, humor, and energy with this chapter; and Roberta Hinds for her help with research.

families who seek therapy. They will likely observe families through their patterns of interaction, power structure, and so on. Ford Sori (1995) noted that in art therapy the structure of family may be assessed through the use of family drawings in two ways: through direct observation of family members as they work on a joint project, and by examining and discussing the artwork itself with the family. Both methods yield valuable information that forms the basis of the therapist's hypothesis and treatment plans.

This chapter presents structural family therapy theory and its application for family art therapists. Additionally, a case study from a structural framework will provide the reader with an example of how a family engaged in art therapy.

DEVELOPMENT AND HISTORY OF STRUCTURAL FAMILY ART THERAPY

One needs to look no further than Minuchin's childhood to understand the origins of his bravado confrontational style and passion for working with people marginalized in the society. Born in Argentina to Russian Jewish immigrants, the young Minuchin lived in a community steeped in antisemitism. He struggled to remain loyal to his Jewish roots and identified with components of the Latino culture, particularly the way one fiercely defended one's honor; he quickly confronted children who hurled unkind remarks about his heritage (Simon, 1992). Minuchin's family was big, loving, and traditionally patriarchal (Wylie, 2005). His father, whom he seemed to revere, left the family when Minuchin was 9 years old to drive cattle across the plains in order to support the family. This had a profound impact on the young Minuchin, who fantasized about his father's life as a cowboy and saw him as a hero and protector of the family. Perhaps this shaped his idea of what all fathers should be: strong, active leaders of the family.

Minuchin attended medical school, specialized and practiced pediatrics briefly before his sense of social purpose drove him to volunteer as a doctor in the Israeli army in 1948. In 1952, he worked with displaced children from the Holocaust and Jewish immigrants from Arab countries (Goldenberg & Goldenberg, 2004). In 1954, wanting to gain a deeper understanding of children's behavior, he went to New York to study psychoanalysis, then the predominant discipline in psychotherapy. Four years later, he practiced as a psychiatrist at Wiltwyck, a correctional facility for boys from lower-income groups. He soon became frustrated with how treatment effects tended to disappear once the boys were returned to their families. Minuchin began to look beyond the individual to an examination of family environments. He and his colleagues, including Dick Auerswald, Charlie King, Braulio Montalvo, and Clara Rabinowitz, experimented with the various techniques they invented, observing and giving feedback to one another as they went along. In 1962, Minuchin visited the then mecca of family therapy, Palo Alto, where he met

Jay Haley, sparking a connection that was to develop into a long, fruitful partnership (Nichols & Schwartz, 2006).

Minuchin became a "heavyweight" in family therapy and is recognized as the pioneer of structural family therapy (SFT). In the late 1960s, he published a groundbreaking book, *Families of the Slums*, which documented his work and findings at Wiltwyck, and made remarkable achievements in his 10 years of directorship at the Philadelphia Child Guidance Clinic. There, he garnered the talents of Montalvo and Haley, as well as those of Harry Aponte, Marianne Walters, Charles Fishman, and Cloe Madanes. As a result of the tireless work of these and other practitioners at the clinic, structural family therapy became the most influential and widely practiced of all systems of family therapy in the 1970s (Nichols & Schwartz, 2006). The year 1974 saw the publication of another classic, *Families and Family Therapy*, which has since been translated into 11 languages and remains the best-selling book ever on family therapy (Simon, 1992).

After stepping down as director of the Philadelphia Child Guidance Clinic in 1975, Minuchin headed its training center until 1981, when he founded Family Studies, Inc. (now known as Minuchin Center for the Family), offering consultative services to community organizations, particularly those dealing with poor families (Goldenberg & Goldenberg, 2004).

CORE CONCEPTS OF STRUCTURAL FAMILY THERAPY

The essence of SFT lies in the view that there is an order, whether explicitly stated or unconsciously recognized, in which family members interact with one another. Salvador Minuchin (1974) defines family structure as "the invisible set of functional demands that organizes the way family members interact" (p. 51). It describes transaction patterns of how, when, and to whom each member relates.

Two sets of constraints maintain these transactional patterns: *generic rules* and *idiosyncratic rules*. *Generic constraints* are universal rules governing family organization, such as the presence of a power hierarchy between parents and children and complementarity of functions between husband and wife. Idiosyncratic or individualized rules, on the other hand, involve the mutual expectations of particular family members through years of explicit and implicit negotiations among these members (Minuchin, 1974). The manner in which the expectations originated may no longer be clear to the persons involved; indeed, expectations may have been fostered through repeated transactions (Nichols & Schwartz, 2006). For example, a family may expect all its members to be home by 8 o'clock for dinner every Friday as a result of years of habitually having dinner together that time of the week.

Families may be oblivious to these sets of innocuous "rules," perhaps in part because they are recreating the rules formed in *their* respective families of origin; these verbal transactions may be compounded in times of stress, creating a sense of stuckness. Statements such as "talking until I'm blue in the face" may describe this pattern. Art therapy may transcend barriers like language and rules and assist families to examine the dynamics through an unsullied lens. It gives a voice in an unthreatening manner to all members of a family, including children, whose voices may previously have been denied by the family's usual controlling mechanisms (Donnelly, 1989). The process of art making also makes the invisible visible as family patterns and rules of interaction surface, revealing the underlying structure that governs day-to-day behavior of various members (Riley, 1994). Family portrait drawings may shed new insights for the family, as the implicit is often made explicit through a medium such as art.

Subsystems

A family carries out its tasks through its various subsystems or groupings of individuals based on generation, gender, and common interests. An individual in the family usually belongs to different subsystems, entering into different relationships with other persons, performing different functions and having a different level of power in each subsystem. This is best illustrated by a husband who plays a complementary and loving role to his wife in the spouse subsystem while being a nurturing yet strict father to his child as a member of the parental subsystem. Among the many subsystems that exist in a family, SFT is primarily concerned with the spouse, parental, and sibling subsystems.

When two people marry or become partnered, they separate from each family of origin and create a new family comprising a *spouse subsystem*. This involves accommodating each spouse's needs, negotiating roles, and establishing rules and expectations governing the behavior of each spouse. At the same time, the couple undertakes the task of negotiating a different relationship with their own parents, siblings, and in-laws. The families of origin, in turn, must adapt to the separation or partial separation of one of its members, the inclusion of a new member, and the assimilation of the spouse subsystem within the family system's functioning (Minuchin, 1974).

Minuchin believes that the ideal family builds on a spouse subsystem in which each member accommodates, nurtures, and supports the uniqueness of the other (Becvar & Becvar, 2003). It is vital that the spouse subsystem develops boundaries around itself so that spouses can have space to meet their psychological needs and receive mutual support without the interference from persons outside the subsystem such as children and in-laws. The spouse subsystem later becomes their child's model for intimate relationships, as the child observes ways of expressing affection, of providing support, and of dealing with conflict. A major dysfunction in the spouse subsystem will reverberate throughout the family through such means as scapegoating a child or coopting a child into an alliance with one spouse against the other (Minuchin & Fishman, 1981). Art therapy may provide insight into alliances and scapegoating, sometimes by the placement of family members in family drawings. Who is the member most alienated from the family? Who is closest? Furthest away? What kind of expressions does each family member have?

With the birth of a child in the family, the couple takes on new functions as a *parental subsystem*. This is the executive unit of the family, primarily concerned with child rearing and socializing functions. A hierarchical structure is established within a clear boundary, allowing the parents to exercise authority over the child from their position of leadership. The parental subsystem is where the child first learns what to expect from people who have greater resources and strength. Minuchin is careful to point out that the parental subsystem varies widely in its composition, in that it may include a grandparent, an aunt, or a parental child (one who is delegated the authority to protect and discipline her siblings). It may also exclude one parent. When families engage in art therapy, it is important to note, in addition to placement of figures, the size of the figures. This also provides interesting insights for the family and art therapist. If a member is remarkably (and unrealistically) larger than the remaining family, this could indicate the level of importance or perhaps who carries the most power in the family. Of course, conjecture is not in the best interest of the client; the best interpreter is the client, not the art therapist.

Problems arise when the couple, unable to separate parenting functions from spouse functions, brings their unresolved conflict within the spouse subsystem into the area of child rearing (Minuchin, 1974). The parental subsystem also needs to have the flexibility to adjust its functions and boundaries as children mature. The unquestioning authority that wields restrictive control over young children must be replaced by a more flexible, rational authority as the children enter adolescence and seek to fulfill an increasing need for autonomy.

In families with more than one child, the *sibling subsystem* is another component of great interest to structural family therapists. This subsystem is where children first experience peer relationships and learn to support, cooperate with, and compete against one another. Within the subsystem's boundaries, children are protected from adult intrusions as they develop their own interests, accommodate to one another's needs, and learn to resolve conflicts.

Complementarity

Complementarity exists in the behaviors and roles of members within a family. Any two family members accommodate to each other in such a way that one develops particular aspects of himself or herself, while the other develops a behavior or trait to complement these aspects, like adjacent pieces of a jigsaw puzzle (Colapinto, 1991). In a well-functioning family or subsystem, complementarity manifests in effective teamwork, such as a mutually supportive couple in the spouse subsystem who divide their responsibilities in the family. In some cases, family balance is achieved by the assignment of complementary roles or functions to different family members (e.g., good child-bad child; tender mother-tough father); complementarity or reciprocity thus provides a generic constraint on the family structure, enabling the family to perform its tasks while maintaining its equilibrium (Goldenberg & Goldenberg, 2004). In other words, a child has to act like a child so that his father can act like a father (Minuchin, 1974).

The notion of complementarity implies that in any dyad, one person's behavior is yoked to the other: each individual's actions are not independent and acted out of free will, but instead are subject to reciprocal forces that support or polarize (Minuchin, 1998). Part of the challenge of structural family art therapists is to disentangle individuals from their automatic yoked reactions when complementarity gives rise to destructive patterns of interaction.

Minuchin illustrates his idea of complementarity by describing a family of two parents and a daughter who was almost mute. When the therapist asked the daughter a question, both parents answered simultaneously. The mother later explained that she did that because her daughter made her talk; the father said he spoke for his daughter because she was always silent; the daughter told the therapist, "They make me silent" (Minuchin & Fishman, 1981). Art therapy levels the playing field for all family members, unlike verbal therapy alone. The family members (often the children) who are least capable of articulating their feelings verbally are often the most likely to fall silent and have their opinions remain unheard. Art therapy equalizes the power differential inherent in most family *because* of the process of art making.

Circular causality often accompanies complementarity. As shown in the example above, one person's behavior causes a second person to react in a certain way, which in turn feeds into the first person's behavior before reinforcing the second person's response. Through time, both are caught up in a vicious cycle, each perceiving his or her own behavior as no more than a reaction to the other person's action.

However, Colapinto points out a subtle difference between the concepts of circular causality and complementarity. For him, circular causality pertains to a *sequential* two-way interaction (A's behavior causes B's behavior, and vice versa), while complementarity designates a *spatial* configuration (A's and B's shapes fit), represented by the interlocking pieces of the puzzle (Colapinto, 1991).

Hierarchy

The rules the family prescribes include not only patterns of interaction, but also differential degrees of decision-making power for various individuals and subsystems (Colapinto, 1991). This gives rise to the hierarchical function of the family. The parental subsystem sits above the sibling subsystem in this hierarchy of power, exercising both leadership and protection. Hierarchy can also exist within a subsystem, typically in the sibling subsystem where the order of birth, for example, determines the amount of power accorded to each child. Therefore, a child who submits to his father may take on executive powers when he is alone with his younger brother (Minuchin, 1974).

In some families, however, age and the subsystem of which an individual is a member are not the only factors in the hierarchical organization. A parental child in a single-parent family may carry more authority than the other children even if he or she is not the oldest of them; children of a parent's previous marriage may find themselves relegated to a lower position with the remarriage of the parent and birth of younger children in the reconstituted family; in some cultures, children of one gender are commonly accorded higher responsibilities than those of the other.

In family drawings, the size and placement of the family members are clues to the hierarchical system: the member placed highest on the page or the largest figure is likely to have the most power. The use of colors may reveal similar information, with more powerful members depicted in dark or vibrant colors and weaker members drawn in lighter or more transparent colors (Ford Sori, 1995).

Boundaries, Enmeshment, and Disengagement

Boundaries play an important role in regulating transactions that take place between individuals or subsystems, or between the family and its external environment. They are rules that prescribe who should be in contact with whom about what (Colapinto, 1991) and can be clear, diffuse, or rigid. *Clear boundaries* are firm yet flexible and permit access across subsystems so that individuals are supported while maintaining a certain level of autonomy. With clear boundaries, the various subsystems can adapt to situational and developmental challenges that the family faces, enabling the family to deal with these challenges by effecting changes in structure, rules, and roles.

In a family with *rigid boundaries*, members are disengaged from one another, as well as from the larger system of which the family is a part. Typically, family members live their own lives, with little or no interference, participation, or support from one another. Though this fosters autonomy, it also breeds isolation. In contrast, families with *diffuse boundaries* are characterized by enmeshed relationships and intrusions of individuals into subsystems of which they are not a part. For example, when the boundary between the parental and sibling subsystem is diffuse, the parents may interfere whenever the siblings have an argument, or become so overinvolved in their children's affairs as to invade their privacy. In some cases, children act like parents, rendering parental control ineffective.

Minuchin clarifies that enmeshment and disengagement are not necessarily dysfunctional. In fact he is of the view that most families have enmeshed and disengaged subsystems, as in the case of a mother who is enmeshed with her children when they are small, while the father takes a disengaged position toward the children. The father may become more involved as the children grow older and the parents gradually grow more disengaged from the children as they enter adulthood. When subsystems are highly enmeshed or disengaged, however, family dysfunction occurs. It is also imperative that the art therapist does not impose his or her own biases regarding culture and how the family defines their culture. This avoids pushing one's own agenda, that is, to promote independence among family members, when the family may be comfortable with their system; enmeshment may not be the reason why they have sought family art therapy.

Coalitions

An *alliance*, whether temporary or permanent, may form between two or more family members who bond through a common interest or goal, such as a father and son who share a passion for fishing. When an alliance is formed between two family members against a third member, it is known as a *coalition*. Though this can happen between two children against another, structural family therapists commonly see cross-generational coalitions, or *triangulation*, such as when a mother unites with the child against the father or when a daughter allies with her aunt against her mother.

Minuchin makes a distinction between stable and detouring coalitions. He defines a *stable coalition* as a rigidly bounded union between one parent and the child in an alliance against the other parent that becomes a dominant part of the family's everyday functioning (Goldenberg & Goldenberg, 2004). For instance, a mother may form a coalition with her daughter against the father, undermining his position of authority in the family and keeping him out of family affairs. Often, when two parents in conflict try to triangulate their child, the child may be made paralyzed and have struggles with loyalty issues and guilt or anger because his or her every movement is construed by one parent as an attack.

A detouring coalition, in contrast, forms between two parents when they deal with spousal conflicts through triangulating the child and uniting to either attack the child because he or she is labeled as bad, or protect the child because he or she is defined as sick or weak. Through this detour, the parents are then able to maintain an illusion of harmony within the spouse subsystem. In all forms of coalition, boundaries between subsystems are weakened and enmeshment between members of different subsystems occurs.

Alliances and coalitions often reveal themselves both through the process of art making and in the product itself, as do enmeshment and disengagement of family members (Ford Sori, 1995). A dyad may subtly exclude a third member from participating in the collaborative family drawing (coalition); a child may constantly look to a parent to complete his or her part of the drawing (enmeshment); a family member may appear distant or uninvolved in the project (disengagement). In the completed artwork, the size of the figures in relation to one another as well as the distance between them similarly may clue the family art therapist in on the alliances and coalitions that exist in the family.

Family Dysfunction

A family's structure determines how the family organizes itself in order to maintain its stability and reacts to tensions arising from changes within the system or in its environment. The structure of a healthy family changes over time, adapting to changing needs generated by its own evolution and in the face of external stressors. It allows boundaries to be redrawn, subsystems to regroup, and hierarchical arrangements to shift (Colapinto, 1991). It is through such processes that individuals within the family system grow, individuate, and meet their needs.

On the other hand, a family becomes *dysfunctional* when it does not have the flexibility to change and realign its transactions in times of stress and conflict. Stressors can be environmental, such as when a parent is entrenched, or developmental, such as when a child enters adolescence. In particular, any changes in the membership of the family, such as when new members are added by birth or remarriage or when a member is removed by death or divorce, can disrupt the homeostasis of the family system, presenting considerable stress. When a family absorbs a new member (such as a stepparent), that new member must adapt to the system's rules, and the old system in turn must be modified to include the new member. However, there is a tendency to maintain the old patterns though they are no longer effective or appropriate, which places a stress on the new member and may cause him to increase his demands (Minuchin, 1974).

Dysfunctional sets, or the persistent use of obsolete transactional patterns by a family in response to adversity, are instrumental to the development of symptoms, usually in the weakest family member who is also a victim of triangulation. Dysfunctional sets often result in the formation of rigid triads to diffuse conflicts or tensions within a subsystem. This typically happens when parents use a child to detour or deflect spouse conflicts through triangulation or coalition.

Minuchin (1974) distinguishes pathology from dysfunction by reserving the label of *pathology* for families that not only maintain but also increase the rigidity of their transactional patterns and boundaries when attempting to deal with a stressful situation and avoid or resist any exploration of alternatives (Minuchin, 1974).

Symptoms serve a purpose of maintaining the dysfunctional homeostasis in the family system. Colapinto (1991) points out that, in addition to directly contributing to the development of the symptom, the family may maintain the symptom when it fails to effectively challenge it and when it benefits from having the symptom protect the stability of the whole system.

Therapeutic Goals

SFT does not consider symptoms as occurring in isolation, independent and removed from its environmental context. Rather, it sees the presenting problems of an identified patient as embedded in the family's dysfunctional rules. The aim of therapy, then, is to bring about changes in the family structure in such a way that symptom resolution becomes a by-product of a systemic goal. Changing the family's dysfunctional transaction patterns is perceived to be the most effective way of eliminating the symptom for good.

With this objective in mind, the art therapist becomes an active change agent who directly challenges the family's patterns of interaction by forcing the members to look beyond the symptom to see how they have each inadvertently contributed to it within the context of the family structure. Through discussing the dynamics of the family in art making and reviewing the creative product, the art therapist helps the family modify its functioning and realign its boundaries so that the members are able to solve their own problems. Throughout the process, the art therapist's focus is on modifying the present and not focusing on or interpreting the past.

Role of the Art Therapist

The therapist plays a decisive role in effecting changes in the family system. Indeed, much more than the techniques, prescriptions, or interpretations, it is the therapist's behavior that helps families change. The following descriptions were written for a structural family therapist. Consider the fusion of art therapy with that described below. Drawing from concepts of theater production, Colapinto (1991) portrays the therapist as playing at different points of therapy the parts of a producer, stage director, protagonist, and narrator. As a producer, the therapist creates conditions for the formation of the therapeutic system; as a stage director, he or she introduces situations that challenge the existing structure and push the family towards more functional patterns; as a protagonist, the therapist takes the place of an additional member of the family and unbalances the family organization; as a narrator, he or she comments on observed interactions and, by questioning each person's attribution of meaning to the behavior of other family members, helps develop new meanings. While performing these various roles, the therapist maintains such qualities as a respectful curiosity, a commitment to help families change, a preference for concrete behavioral modifications over talk about changed feelings, a constant readiness to formulate and modify hypotheses based on information received, and the ability to imbue the sessions with intensity while keeping the clarity of the therapeutic goal.

Techniques

An important first step in family therapy, *joining* involves gaining the family's trust and support for the therapist to achieve a positive therapeutic relationship with the family. Minuchin (1974) emphasizes the need to understand and know a family in an intimate, experiential way:

To join a family system, the therapist must accept the family's organization and style and blend with them. He must experience the family's transactional patterns and the strength of those patterns. He should feel a family member's pain at being excluded or scapegoated, and his pleasure at being loved, depended on, or otherwise confirmed within the family. The therapy recognizes the predominance of certain family themes and participates with family members in their exploration. (p. 123)

To join a family, the therapist is also required to *accommodate*, or adapt to, the family system. He or she temporarily refrains from imposing changes to the system and instead encourages and accepts the communications that take place in his presence. Accommodation typically involves the use of maintenance, tracking, and mimesis. *Maintenance* refers to deliberate acts to preserve certain transactional patterns, such as when the therapist makes remarks that confirm and support a member's strength and potential. In *tracking*, instead of challenging what is being said, the therapist follows the verbal and nonverbal content of the communication, asking clarifying questions, making approving comments and showing an interest in the process. To adapt to a family's communication style and affective range, the therapist uses *mimesis*, matching its tempo, tone, and rhythm. For example, with a family whose communication is characterized by long pauses and slow responses, the therapist deliberately slows his or her pace; with a jovial family, the therapist becomes jovial and expansive (Minuchin, 1974).

In joining the family, the therapist observes the dynamics of communication among members, from which he or she formulates hypotheses about the underlying structure. He or she pays attention to who talks to whom, whether transactions are completed or interrupted, whether communications typically take place between two members (a dyad) or includes a third person. The therapist also notes nonverbal behavior, such as when the wife looks nervously at her husband whenever it is her turn to speak.

Family mapping is a useful tool in organizing schema about the complex interactive patterns within the family. It reveals such structural information as coalitions, affiliations, the nature of family conflict, roles of individual members in the family, and delineation of boundaries between subsystems (see Figure 5.1 and Figure 5.2). With a family map, the therapist can formulate hypothesis about areas within the family that are functioning well and areas that need restructuring. The first map (with arrow) in Figure 5.2 indicates that the marital subsystem (M for mother and F for father) detours their conflict by attacking the child (C). "This reduces the danger to the spouse subsystem, but stresses the child" (Minuchin, 1974, p. 61). The second map demonstrates a *coalition* of a mother and child against a critical husband/father. "The boundary around the spouse subsystem thereby becomes diffuse.

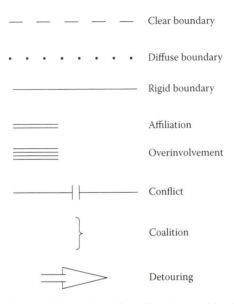

Figure 5.1 Symbols for family mapping. (From *Families and family*, by S. Minuchin, 1974, p. 53. With permission.)

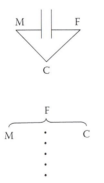

Figure 5.2 Examples of family maps. (From *Families and family*, by S. Minuchin, 1974, p. 61. With permission.)

… A cross generational dysfunctional transactional pattern has developed" (Minuchin, 1974, pp. 61–62).

If in the process of joining the therapist is like an actor in the family play, then in *restructuring* the therapist takes on the role of the director-actor who creates scenarios, instructs the family members in playing out alternative scenes, and at the same time uses himself or herself to enter into alliances and coalitions with a family member to create, strengthen, or weaken boundaries and unbalance the structure so that the family is forced to seek out new transactional patterns (Minuchin, 1974). All this while, the therapist maintains his or her position of leadership and therapeutic control, resisting any overt or covert attempts to be triangulated by the family.

In SFT, the therapist strives where possible to have the family *enact* their real dysfunctional transactions instead of relying on their descriptions. The SFT facilitates the interaction of family members with each other in the sessions, to experience the family reality as they define it. Enactment is usually the first step towards restructuring, as it gives the therapist an opportunity to observe the verbal and nonverbal ways in which family members signal to each other and monitor the range of tolerable transactions. He or she can then intervene in the process by increasing its intensity, involving other family members, introducing alternative responses, and reframing the issues.

In a case where a mother sought therapy because the tantrums of her 2-year-old daughter were embarrassing her in public (cited in Goldenberg & Goldenberg, 2004), the therapist saw the opportunity for enactment when the daughter asked the mother for a candy. The therapist asked the mother not to give in to the daughter's request; consequently, the daughter threw a temper tantrum that proceeded from crying to falling on the floor and undressing herself. Though the mother was tempted to give in, the therapist promptly stopped her, thereby increasing the intensity by prolonging the tantrum. After an exhausting half an hour, the child came to a whimpering stop. The mother had asserted her control during the enactment, generational boundaries were reestablished, proper hierarchical order was restored, and alternative transactional patterns were learned.

Enactment in structural family art therapy takes place in the process of collaborative art creation, such as a joint family holiday drawing (Jordan, 2001) or a family mural painting. By focusing on the process instead of the content in art making, the family art therapist notes who initiates discussions, who is ignored, who interrupts whom, and whether the family members work as a team, take turns, or are uninvolved in what other members do.

To emphasize a particular dysfunctional pattern, a therapist may also increase the *intensity* of a remark by heightening its affective component (e.g., "When did you divorce your wife and marry your job?") or repeating a message over and over again (e.g., "Your daughter is no longer a child. She can look after herself").

A structural family therapist is perpetually looking for ways to realign the boundaries within a dysfunctional family. This sometimes involves a move as simple as asking the child to change seats with the father so that both parents can be next to each other. This *boundary-making* gesture is an effort to create greater psychological distance between the enmeshed mother and child, at the same time strengthen the parental subsystem by clarifying its boundaries. Besides concrete spatial maneuvers, a therapist may also introduce rules forbidding interruptions from other family members when one member speaks, thereby blocking intrusions, affiliations, or coalitions (Minuchin & Fishman, 1981). Sometimes the therapist assigns different tasks for different subsystems to work on, again with the aim of strengthening boundaries around each subsystem.

One of the most striking art therapy interventions to strengthen boundaries involved the use of old, discarded chairs that my mentor, Dr. Nancy Knapp, had rescued from the garbage dumpster. Two art therapy interns were working with a family to realign and strengthen boundaries by assigning the family to work in dyads to design and paint chairs. The family scapegoat, an adolescent boy, worked with his father, who consistently criticized his son. Prior to seeking art therapy, they had reached a noncommunicative stalemate. The art therapy directive provided the impetus to communicate in a different way; they had to agree upon a direction with the chair. They shared power and decision making. They engaged in the art process and found laughter and enjoyment with each other. This simultaneously strengthened the father/son subsystem and decreased the enmeshed mother/son subsystem.

Whereas boundary making entails changing family subsystem membership or altering the distance between subsystems, *unbalancing* provides the therapist a chance at changing the hierarchical relationship of the members within a subsystem (Minuchin & Fishman, 1981). Here, the therapist joins and supports one individual, usually a peripheral member or one low in position, empowering this person while ignoring existing family rules about the way other members should interact with this person. The focus on one family member compels the other members to change their positions around him or her. Used effectively, unbalancing introduces a new reality to this member and the rest of the family, as this person begins to experiment with expanded roles and functions made possible by his or her alliance with the therapist. In structural family art therapy, the therapist may assign a collaborative family drawing and then throw his or her weight and support behind a parent to help this parent take charge of the project, blocking interference by other family members to facilitate the parent taking control (Ford Sori, 1995).

Another useful technique in challenging the family structure is *reframing*. This takes place when the therapist attaches a new meaning to an old behavior or situation, with the aim of changing family perspectives and family behavior patterns. Usually, when a problem is relabeled as a function of the family structure, what is previously seen as a member's problem now becomes a reflection of poorly working family structure, an issue that every member in the family has a responsibility to deal with. For example, a therapist may reframe a girl's eating disorder as disobedience and as making her parents incompetent, thus challenging the parents to restore the hierarchical organization in the family and assert their authority from their position of leadership (Minuchin, 1974).

Creative techniques and metaphorical interventions can be used to complement verbal reframing. A child who sees himself or herself as the family problem may be helped to view his or her role in bringing the parents together in dealing with the child, thus strengthening the spouse subsystem. The therapist may then direct the child to make a family drawing and tell him or her to "cut yourself out" of the family. The child is then encouraged to reflect on how the child's separation from the family will change the way remaining members relate to one another and what the child can do now that he or she is liberated from the family frame. This is useful in addressing the neglected developmental task of individuation (Riley & Malchiodi, 2003).

CASE EXAMPLE

There seems to be a trend and increasing societal flexibility toward career change during one's life. I find this interesting to consider how some careers become seemingly stale while others, like being a couple and family art therapist, never fail to keep you stimulated, engaged, and most of all humble. Families are like snowflakes—all are unique, no two are alike, yet their infrastructures are remarkably similar. We are all children of some family unit, who in turn are products of their family unit. There is some truth to the statement that when you treat a family, it at times feels like you are treating several generations of ghosts. These ghosts inform, influence, and may, at times, seem as alive as (or perhaps even more alive than) the living, breathing family that sits in front of you in the therapy room. Such is the case of the family case study below.

Lauren's Journey: Sessions 1 and 2

The owner of the clinic where I maintain my part-time private practice left a voice mail on my answering machine. "I've been seeing Elliott, a self-made 51-year-old man off and on for a couple of years; I've seen him both alone and with his wife from time to time, while his wife was alive. He is quite concerned about his daughter … and I thought you would be a good match for her." Lauren, a 30-year-old, neatly dressed White woman, came into the first session with a bright smile, a big "hello," and a very engaging demeanor. As we sat down, this sunny façade quickly disintegrated after I asked the simple question of what brought her into therapy. Tears quickly flooded out, and her pain was palpable. She cried, "I lost my mother, my very best friend, who meant everything to me and no one seems to understand … everyone has moved on with their lives and I feel so stuck, so very alone." As the session progressed, she struggled to talk about her mother's death. Her mother Paige had died of melanoma 2 years prior; her prognosis to live 6 months extended into 2 years. Her death was difficult and extremely agonizing for both her and the family caretakers (see Figure 5.3).

Lauren was distressed that she seemed to be the only one who remained depressed, while her brother Lance and stepfather Eli (whom she referred to as "father," because he raised her from the time she was very young) appeared to have moved on effortlessly with their lives. She was especially angry that her father had "dated" several women soon after Paige's death and had recently invited his latest girlfriend to move into his estate. Lauren felt his actions conveyed both a disregard and disrespect for the legacy of her mother. How could he have truly loved his wife if he did not take time to mourn? How could he have gone off and done "his own thing" for hours during the last days of her life when she was dying? How could they *all* pick up the pieces and define or redefine "family"? What *was* their family system? It felt like the thread had been ripped from the tapestry of this family, this family who shared eternally the

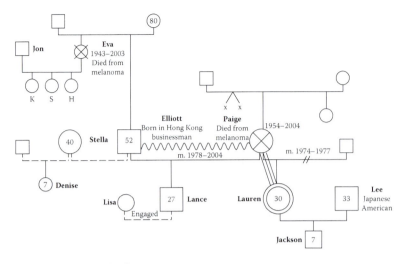

Figure 5.3 Lauren's family genogram.

same fabric was disintegrating at the seams, and was in jeopardy of becoming separate garments, separate strips of cloth fluttering and dancing in the breeze of a ghost named Paige. Lauren's despair and loneliness extended beyond her family of origin—she felt Lee, her husband, had become increasingly impatient, and did not understand the depths of her grief. She also had a couple of rifts with her friends and subsequently felt they had also largely abandoned her. Although she desired their support and a shoulder on which to cry, she sensed their discomfort—in turn, she disengaged even further. She also resented the simplicity of their lives, their seemingly uncomplicated and pain-free existence. She struggled to get out of bed in the morning while they planned simple tasks like where to go to dinner. She labored to get through a day of work, while they had a life that she perceived had few worries and no baggage.

She further felt others were less sympathetic due to the stigma around her mother's death. Some individuals had commented that had Paige stayed out of the sun, she would not have contracted melanoma. This covert accusation that somehow her mother *caused* her own death was extremely painful.

Death in a family can have an enormous impact on the structure of the family, exposing role flexibility or rigidity within the family system and subsystems. The permanent removal of a member from the family poses a challenge for the subsystems and boundaries to exist as they previously did, necessitating reorganization. However, less functional families may feel a need to maintain the status quo and make as few changes as possible or change the structure while remaining emotionally stuck with sadness, depression, or anger (Lamberti & Detmer, 1993). Where the deceased used to be a part of an enmeshed dyad, the surviving member of the dyad may pose a resistance to systemic changes by grieving for an extended period or a lifetime. In Lauren's case, the perceived "indifference" from other family members further fueled a need to mourn for her deceased mother, as she desperately clung on to the memory of her mother that the cold, unfeeling tides of time threatened to sweep away.

Lauren stated the relationships between herself and her husband within the spouse subsystem, and between herself and her father in the parent-child dyad were problematic. Beyond the dyadic (i.e., Lauren/husband and Lauren/father) problems, Lauren felt the triadic relationships between herself, husband, and father also needed to find a more satisfying ground for growth. Because she felt her relationship with her husband needed more immediate attention, she agreed to bring her husband into the second session.

Lauren was reluctant to draw during this session, but did attempt to depict her feelings, or grief, through an abstract representation. She completed a rather vague, fainted, cloud-like depiction of "grief." She reiterated her aloneness, her journey through endless waves of despair and depression.

Session 3: Lauren and Lee—The Couple's Story

During the second session, Lauren filled in the details of her family of procreation. She was married to Lee, a 35-year-old, third-generation Japanese-American male, and together they had Jackson, a 9-year-old son. The couple had been together for 12 years. Lauren worked as an administrative assistant for a dentist, a job she enjoyed for the time being. Her husband Lee was employed as a human resource officer. Although they were a dual-income family, she acknowledged her father had helped them out financially with their down payment for a home and other expenses along the way. She felt both appreciative of and frustrated with her father's "gifts," which she saw as a double-edged sword; on one hand they lived and enjoyed a lifestyle well beyond their means, and on the other, the sacrifice for these gifts was that they felt "controlled" and at times "manipulated" by Elliott and his influence in many of their financial decisions.

Lee was a soft-spoken man who was engaged and friendly. He was concerned with the level of Lauren's despair, but admitted he could not understand because he had not experienced a death of a loved one. Lauren admitted her resentment in feeling her need to defend her grief process and that she was alone in this journey. She stated she wanted his support; he felt he *was* supportive, but felt it was time for her to resume her roles as wife and mother.

Both admitted that the relationship had suffered significantly since her mother's death. They cited several problematic issues, including communication, differing parenting and discipline styles around their son Jackson, and their relationship with Elliott. However, both expressed their commitment to the marriage, their love for each other, and their motivation to improve their relationship on all fronts. Although both admitted that their communication could escalate during a fight, they were respectful and able to listen to each other in session.

Figure 5.4 Structural mapping of Lauren's family as presented in session 1.

The structural map presented in Figure 5.4 conveys a family system where Lauren (D) and Paige (M) form a coalition through their enmeshment and relationship that largely excluded their respective spouses. Elliott (F) resides at the top of the hierarchy, disengaged from his family because of his excessive work habits. Though Lee (Husband) holds a position that is more or less equal to Lauren's, he is also excluded due to Paige and Lauren's coalition.

They were asked to draw a picture of themselves and write a few thoughts about how they would describe themselves. Lauren drew herself and Lee holding hands and entitled the picture "best friends." She wrote they are "the perfect couple." Descriptive words included "thoughtfulness, argumentative, encouraging, and same sense of humor" (see Figure 5.5). Lee also drew a very similar drawing of the couple holding hands, which he entitled "a walk in the park." He wrote as descriptive words, "comforting, fun, exciting, lasting, and

Figure 5.5 Lauren's drawing of herself and Lee.

Figure 5.6   Lee's drawing of himself and Lauren.

warmth" (see Figure 5.6). The couple drew independently, without viewing the other's drawing, so the uncanny similarity in the placement of the figures, mood, and content of the drawing is notable. Both felt pleased with the content of each other's drawings—the positive content and connection was a reassurance of their commitment to each other. Because of the recent escalation in fighting and level of disagreement, both agreed they could benefit from couple's therapy and scheduled a third appointment together.

The couple's commitment and motivation during this session seemed promising—it often seems that individuals seek therapy while problems are significant but not necessarily overwhelming. On the other hand, couples and families often choose to come into therapy only after problems have been festering for a much longer period of time. Consequently, they are more likely to be in a state of crisis, and sometimes only seek therapy when an ultimatum, such as divorce, has been threatened. Although a structural approach can be effective at various points on the relationship continuum, intervention may be likened to cancer treatment: early intervention and treatment may produce the most positive results.

Minuchin (1974) felt the spouse subsystem builds on accommodating each other's needs, negotiating roles, establishing rules and expectations of each other. Additionally, the couple reaches an agreement on a different relationship with their perspective families of origin. Although this couple was not without their challenges, a pivotal point in their relationship occurred when Paige died. Lauren not only lost her mother, she lost her best friend, confidant, and person she felt most connected to. Her attachment to her mother may have impeded her ability to fully regard Lee as her partner. Often, when Lauren was having a hard day, she would turn to Paige, not Lee. Additionally,

Lauren and Paige often coalesced about their problems, including not only work, but also relationships. Lauren was acutely aware of the struggles and turbulence in her parent's relationship. I questioned whether this might have provided a ripe opportunity for Lauren and Paige to form a coalition against Elliott. Coalitions may also provide the opportunity for the "odd person out" to further disengage from the family system.

Session 4: Lauren and Elliott

As an art therapy educator, I espouse the necessity for students to attend to the *process* of the client. Further, as family art therapists, we discuss how to set boundaries, be aware of triangulation, and to not engage in coalitions in cases where one feels a stronger connection to one of the family members. My former professor, James Framo, often reminded students that he would work with the *system*, not the individual, in an effort to avoid coalitions and triangulation; his role as a family therapist was to set the boundaries of therapy.

As Kim, an art therapy intern, and I waited for the couple to arrive, we discussed possible art therapy directives for the session. Imagine our surprise when Lauren arrived with her *father*, not her husband. She explained that their son had soccer practice, and her husband needed to take him. She felt because she and her father also had their issues, she would use this opportunity to bring him in! Although this was not the plan, working with this father/daughter dyad seemed useful.

Lauren and Elliott quickly settled into the session. Elliott was pleased Lauren was in therapy; he had been at the same clinic for couples therapy and individual therapy in years past. Elliott expressed his feelings of concern that Lauren seemed so depressed and stuck in her grief; he was pleased she had sought therapy and was hopeful that she would be able to get on with her life. Lauren rolled her eyes and then confronted her father with her anger and disappointment about how he did not seem to grieve the loss of his wife. Lauren declared, "You started dating very shortly after her death! How could you move on so soon? And now you're moving this woman into your home? [her voice escalated] The home that Mom designed? The home that Mom helped build? That home that was supposed to be hers, not this gold-digger's!" Elliott calmly attended to Lauren, stating he felt misunderstood and that he did indeed grieve for Paige.

Elliott calmly talked about himself. He grew up very poor in the ghettos of China and was strongly disciplined by his mother. He worked tirelessly to educate himself, relocated to the United States, and became a highly successful businessman at a young age. Although he formally retired at the age of 42, he related how he continued to feel responsible for everyone's well-being: "the children are vulnerable, I take care of my mother, and look after the family"; this constituted his current several "jobs." His success was achieved through his self-control, high energy, and excessive drive. No doubt that he tackled his current "jobs" with the same zeal.

The artwork they created in this session was revealing; I asked them to create first a " geometric family drawing" and next, "an ideal geometric family drawing." This directive, to choose shapes and colors to represent oneself and other members of the family, is often less threatening than realistic family portraits and may provide a window into helping a family to examine their family system. Lauren thoughtfully drew several small shapes on top of the paper, then created her family drawing (see Figure 5.7). She drew her son as a "yellow ball, because he was sunny," her husband was a "purple triangle because he was laid back," her brother was a red diamond because she found him "unpredictable, grumpy, and with a really bad temper," her father was a green trapezoid because he "was hard to fit in in certain situations." The color green represented "successful and [being] environmentally concerned." She drew herself as a blue square to "represent the way I feel—blue ... I'm not a fun person lately." When questioned about the crossed out octagon, she said it was a "mistake," not her mother. Lauren drew most of the figures the same size, and found separate, but meaningful shapes and colors for each individual. The figures were approximately the same proximity apart.

Elliott drew himself in the middle of the drawing—all figures were connected to him, and he was clearly the central force in the family (see Figure 5.8). He wrote some of his feelings around certain family members; for Lauren and Lee, he wrote, "turbulence, anger, frustration." His words to his son were, "disconnected, anger, independence, not aware of my needs." For his mother, he wrote "dependence on me, aging, survival, daily decision." This meant he felt a need to take care of her. He expressed a desire to "renew relationship" with his sister. Last, he placed his girlfriend in the upper right corner and wrote, "new relationship, constantly being judged, like walking on eggshells. Receive good support." He explained he felt judged by all of his

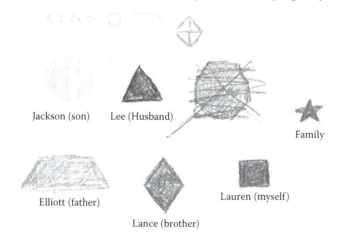

Figure 5.7   Lauren's geometric family drawing.

Figure 5.8 Elliott's geometric family drawing.

family, but not his girlfriend. Last, he placed a question mark between himself, his deceased wife, God, and his deceased sister.

From a structural framework, these drawings seem to convey different views of the family system—Lauren's drawing reveals shapes that are different from each other, but solid, relatively equal in size and proximity. However, there is no indication of interaction from one figure to the next, which may coincide with her feeling of separateness from herself and her family. Elliott, on the other hand, placed himself in the center of his family and extended family. This may be an interesting glimpse into the family system and hierarchy—as the center of the family, he would maintain the most power and control, as everything filters through him. This parallels with Lauren and Lee's frustration that she and her husband often felt "controlled" by Elliott.

The second drawing was an "ideal geometric family portrait." Lauren drew a large blue star, which she also included in her first drawing, and had it entitled "family." She wrote this family had "different directions, ideas, and personalities … [but] all are striving to fulfill dreams together" (see Figure 5.9). Elliott again placed himself in the middle of the drawing; surrounding him were his children and extended family. He drew a line toward the bottom of the page to represent his wife, deceased sister (who had also died of melanoma), and God. He explained that all members were now equally distanced from him, and the line meant he had resolved his grief with his wife, who remained part of his life (see Figure 5.10).

Different Directions, Ideas & Personalities all striving to fulfill our dreams together.

Figure 5.9 Lauren's ideal geometric family portrait.

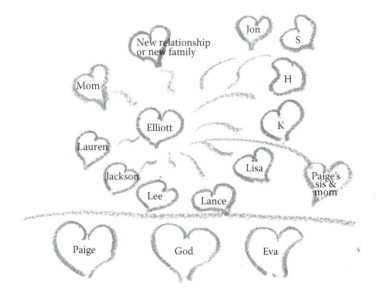

Figure 5.10 Elliott's ideal geometric family portrait.

It is compelling to consider this on the lines of gender. Lauren is surrounded by males in her family—her husband, father, brother, and son, with her only female connection being her mother. Interestingly, Elliott is surrounded mostly by females in his family—his daughter, mother, sister, deceased wife, girlfriend, with his son as his primary male connection. Culture also needs to be considered in this (and every) family system—Asian families tend to regard males as dominant and more powerful members. Males are generally given more privilege in Asian families, especially the oldest son. In this family, Elliott was the only son; Elliott's son, Lance was also his only son. Both Elliott and Lance seem to maintain a position of power and authority in the hierarchy of the family. Lauren did express her resentment that her inheritance was roughly one-sixteenth of her father's estate; Lance was to inherit half of the estate. Elliott's explanation was that this was a traditional practice in his culture; Lauren felt she and her brother were both Americans and desired a more equal division of the estate.

It seemed a useful directive on several levels—first, using geometric shapes may be less threatening, but not less revealing than a directive such as a realistic family portrait. Next, the dynamics of comparing a realistic versus ideal family through artwork is imminently more valuable than verbal descriptions. Families are often skilled at their "verbal dance," or repetitive exchanges, which may deteriorate into bantering and accusations—therefore no one takes responsibility, and the family remains stuck in their repetitive dialogue. Next, artwork may often reveal dynamics more transparently than verbal therapy; structural concepts such as *boundaries, coalitions,* and *hierarchy* may be demonstrated through placement, closeness, size of the figures, and color utilization. Further, it provides the opportunity for families to consider these dynamics through a fresh lens; the concrete nature of artwork may reveal perceptions of the system that were unspoken, denied, or transferred to the scapegoat of the family. Directives that involve the *system* may enlighten the family view from "the other" to "the system" as the problem.

This dyad was an interesting dichotomy; one who did not grieve, and one who felt nothing but grief. Yet both were oddly in the same space. Both felt misunderstood. Both felt justified in their feelings. Both wanted things to improve, but were clueless as to how. Both wanted a sense of family but did not know what that meant—one of the great challenges with death is the necessity for systemic shift. This can be demanding, redefining and reorganizing a system that is both strained and in limbo.

I reframed to the family their part of their dilemma; all were in some way trying to protect the others. Elliott felt his children were too "fragile" to talk with regarding his grief. Lee, frustrated that he could not "fix" the problem of Lauren's sadness, ignored her so as to not agitate their relationship further. And Lauren remained stuck in her grief, because she thought all members had moved on with their lives ... this "stuckness," in essence, protected her mother's legacy. I asked Lauren what might happen if she were able to give up some of her grief; she tearfully replied that no one would remember her mother.

Because this family had not found a venue to grieve, I suggested a celebration of Paige's life. They embraced the idea and decided to include only the family of origin—Elliott, Lauren, and brother Lance. In preparation for the session celebrating Paige's life, I conveyed that I would e-mail them instructions. I sent them the following e-mail: "We will convene on October 15, 2005, to celebrate Paige's life. In preparation, you may want to bring some of her favorite memorabilia, music, flowers, candles, or any other items that you would like to share. I would suggest that you think of or write down some of your favorite memories or stories." A 2-hour session was scheduled. When anxiety runs high in families, that is, when discussing how to celebrate a loved one's life, words may evaporate easily; therefore, written instructions may provide a more concrete framework in which to prepare.

Session 5: A Celebration of Paige's Life

Lauren and Elliott arrived for the first time on time. Brother Lance arrived with them. They seemed anxious to start the session. I provided a variety of art materials for the family to engage in. We all sat in a circle and used the floor as a space of containment. Lauren brought out a four-page typewritten paper that was filled with the many memories and stories she cherished. Lance brought a couple of his mother's items, most notably a book she had written and published a couple of years before she died. And Elliott had a scrapbook that contained many pictures of Lauren when she was a young woman.

I thanked the family for their efforts and asked who might want to share what they had brought in. Lauren seemed anxious to begin—she pulled out her paper, obviously a labor of love, and started to read from the script. Over the next hour, the family engaged in an intense dialogue of these stories. They cried. They laughed. And they all attentively relished in the memories of the life of this remarkable woman. Next, Lance talked about how proud he was that his mother had met one of her dreams of not only writing, but publishing a book. All acknowledged her creative, bright spirit. Elliott held back until the latter part of the session to open up the scrapbook, which contained pictures of a very young Paige. Lauren and her brother had many questions about her early life and had not seen many of these pictures. They seemed thirsty to meet a young Paige. Elliott tearfully talked about their early days, how they met, what they liked to do. Lauren remarked, "She looks so *healthy!*" So much of the pain of Paige's death was seeing her in pain and helplessly watching her die a difficult death. I mentioned that the painful memory of her death had overshadowed the fact she was a vibrant, healthy, energetic woman most of her life. Lauren nodded, stating she had only been able to obsess about her mother's death. Could healing start when one remembered the healthy person as well?

Several systemic shifts occurred in this session. Perhaps most important was the real *joining* of the family system for the first time since Paige's death. The animosity and blame over decisions made around Paige's last stage of life gave way to amalgamation. Elliott somehow became more human, more compassionate, and his tears over Paige's death conveyed an emotional side not typically seen; Lauren seemed to grasp his grief and sorrow for perhaps the first time. He was no longer at the top of the hierarchy; he became simply a piece of the family pie. Lauren, by sharing in her grief with the family, was no longer the sole person charged with keeping her mother's legacy. She was able to share her legacy with the new traditions they all committed to in honoring Paige's life. Lauren left the session with her eyes filled with tears and a huge smile. She somehow seemed softer. She thanked me, and I, in turn, thanked all of them for allowing me to be a part of honoring Paige.

OTHER ART THERAPY SESSIONS

Changes in families can progress at a different rate, as we are not only dealing with the current system, but the ghosts of systems past. It is imperative to remember that change for all of us is usually discontinuous. Early family therapists coined the term "homeostasis" to characterize the status quo, regardless of how dysfunctional, that each family sustains, especially when confronted with change. Change in families may be less obvious and less timely than the therapist might envision at times; of course, the opposite is true as well

This family remained committed to confront their challenges; despite the frustrations, their love and allegiance towards change was laudable. During our last session, Lauren emphatically stated that she was "doing so much, so very much better." She confronted Lee to both recognize her improvements as well as allow for the occasional blue days she continued to have. Lauren and Lee stated they wanted to improve their parenting and communication skills. Prior to Paige's death, Lauren and Paige were "everything to each other ... best friends, confidants, talked all the time." One might suspect that Paige and Lauren formed first an alliance, and later a coalition, leaving both of their respective spouses as the "odd man out." This leaves several questions: were Lauren and Lee truly able to build a spousal subsystem, given the fierce attachment between Lauren and her Mom? Did their enmeshment further fuel Elliott's disengagement from the family, particularly with his wife? If so, could this account for the differences in how each grieved? In other words, Elliott's disengagement provided a venue for anticipatory grief, whereby grieving begins prior to the person's death. Paige's death challenged the entire family system to reorganize, shift hierarchical power, and restructure the boundaries.

These shifts, however painful, may enable Lauren and Lee the freedom to build a spousal system, one Minuchin identified where each member would ideally accommodate, nurture, and support the uniqueness of the other (Becvar & Becvar, 2003). It is fascinating to examine their last two directives, a kinetic family portrait, and a wishful, future family portrait. They were given the option to include extended family members like Elliott; note that all included only the immediate family and family dog. As the family drew, they laughed and bantered back and forth about their skill level; this free exchange elucidated a spontaneity not seen in previous sessions. The similarity is striking between their drawings, given they drew independently without viewing and prompting each other. The first set of drawings, the kinetic family portrait, similarly depict the family outside, near water, either hiking or walking around. Both parents placed the family in an identical fashion, and overall, the family appears close and happy (see Figure 5.11, Figure 5.12, and Figure 5.13). The future drawing again was remarkably similar; all depicted a new home (note how similar Lauren's and her son's are) and a new baby (see Figure 5.14, Figure 5.15, and Figure 5.16). Evaluating current and future family drawings often reveals the level of harmonization within the family system. This family, despite their challenges, seems very synchronistic in both their current view and future desires for the family system.

Figure 5.11   Lauren's kinetic family portrait.

Figure 5.12   Lee's kinetic family portrait.

A perfect way with a.k.

Figure 5.13   Jackson's kinetic family portrait.

DEBT

BABY

HOME SWEET HOME

Figure 5.14   Lauren's future family portrait.

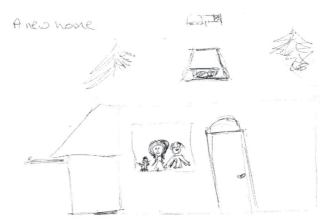

Figure 5.15   Lee's future family portrait.

Figure 5.16   Jackson's future family portrait.

How often have we observed that the person at the top of the hierarchy, who maintains the power in the system, is the one most reluctant to relinquish or share in their power? This seems true for Elliott as well. His control over the family system has been simultaneously an irritant and a triumph financially for the family. His success as a businessman resulted from his self-discipline and hegemony. Part of his challenge is to not "run" his family as he ran his business. In an effort to utilize Elliott's high energy, the therapists suggested he form a closer relationship with his grandson (this provides an opportunity for connection or alliance, and may form a new subsystem). To his credit, Elliott has followed through by picking Jackson up at his school on his early release day, and spending quality time with him. He has attempted to dictate less and support more with Lauren and Lee, with mixed results. He has generously booked a family vacation for him and his girlfriend, and Lauren, Lee, and Jackson, in a gesture of kindness; hopefully, this will also provide an opportunity for the family to relax and perhaps find new transaction patterns.

Minuchin and Fishman (1981) state:

> A family which has experienced death … may have problems reassigning the tasks of the missing member. Sometimes a family will establish the attitude that if the mother had lived, she would have known what to do. Taking over the mother's functions becomes an act of disloyalty to her memory. Old coalitions may be respected, as if the mother were still alive. (p. 57)

The case example paralleled the description above. The family continues to realign boundaries and work on strengthening the system.

Perhaps the last drawing created by Elliott speaks to the new beginnings desired by himself and all of the family members. Entitled "Rising Sun," it depicts a figure reflecting and relaxing by the mountains and water (see Figure 5.17). Elliott stated this was a hopeful picture, depicting a future that was more settled, more harmonious, more serene. Despite the pain and anger, all family members invested considerable energy into the art therapy process, and were motivated to follow through with assignments and suggestions.

Structural family art therapy seemed valuable and well suited for this family's needs. Ultimately, there were positive shifts in the family subsystem, more direct communication, and work continues on the development of an evolving family hierarchy. The evolving family system has a spouse subsystem that is clearly delineated, and a more fluid relationship between the generations. Absent are the coalitions, which allows for the spouse subsystem to make decisions appropriate for the family, and frees Lauren from being stuck in her family of origin (see Figure 5.18).

Retrospectively, Lauren's family tapestry has been altered. Paige's death has frayed the fabric, creating holes. The fabric will never have all the original colors and the design has been permanently tainted. By realigning the family structure, the family has created new threads to weave into the tapestry. The resulting tapestry will hopefully reflect new resilience, strength, and stability despite the tatter and holes. It is the family's task to keep the colors of the original tapestry vibrant in the memory of their current system and in systems of generations to come.

Figure 5.17 Elliott's last drawing.

Figure 5.18 Structural map of Lauren's evolving family system.

REFERENCES

Becvar, D. S., & Becvar, R. J. (2003). *Family therapy: A systemic integration* (5th ed.). Boston: Allyn & Bacon.

Colapinto, J. (1991). Structural family therapy. In A. S. Gurman & D. P. Kniskern (Eds.), *Handbook of family therapy* (Vol. 2, pp. 417–433). New York: Brunner/Mazel.

Donnelly, M. (1989). Some aspects of art therapy and family therapy. In A. Gilroy & T. Dalley (Eds.), *Pictures at an exhibition: Selected essays on art therapy.* London: Routledge.

Ford Sori, C. E. (1995). The "art" of restructuring: Integrating art with structural family therapy. *Journal of Family Psychotherapy, 6,* 13–31.

Goldenberg, I., & Goldenberg, H. (2004). *Family therapy: An overview* (6th ed.). Pacific Grove, CA: Brooks/Cole.

Jordan, K. (2001). Family art therapy: The joint family holiday drawing. *The Family Journal: Counseling and Therapy for Couples and Families, 9,* 52–54.

Lamberti, J. W., & Detmer, C. M. (1993). Model of family grief assessment and treatment. *Death Studies, 17,* 55–67.

Manicom, H., & Boronska, T. (2003). Co-creating change within a child protection system: Integrating art therapy with family therapy practice. *Journal of Family Therapy, 25,* 217–232.

Minuchin, S. (1974). *Families and family therapy.* Cambridge, MA: Harvard University Press.

Minuchin, S. (1998). Structural family therapy. In F. M. Dattilio (Ed.), *Case studies on couple and family therapy: Systemic and cognitive perspectives* (pp. 108–131). New York: Guilford Press.

Minuchin, S., & Fishman, H. C. (1981). *Family therapy techniques.* Cambridge, MA: Harvard University Press.

Nichols, M. P., & Schwartz, R. C. (2006). *Family therapy: Concepts and methods* (7th ed.). Boston: Allyn & Bacon.

Riley, S. (1994). *Integrative approaches to family art therapy.* Chicago, IL: Magnolia Street Publishers.

Riley, S., & Malchiodi, C. A. (2003). Family art therapy. In C. A. Malchiodi (Ed.), *Handbook of art therapy* (pp. 362–374). New York: Guilford Press.

Simon, R. (1992). One on one: Conversations with the shapers of family therapy. Washington, DC: Guildford Press.

Wylie, M. S. (2005). Maestro of the consulting room. *Psychotherapy Networker, 29*(3), 40–50.

CHAPTER 6

Experiential Family Therapy and Art Therapy

CHRISTINE KERR

INTRODUCTION

When I began studying family therapy, the first book on the required reading list was *The Family Crucible* by Gus Napier, Ph.D. with Carl Whitaker, M.D. (1978). The professor was clear in stating that this book had *most* influenced his development as a family therapist. Before I began reading this book, I glanced at the dictionary to refresh my memory; what was a crucible? I remember thinking that the use of this word in the title of a book was unusual. *Crucible* can be defined as "the state of pain or anguish that tests one's resiliency and character" (*Webster's*, 2003). While I was reading *The Family Crucible*, I began to understand the reason for these unusual words in the title. As I read the book, I felt that the author was allowing the reader a personal look into the lives of others, as well as the counseling experiences of two therapists with a couple and their children. In reading this book, I was allowed a lens into the characters and their struggles with family issues. The scenarios of the interior lives of husbands, wives, fathers, mothers, sons, daughters, siblings and their patterns of intimacy and discord were rich and descriptive. *The Family Crucible* was truly a page turner. As I have continued my work in family therapy and family art therapy, I still require my students to read *The Family Crucible* (Napier & Whitaker, 1978). The rationale for continuing this tradition is the descriptive quality of the author's words as well as the creativity, freewheeling and intuitive approach of Carl Whitaker as a family therapist. Whitaker's spontaneity, expressive and metaphorical approach speaks to all of us in the creative arts.

This chapter focuses on a unique form of family therapy and family art therapy that is "not based on intellectual understanding, but rather upon an interactive process, metaphorical language, and personal interaction" (Keith, 1982, p. 331). Experiential family therapy is a branch of family therapy treatment that was developed in the 1950s and 1960s. The tenets of both existential therapy and humanistic psychology exerted significant influence on the theoretical orientation of this form of family therapy. Additionally, the use of the expressive therapies to augment the family therapy process was introduced with the work of Kwiatkowska (1967).

In this chapter, the role of existential and humanistic psychology are discussed. In the second portion of this chapter the role of the family therapist as it relates to experiential family therapy and family art therapy is discussed. The accomplishments of Carl Whitaker (1988) and Virginia Satir (1988) are highlighted. Both of these charismatic individuals were pivotal in developing experiential family therapy. In the final section of this chapter, a dynamic case study will illustrate how this form of family therapy clearly intersects with the art therapy process.

THE EXISTENTIAL AND HUMANISTIC INFLUENCES ON EXPERIENTIAL FAMILY THERAPY

The existential and humanistic traditions in psychology were major influences in family therapy. The existential approach to psychology arose out of an objection to Freud's model of psychic functioning and his efforts to understand human behavior by way of reductionism, tracing all human behavior to a few basic drives. Second, the existential movement objected to Freud's determinism, in noting that Freud (1914) viewed all mental functioning as being caused by identifiable factors already in existence.

Existential psychology is not a comprehensive psychotherapeutic system but rather a frame of reference by which both the therapist and the client/families begin to understand each member of a family as "an existing, immediate person, not as a composite of drives, archetypes, or conditioning" (Corsini & Wedding, 1995, p. 290).

Additionally, the significance of existential psychology is in its reaction against the therapist's tendency to view therapy as a pattern of well-defined techniques or the projection of a particular therapist's theoretical viewpoint.

Existential Theory's Influence on Family Therapy

According to Nichols and Schwartz (2004) existential thought contributed to the experiential family therapist's emphasis on unblocking emotional expression, which continues to be a useful counterweight to the reductionistic emphasis on behavior and cognition, common to today's problem-solving approaches. Consequently, basic family conflicts are not viewed as suppressed instinctual drives or a result of unresolved conflicts from early childhood experiences. Instead, family dysfunction emanates from those universal human conditions such as *conflict, anxiety, isolation, meaninglessness,* and questions about *love and creativity.* These universal conditions are the basic dimension of all human questioning and often human struggle. According to existential thought, every individual will experience some conflict regarding these *givens* at some point in their existence (Buber, 1970; Bugental, 1976; Frankl, 1963). Second, the existential approach emphasizes a view of human nature where the family members have the ability to strive towards self-determination. This has been defined as "I-AM" experience or the ontological experience (May, 1965; Yalom, 1995). The client/family unit becomes responsible for making gains during treatment. Within the therapeutic relationship, this construct emphasizes the therapist's need to understand the client's current experience and worldview. May (1961) and Van Duerzen (1983) agree on one fundamental procedural point: the family therapist must approach the patient phenomenologically. The family therapist must enter the patient's experiential world and listen to the phenomena of that world without presuppositions. From an existential perspective, Bugental (1976), observes that the best experiential therapists are those who have gained some mastery over their own inner turmoil. This mastery allows the therapist to accept the client's therapeutic gains and losses without personal bias. Jourard (1976) concurs with Bugental (1976), when he writes, "a therapist cannot himself lead a person to a freer existence than he himself has attained" (p. 40).

Humanistic Psychology Influence on Experiential Family Therapy

Humanistic psychology grew out of the philosophical background of the existential tradition (May, 1961; Rogers, 1961, 1980). Humanism is grounded in a positive view of humanity that views the potential of every person to innately strive towards becoming fully functional or *a self-actualized individual* (Rogers, 1980). A client's ability to *self-actualize* can be *synergized* when the therapeutic alliance is strong between a caring therapist and family members. When the client family is given the opportunity to experience a caring therapeutic alliance with a family art therapist, often the family art therapist's support can reframe the family's distorted feelings.

Second, it has been argued that the therapeutic relationship empowers clients and their families. The therapeutic alliance can also be defined in terms of the therapist's *affective responsiveness* to the client within that relationship. Within the humanistic tradition there is a strong emphasis on what Buber (1970) termed the "I-thou relationship" or the personal relationship that the therapist strives to authentically establish with the client. Clients are more apt to actualize their potential for growth, creativity, wholeness, and inner directedness when the therapist is cognizant of his or her obligations to the therapeutic relationship (Rogers, 1961). The affective qualities of genuineness, nonpossessive warmth, empathy, unconditional regard, and respect for the client are quintessential emotional qualities that the therapist is obligated to provide for his or her clients (Rogers, 1951).

Humanistic Psychology Influence on Family Art Therapy

Creative expression goes hand in hand with the constructs of existential philosophy and humanistic traditions. From a humanistic tradition it is essential that all clients' art making be received in a *nonjudgmental* manner by the family art therapist. Art skills of the clients are secondary to the therapeutic making of the art piece. Second, the family art therapist's therapeutic stance must be action oriented and dynamic (Landgarten, 1987). By understanding the interface between media and art materials, affective responsiveness additionally underscores the humanistic tradition.

KEY THEORETICAL CONSTRUCTS OF
EXPERIENTIAL FAMILY THERAPY

Brief Biographical Background of Carl Whitaker, M.D.

Carl Whitaker (1918–1995) was a psychiatrist who was active in family therapy, well before the field was formally recognized in the early 1950s. His model of family therapy has been called symbolic-experiential family therapy (Whitaker & Keith, 1981). Whitaker stated that he began to formulate his ideas about how to treat families from his early experiences in World War II, where he administrated a small psychiatric hospital and received training in child therapy and play therapy (Nichols & Schwartz, 2004).

From these experiences, Whitaker began to observe that his patients in treatment appeared to respond more authentically and with less resistance when he spontaneously engaged them in therapy sessions. Whitaker began to view "psychologically troubled people ... as being alienated from feelings and frozen into devitalized routines" (Hoffman, 1981, p. 51).

In 1946, Whitaker became chairman of the Department of Psychiatry at Emory University, where he began working with schizophrenic clients and their families. During this time, Whitaker became instrumental in organizing this fledgling field of family therapy. He organized conferences. These early conferences allowed other therapists to share their experiences and discuss this innovative type of clinical treatment. He remained actively involved in treating families, conducting workshops until his death in April 1995.

The work of Carl Whitaker is difficult to operationalize from a clearly theoretical perspective. The reason for this difficulty is noted by Whitaker's emphasis on *the person of the therapist* as the primary agent for change within a family system, as well as his insistence on teaching family treatment by apprenticeship. Whitaker was an advocate of co-leadership because of the family therapist's intense involvement with client families (Napier & Whitaker, 1978).

Additionally, Whitaker & Keith (1981) believed that family therapists could not learn to conduct family therapy in a purely intellectual manner that proscribes set definitions of diagnosis or treatment interventions. In fact, Whitaker denied that he adhered to any theory or proscribed to any technique. Whitaker (1976a) summed up his antitheoretical view of psychological theory in a paper entitled, "The Hindrance of Theory in Clinical Work."

Whitaker's creative and spontaneous thinking formed the basis of his bold and innovative approach to family treatment. Instead of relying on theoretical constructs to guide his therapeutic orientation, Whitaker (1976a) attempted to engage his client families by using metaphors and his own repertoire of personal stories to open up communication. His style was unpretentious and emotionally responsive. Whitaker deliberately created tension by confronting families. He often used paradoxical injunctions. He believed that confrontation would result in *unfreezing* the family. Confrontation often created stress for individual family members. Stress was necessary for change (Whitaker, 1976a). He also encouraged his families to share their fantasies, to free associate and recall their dreams in therapy.

In 1981 Whitaker and Keith listed principles designed to help the therapist avoid errors. As a family art therapist and psychotherapist, I have found these principles most useful.

- Do not become so much a part of the family that it affects your ability to help.
- Do not become aloof from the family that you operate from only a technical perspective.
- Do not pretend that you don't feel stress or feelings of inadequacy.
- Do not employ a technique for change if you will only create another serious problem in a family member.
- Move at the appropriate pace for the family.
- Do not expect insight to produce change. Therapists often move too fast and expect insight to produce change.
- Do not expect the family to operate from your value system.
- Do not revere your intuitive leaps. Intuition is only intuition, and it may not be appropriate for your family. If the family resists, back off quickly.
- Recognize when you have the family's trust. If you don't, you may waste time in the relationship-building phase when the family is ready to work.
- Do not create a scapegoat in the family. Help the family understand that each person has a part in the problems within the family.
- Realize the benefits of not treating someone. Not all families need therapy and not all families will benefit from therapy.

The Need for Professional Growth Work for the Family Therapist   Whitaker (1976a) described his belief that the family therapist actually begins preparing for his or her professional role within his or her own family of origin. For Whitaker (1976a), the self-concept of a therapist is far more important than specific interventions or techniques. Because his approach emphasizes the therapist's personal characteristics over the use of techniques, personal therapy for the therapist is viewed as being essential. This therapy may include marital or family therapy for the trainee or individual therapy. The goal of personal growth work is to increase the therapist's access to his or her own personal creativity.

Brief Biographical Background of Virginia Satir

A member of the Palo Alto Group, Virginia Satir began treating families in 1951 and established a training program for psychiatric residents at the Illinois State Psychiatric Center. Like Carl Whitaker, she was also a charismatic family therapist. Also like Carl Whitaker, Virginia Satir was known more for her clinical style of communication than her theoretical contributions to the field of family therapy. The quality of her therapeutic artistry was in her ability to communicate to her client's families.

Satir (1988) believed that families were trapped in narrow and often redundant roles, such as *victim, placator, defiant one,* or *rescuer.* For example, the victim was often the scapegoat. The *victim* communicates passively and often negatively. The placator communicates in a style where he or she attempts to keep others from getting upset. *The defiant* one communicates in a way that is aggressive and often finds fault in other family members. The rescuer communicates as a caretaker. Often the caretaker attempts to explain why family members feel and say the things that they do. Based on individual communication styles, Satir attempted to work with her families to eliminate these ineffective styles and replace them with more open, congruent, and direct communication (Satir, 1983). Because Virginia Satir held an optimistic worldview, she believed that each individual had the potential for growth. She advocated that family members had the potential ability to share their thoughts and feelings. She created a therapeutic environment where family members could experience a sense of self-worth and congruency with the family therapist. Her approach was flexible and often variable. Her flexibility has been noted in family sessions lasting 45 minutes to day-long marathons. Her variable repertoire includes the use of drama therapy, religion, and dance.

Based on this experiential approach, Virginia Satir (1983) incorporated the use of expressive therapies with her family/clients. She utilized family reconstruction as a method for families to reveal the source(s) of their own belief systems. The goal of family reconstruction was to assist the families in further understanding their own nuclear family. It is a form of psychodramatic reenactment, where the family explores significant events spanning three generations of the family life cycle. This technique often incorporates ropes and blindfolds to dramatize the constricting roles family members often become trapped in. This technique guides the therapist in unlocking dysfunctional patterns that stem from the family's family of origin. The goals of this experiential reenactment are to enable families to identify the roots of old learning patterns, to assist them in reformulating more realistic assessments of their parents, and to assist them in further integrating their own self-actualization (Satir & Baldwin, 1983).

THE FAMILY ART THERAPY PROCESS:
AN EXPERIENTIAL APPROACH

The art process in family treatment may increase *relationship building* for family members (Landgarten, 1987; Linesch, 1993). In all forms of family therapy, an increase in relationship building requires that communication among family members are allowed to increase. As noted by both Whitaker and Keith (1981) and Virginia Satir (1983), dysfunctional communication in families are often a result of family members engaging in redundant roles, nonproductive rituals, and behaviors that compromise the expression of authentic emotion. The art therapy process offers a unique opportunity for both the family therapist and family art therapist to circumvent highly rigid patterns of behavior and ritual by utilizing the visual arts as a tool for unlocking underlying thoughts and feelings. It is important to note that the process of art making is innately intuitive and often nonverbal. When the family is given an art directive, this task involves a unique effort and intent on the part of the client(s). Consequently, the nonverbal nature of the art process may offer a means for liberating bound and redundant interpersonal styles that often make relationships stale and rigid (Landgarten, 1987). As noted by Landgarten (1987) and Linesch (1993) the art process often assists the treatment process. Art making may act as a catalyst for the facilitation of *energy* and *empowerment*. According to Linesch (1993), "the making of art is by definition a creative and productive endeavor; as such, it promotes a sense of self and of accomplishment for families entrenched in failure and impotence, the initiating process of creativity can be liberating and constructive" (p. 24). Finally, efficacy in utilizing the visual arts working may denote the availability of clinical data that can economically be transferred from the visual art product into clinical assessment and treatment (Landgarten, 1987; Linesch, 1993).

Consequently, the introduction of the art process into family treatment can be a creative, proactive, and transforming approach to family treatment. Art interventions have been developed that have the potential to parallel many of the practices of conventional family therapy. Specifically within the experiential family art therapy tradition, Kwiatkowska (1962), Rubin (1987), and Landgarten (1987) all developed family art-based tasks for evaluative purposes. These art-based assessments provide the family with an opportunity to creatively explore and collaborate through the process of making art together.

When the family art therapist engages in art making, the family art therapist is given the opportunity to view family boundaries, communicative patterns, hierarchies, and resistances (Landgarten, 1987; Rubin, 1987). According to Landgarten (1987), within the limitations of a single family session, the family art therapist may witness *family blueprints* that often are indicators of overall family functioning. Examples of a family *visual blueprint* are indicated in the numerous dialogues between family members and the therapist, as well as in an individual or the communal drawing experience. Family dynamics may be revealed in the use of the family's symbols (Rubin, 1987). The size and placement of images may visually mirror family roles and forms of family communication (Landgarten, 1987; Rubin, 1987; Satir, 1971; Whitaker, 1976a). A family's system and subsystem are often gleaned by observing who leads or follows in the execution of a group art mural.

A group mural is an art task that requires a large piece of butcher paper and various types of art media; preferably art media that has the ability to cover a large space such as paints or chalk pastels. Jointly, the family makes art on the mural paper. Prior to the art-making phase of the process, there is often a time during which the family discusses and plans the execution of the group mural. Often during this time, family dynamics and alliances may be evident in the discussion period prior to implementation of the mural. Family members who are reserved or shy may choose to work on the outlying reaches of the drawing or suggestively add only a minimal effort to the overall drawing task. Assertive family members may draw over most of the mural paper; therefore not respecting other family members' drawing space (Landgarten, 1987; Linesch, 1993).

CASE STUDY

Both Carl Whitaker (1976a) and Virginia Satir (1983) were concerned with effective outcomes for their clients and their families. Both of these experiential family therapists believed that the goal of family treatment was to provide each individual family member with a *personal growth experience* as well as to increase each family member's sense of belonging to each other. Both Whitaker (1976b) and Satir (1983) felt that enhancing communication through creative therapeutic interventions "unblocked" emotions and ultimately assisted the family to change, often to weather developmental life crisis. As noted by family art therapists (Landgarten, 1987; Rubin, 1987; Linesch, 1993), family emotions are often intensified by the directness of the art experience. The art experience may support the tradition of the experiential family therapy movement. The following case study explores the family process during three family art sessions.

The Family

This family was in treatment for approximately six months. The family was in traditional verbal family therapy for one month with a practicing psychologist who specialized in family therapy. This clinician asked that I co-participate in the treatment of this family. This psychologist was interested in using family art therapy interventions to augment the therapeutic process. He also believed that co-therapy would be helpful to modulate nonproductive resistances that the family exhibited.

In experiential therapy, there are no techniques, only people (Kempler, 1968). According to Nichols and Schwartz (2004), "this epigram neatly summarizes the faith in the curative power of the therapist's personality. It isn't so much what therapists do that matters, it's who they are" (p.145). This treating family therapist was lively and an engaging individual. We had previously consulted on various cases as well as jointly participated in a supervision group. I enjoy his storytelling and his ability to share his thoughts about his clients in an open and thoughtful way. But most of all, I enjoyed his humor. He appeared to be able to reframe negative statements by using humor. He was evocative and creative. I welcomed the opportunity to co-lead in the treatment of this family.

My co-therapist had already completed the initial assessment of this family. The family was asked if they would like to participate in family art therapy and whether they would be willing to agree to participate in co-therapy with me over the middle phase of treatment. Dr. A had told this family that he was feeling uneasy about each family member's need for attention. He felt that the nonverbal approach might be productive and that I too had a *New York sense of humor*. I remember appreciating this compliment and his vote of confidence. As noted by Kemplar (1968):

> The family therapist becomes a family member during the initial interviews, participating as fully as he is able, hopefully available for appreciation and criticism as well as he is able to dispense it. He laughs, cries and rages. He feels and shares his embarrassment, confusion and helplessness. (p. 97)

Working in tandem with another co-therapist is a hallmark of Whitaker's therapeutic techniques. "A strong investment in co-therapy relationship (or treatment team) keeps therapists from being inducted or drawn into families" (Nichols & Schwartz, 2004, p. 147).

At our first session together, the family was introduced to me. The session was scheduled for a longer period of time versus the traditional 50-minute treatment hour. We asked the family to schedule for an hour and a half. This allowed for my introduction into the treatment process as well as the art making session and verbal processing of the art experience.

The family came into the art studio. The mother was a teacher, the father a computer analyst. Their oldest son had graduated college and moved away from home. He was employed and was making a successful start at a career in a publishing house in San Francisco. The oldest son had communicated to Dr. A that he would be available for therapy. The second child, Elizabeth was 20 years old. She had been treated for depression and addictions when she was 18. She was currently in a local community college. She was a freshman. She stated her frustrations about continuing college due to her lack of academic motivation. Her scholastic accomplishments were marred by her indecisiveness and feeling that "her older brother gets all the attention."

Her mother, who I will call Mary, verbalized frustrations at her daughter's lack of accomplishment. I recall Mary saying, "Just get up and go to school. We don't want a repeat of you going back to the hospital." Elizabeth's father was much less direct. He stated, "Leave Elizabeth alone, she'll find her way." Dr. A and I began to explore the *communication patterns* and the *family roles* that each member of this family displayed. My co-therapist and I began to role-play with each other. We dramatized the role of placator, defiant child, and angry mother in an evocative and verbal manner. The family appeared amused and probably a little stunned. When the role-playing was finished, each family member commented, "You seemed to have us nailed down to a tee."

Being an educator, sometimes I find it hard to take the professor out of the session. During this session, I felt it would be useful if I explained certain basic concepts of family therapy. I remember talking thoughtfully with them about (a) *developmental life cycles of the family*; (b) the concept of the *identified patient*; (c) some of the underlying reason why adolescents act out; and finally, (d) why these behaviors are often *symptomatic* of the need to draw attention to adolescent fears that may emanate from possible *spousal discord*. Some of what I said appeared to resonate with Elizabeth, the youngest child. I remember moving towards her. I moved my chair next to her. I offered her some paper. I said, "Are you ready to draw and tell us *your story?*" She said yes. Her parents remained thoughtful but were not willing to engage in the art process with Elizabeth. Dr. A and I both felt that this reluctance would ultimately benefit Elizabeth. She had displayed immobility and fear about opening herself up to her parents and to Dr. A. Elizabeth drew "My life." Her parents watched, and their daughter began to tell *how* and *why* she felt as she did.

Elizabeth drew in a storyboard format (Figure 6.1). She carefully drew the eight boxes as she executed key life events within each drawn box. We all watched her choose her markers. She appeared very intent and well prepared to complete this task. The resulting life story disclosed aspects of her life that her family had omitted in the initial assessment phase. The brain surgery in 1991 had been overlooked as a key stressor in Elizabeth's development. Both Dr. A and I found this omission to be significant. I asked both Elizabeth and her parents why they had failed to communicate this event. Her mother replied, "Because she's fine." When I asked Elizabeth, she looked at her draw-

Figure 6.1 Experiential family art therapy case study.

ing and then turned away. She seemed to stare at a photograph of mine on the wall. It was my favorite Mary Cassatt drawing of a mother and child. She said, "It happened a while ago … I am fine." She looked towards her father. Their glances met, but they quickly averted their eyes.

At this point, Dr. A asked Elizabeth to physically arrange her parents in relationship to how she was feeling about them. Reluctantly, she stood up and walked towards her father. She took his hand and requested that he stand near her. She wanted to include her brother in this dramatic reenactment but he declined. I asked him why? Unable to give a reason, I asked "could I step in for her brother now?" Elizabeth said, "yes."

Finally, she glanced at her mother. Rather than approaching her, Elizabeth pointed, "You stand there Mother!" She pointed to the door. Her mother appeared shocked and somewhat indignant. Dr. A escorted Elizabeth's mother to the far corner of the room. Dr. A stated, "I'll stand with you. I know that you are uncomfortable and this process hurts." He took her hand. Together they quietly took their place at the opposite side of the room near the door.

Elizabeth was able to share after the *drama reenactment,* that she was furious with her mother. She was not able to fully articulate her feelings, but the placement of her mother, father, and brother were a clear indication of her discomfort. This dramatic family constellation appeared to state nonverbally her feelings of failure, low self-esteem, and disharmony between her mother and herself. However, it is important to note that in Elizabeth's *visual storyboard,* she was able to draw herself with a hopeful ending. Not only had she actively become empowered by the art-making segment of this session, it may be suggested that the process of initiating her solo art making allowed her to physically engage in the *family sculpting* portion of the session.

In experiential family therapy and family art therapy, spontaneity is necessary. As noted by Weinhold and Fenell (2003), it is essential within experiential family therapy and experiential family art therapy to encourage feedback among family members. This feedback often allows individual family members to explore how they think, feel, and react towards each other. An art directive was given to each family member to complete over a two-week period. We asked each member to draw themselves in relationship to *how they feel despair within their family*. According to Weinhold and Fenell (2003), when a therapist heightens the despair a family member feels, the others will rally to provide support that was not present before (p. 248). From an existential tradition, despair is part of life, what has been called *a given*. Despair is often and, yes, unfortunately part of family life. However, denial of negative feelings, the denial of sadness, often intensifies emotionality. In noting the "closed" and aloof presentation of this family, both Dr. A and I felt that it would be beneficial to have each family member draw their representation of themselves in *"despair."*

According to Whitaker and Keith (1981), it is important for the family therapist and family art therapist to avoid becoming enamored by *intuitive leaps*. In assigning this art directive as a homework assignment, we were hoping that the family would become less resistive to sharing their thoughts and feelings. The patterns of this family's communicative repertoire were limited and constricted. But, "intuition is only intuition and it may not be appropriate for the family. If the family resists, back off *quickly*" (Weinhold & Fenell, 2003, p. 249). In this case, this particular art directive was a positive stimulus to forthcoming sessions that opened up both communication and emotions that had been suppressed for many years. In noting the resistance of the parents in the initial art therapy session, both Dr. A and I felt the need to allow the family to complete the exercise within their own time frame. The family brought in the drawings after three weeks.

The daughter shared her drawing. Elizabeth displayed obvious artistic skills in life drawing. Elizabeth was proud of her accomplishment. She stated, "This is how I have felt with all of you." In Figure 6.2, Elizabeth's drawing depicts a young person sitting in a crouched position. The drawing speaks to Elizabeth's despair. One tear defines her sadness. In many ways, the *one tear* is possibly symbolic of Elizabeth's caution in expressing too much emotion.

In Figure 6.3, the father has depicted his feelings towards his wife. The use of perspective is evocative and profound. The wife is depicted in the picture within the self-portrait. Anger and tension appears to permeate this drawing as well as the use of heightened affective color usage. When displayed to his wife, Mary, she stated, "I am speechless." The last drawing, drawn by Elizabeth's mother, appears larger then life (Figure 6.4). Though the size of the drawing denotes importance, the feeling of the drawing appears to indicate constriction. In this drawing, she has drawn her hands encircling her body, unable to be responsive or physically intimate. She indicates a lack of

Figure 6.2   Experiential family art therapy case study.

feet (Oster & Gould, 1987). This may suggest a lack of mobility or emotion in the environment. Her self-portrait is extremely large. In fact it appears to come off the page. Perhaps she is saying, "Maybe I am that inadequate?" (Hammer, 1958; Oster & Gould, 1987).

From this drawing initiative, the family began to *see* each other, both through their artwork and their communication. Elizabeth began to talk about her brain surgery and her fears of "not being complete and a disappointment." Mary began to understand her

Figure 6.3   Experiential family art therapy case study.

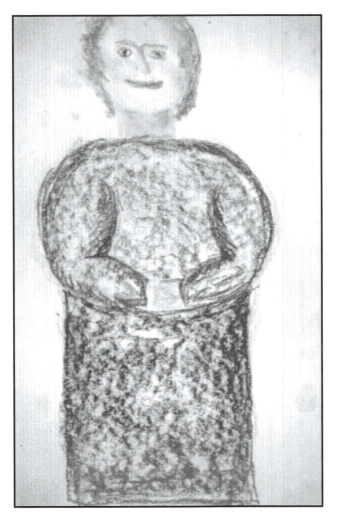

Figure 6.4 Experiential family art therapy case study.

role within the family system. She was able to express her family of origin concerns.

As Mary recounted her family of origin, she became softer and more expressive. She told a story of a young girl growing up with an ineffectual mother. Her mother's passivity had only placated her father, whom she saw as domineering and emotionally distant. Eventually, this impasse had lead to her parents' divorce. Mary was 19 years of age. Additionally, Mary shared that as a young adult, she had to endure repeated hospitalizations of a brother who eventually died. Her fears for her own daughter and her lack of grieving for her brother had clouded her emotional responsiveness to her own daughter, Elizabeth.

Figure 6.5   Experential family art therapy case study.

In the final drawing, Figure 6.5, the family was open and willing to make a group mural. As I recall, this was a type of celebration after many months of treatment. Dr. A and I carefully prepared the studio. We had refreshments. The family was ending treatment. Elizabeth had successfully completed community college and she had done extremely well. Mary and her husband had entered individual treatment. They were making gains in both their marriage and their emotional responsiveness towards their daughter. Their son had requested that he be present for this final session. Both Dr. A and I welcomed his presence. He had been actively involved by either correspondence or by telephone with all family members during treatment. They chose the theme of *the wall* as a metaphor for their family journey. Both Dr. A and I watched as they handily poured paint and discussed the execution of this mural. They mixed paint. They negotiated and they withdrew. They kept saying individually and collectively, "I am no artist." They all participated. They continued to paint. They drew the wall of their emotions. They broke the wall with a waterfall. I believe that *they* and *us* all grew.

REFERENCES

Buber, M. (1970). *I and thou* (W. Kaufman, Trans.). New York: Scribners.

Bugenthal, J. F. T. (1976). *The search for existential identity: Patient therapist dialogues in humanistic psychotherapy.* San Francisco: Jossey–Bass.

Bugenthal, J. F. T. (1981). *The search for authenticity: An existential-humanistic approach.* Reading, MA: Addison- Wesley.

Corisini, R., & Wedding, D. (1995). *Current psycotherapies.* Itasca, IL: F. E. Peacock.

Frankl, V. (1963). *Man's search for meaning.* Boston: Beacon Press.

Freud, S. (1914). The history of the psychoanalytic movement. In *The complete psychological works of Sigmund Freud* (Vol. 14, James Strachey, Ed.). London: Hogarth Press.

Guerin, D. J. & Pendergast, E. (1976). Family therapy: Theory and practice (pp. 450–465). New York: Gardner Press.

Hammer, E. (1958). *The clinical application of projective drawings.* Springfield, IL: Charles C. Thomas.

Hoffman, L. (1981). *Foundations of family therapy.* New York: Basic Books.

Jourard, S. (1976). Changing personal worlds: A humanistic perspective. In A. Wandersman, P. J. Popper, & D. F. Ricks (Eds.), *Humanism and behaviorism: Dialogue and growth* (pp. 69–83). New York: Pergamon.

Keith, D. V. (1982). Symbolic-experiential family therapy. In J. R. Neill & D. P. Kniskern (Eds.), *From psyche to system: The evolving therapy of Carl Whitaker* (pp. 196–211). New York: Guilford Press.

Kemplar, W. (1968). Experiential psychotherapy with families. *Family Process, 7*(1), 88–99.

Kwiatkowska, H. Y. (1962). Family art therapy: Experiments with a new technique. *Bulletin of Art Therapy, 1*(93), 3–15.

Kwiatkowska, H. Y. (1967). Family art therapy. *Family Process, 6,* 37–55.

Landgarten, H. (1987) *Family art psychotherapy.* New York: Brunner/Mazel.

Linesch, D. (1993). *Art therapy with families in crisis.* New York: Brunner/Mazel.

May, R. (1961). *Existential psychology.* New York: Random House.

Napier, A. Y., & Whitaker, C. (1978). *The family crucible.* New York: Harper & Row.

Nichols, M., & Schwartz, R. (2004). *Family therapy: Concepts and methods* (5th ed.). New York: Allyn & Bacon.

Oster, G., & Gould, P. (1987). *Using drawings in assessment and therapy.* New York: Brunner/Mazel.

Rogers, C. (1951). *Client-centered therapy.* Boston: Houghton-Mifflin.

Rogers, C. (1961). On becoming a person: A therapists view of psychotherapy. Boston: Houghton-Mifflin.

Rogers, C. (1980). *A way of being.* Boston: Houghton-Mifflin.

Rubin, J. R. (1997). Approaches to Art Therapy: New York: Brunner-Mazel.

Satir, V. (1971). The family as a treatment unit. In J. Haley (Ed.), *Changing families* (pp. 127–183). New York: Grune & Stratton.

Satir, V. (1983). *Conjoint family therapy* (3rd ed.). Palo Alto, CA: Science and Behavior Books.

Satir, V. (1988). *The new people-making.* Palo Alto, CA: Science and Behavior Books.

Satir, V., & Baldwin, M. (1983). *Step-by-step: A guide to creating change in families.* Palo Alto, CA: Science and Behavior Books.

Van Deurzen, E. (1983). *Existential counseling in practice.* Thousand Oaks, CA: Sage Publications.

Weinhold, B., & Fenell, D. (2003). *Bridging individual and systems theories* (3rd ed.). Denver, CO: Love Publishing.

Whitaker, C. A. (1976a). The hindrance of theory in clinical work. In P. J. Guerin, Jr. (Ed.), *Family therapy: Theory and practice.* New York: Gardner Press.

Whitaker, C. A. (1976b). A family is a four-dimensional relationship. In P. J. Guerin, Jr. (Ed.), *Family therapy: Theory and practice.* New York: Gardner Press.

Whitaker, C. A., & Brumberry, W. M. (1988). *Dancing with the family: A symbolic-experiential approach.* New York Brunner/Mazel.

Whitaker, C. A., & Keith, D. V. (1981). Symbolic-experiential therapy. In A. S. Guerin & D. P. Knisker (Eds.), *Handbook of family therapy* (pp. 187–225). New York: Brunner/Mazel.

Yalom, I. (1995). The theory and practice of group psychotherapy. New York: Basic Book.

CHAPTER 7

Adlerian Family Art Therapy

JUDY H. SUTHERLAND

CORE CONCEPTS

As an art therapist trained in Adlerian theory, I find that when I can observe the family at work on a drawing, I can begin to understand the world they have created for themselves. The family members, too, through the active involvement of making art, begin to understand the purpose of their own behavior. The art product gives form to how they each experience life.

With a simple art directive, "Draw yourself as you want others to see you," the family members gain understanding of how each family member sees the world. Sometimes it is a matter of changing mistaken beliefs and attitudes before they can learn the practical requirements for living in harmony with each other. For instance, mother thinks she has painted a picture of caretaking and warmth, while other family members may see overprotection and control. The children may feel resentful or smothered because mother allows little freedom for them to do things for themselves. Father may feel alienated and angry because mother spends her time with the children, over-involved with their lives instead of with him. If encouraged, family members become ready to find new responses to life to replace the old behaviors that were creating difficulties for them.

IDENTIFYING THE LIFE STYLE PATTERN OF THE COUPLE/FAMILY

The Adlerian systems theory (holistic, purposive, cognitive, and social) focuses primarily on the process of change as found in Sherman, Oresky, and Rountree (1991). In a systems approach, the family is conceptualized as a homeostatic system in which change in one part affects every other part. First, the central organizing factor of the life style pattern (LSP) needs to be identified. Different styles of interacting and coping can be observed in the way family members communicate with each other verbally and/or while participating in an art experiential. Bitter (1993) describes what can be thought of as portraits of coping processes based on integrating Satir's communication in stress with Kefir's personality priorities. These include placating/pleasing (those who are willing to sacrifice themselves in an effort to please others); blaming/significance (those who sacrifice others to stay in power); super-reasonable/control (those who sacrifice themselves and others in favor of controlled emotions); distracting/comfort (those who try to stay in situations that lack stress or pain) (Bitter, 1993, pp. 334–335). Four priorities that Sherman and Dinkmeyer (1987) consider are "comfort, pleasing, control, and superiority" (p. 44). These patterns and priorities are fairly easy to recognize and give the therapist a starting place in understanding the family's LSP.

Each person is looking for a feeling of significance. Many choices we might make about how to live our lives could also be influenced by the stories we've heard from parents or grandparents. Recalling these stories can offer dimension to the LSP. As well, each of us, whether one is the husband, the wife, the parent, or the child, is a participant-observer in each other's lives. In families, pathological patterns can develop around issues of dependence-independence or domination-submission, which may result in overt hostility and conflicts where one person tries to win out over the others. Sometimes how family members see each other depends on how they see themselves.

An art experiential that can help to understand the LSP of the family is to have the parents think back to the prevailing mood in their family of origin and draw the family atmosphere as they remember it. The relationships between the parents and between the parents and the children create the family atmosphere (Dinkmeyer, McKay, & McKay, 1987). They suggest that the atmosphere may be overprotective, overindulgent, rejecting, authoritarian, permissive, or depressing. These handy labels for particular styles of relating with one another can help in the process of recognizing the sometimes discouraging attitudes that could be bringing the family into therapy and possibly can give them a starting place for change. This takes time. There is a purpose for the patterned behavior of the family, and it is difficult first to understand it and then to change it. Roles are played without awareness and changing the roles or the symptoms will definitely upset the equilibrium. Family defenses are strong and so revealing the conflicts through the art process can be less threatening. By itself, the art process will not necessarily effect a change.

In a systems perspective, the individual members are observed within the context of the group process while completing the art task. "The value of the art task is threefold: The *process* as a diagnostic, interactional, and rehearsal tool; the *contents* as a means of portraying unconscious and conscious communication; and the *product* as a lasting evidence of the group's dynamics" that the family may see for themselves (Landgarten, 1987, p. 5). The family creates a *"metaphoric blueprint"* of their dynamics and ways of communicating with each other. Landgarten (1987) makes it quite clear that

> the invading device is the art directive, which contains the appropriate media and is clinically sound…the therapist's constant vigilance for the covert and overt messages that are revealed through the art work, as well as the subtle nuances displayed while family members execute their art. (pp. 5–6).

THE THERAPEUTIC CHALLENGE FOR THE ART THERAPIST

Here again, the art materials can be used to help the family members clarify roles and perceptions they have of each other, to highlight patterns of interaction, and to explore the process of coming to an agreement before creating an art piece together (Dreikurs, 1986); and to encourage understanding of self and others. The process of making art together invites participation and encourages a feeling of belonging through increased self-awareness. Using Landgarten's (1981) work, DeOrnellas, Kottman, and Millican (1997) found that with the family art assessment techniques, the family seems to "forget" that the therapist is observing and as a result, presents more of the "real" inner workings and communication patterns of the family, rather than what they want the therapist to hear and see. This is the greatest strength in using art to change communication patterns, because the true patterns emerge and it is difficult to deny them. The artwork evokes and gives form to how members subjectively experience family life and then creatively respond to those situations. The meaning evolves out of the words they use to explain both their process and their artwork. Once acknowledged, there is a choice (guided by the therapist) in how to change the pattern to one that is more satisfactory.

The meaning the family members give to their process and the artwork will come much closer to the truth than anything the therapist might have to offer. Being silent at times may provide the space the family needs in order to understand what is actually going on in the family dynamics. Sometimes the hardest task for the therapist is learning to wait for the meaning of the artwork to come from the family. However, Landgarten (1987) makes a very strong case for the ease with which the therapist may make observations and the potency for using them. Selective use and timing are all important in effecting any change.

Once a relationship with the family members has been established, and the LSP has been identified, Adlerians use encouragement to foster therapeutic growth. To actively listen, to validate feelings, and to show understanding that, given their belief systems and situations, what they are doing in their

lives makes sense, are all facets of encouragement. Sometimes just understanding the choices a client makes can make the difference in therapy.

The therapist needs to continue to pay attention to the individual while
still reflecting on the system the family has created. Providing affirmation
and assigning good intentions to each member models respect, for example,
"the trait of anger might really indicate involvement and desire for change"
(Sherman & Dinkmeyer, 1987, p. 51). Humor can sometimes help to reframe
a minus situation to a plus situation by pointing out useful aspects of behavior. Trusting the family to find solutions to their own problems helps the
members learn to take responsibility for their own behavior and is training in
"social interest," the ability to care about others with trust and respect and to
cooperate with the social order of life.

The therapist's job is one of joining with the family without being absorbed
into it, all the while working toward changing the system by being a caring
witness to their process. At this point the therapist and the family members
might find it helpful to draw how they see themselves in relationship with
one another in the therapeutic process. Once the experience is made visible it
provides a nonthreatening way to reflect what is going on in the therapeutic
session. The therapeutic arrangement must be set up so that it is clear that the
therapist is not the rescuer, but still someone who is invested in the process.

While agreeing that a model of appropriate family life does not exist,
some challenges to the therapeutic alliance may include totally different life
experiences than those known to the therapist. As mentioned in Carlson,
Sperry, and Lewis (1997), these models can include "nuclear families, staying
single, non-marital heterosexual and homosexual cohabitation, single-parent
families, remarried and stepfamilies, foster and adoptive families, childless
families, and multi-adult households" (p. 5). Variations of the dual-career
couple can "include the commuting couple, the military couple, the executive couple, and the family-business couple" (Sperry & Carlson, 1991, p. 17).
Other variables to deal with include socially enforced gender stereotypes,
ethnic diversity and multicultural issues, court-ordered mandated treatment,
and the managed care environment. In every family situation, the therapist
will be faced with a possible changing value system that underlies much family behavior: male domination and conformity to old stereotypes in contrast
to flexibility and resilience.

ASSESSING THE FAMILY SYSTEM

The individual or family system is organized for two purposes: to maintain
itself and to accomplish either conscious or unconscious cognitive goals.
As mentioned before, the therapist looks for both useful and dysfunctional
behavior by listening to and observing both the verbal and nonverbal behaviors in the session. To assess patterns of dysfunctional behavior, the therapist
might observe the seating arrangements, such as an overly dependent child

not talking and sitting close to a caregiver; the roles assumed: one child who talks for the whole family; alliances: one caregiver and child against the rest of the family; one or more of the children against the caregivers; or a whole family against a child (scapegoat). It is also important for the therapist to pay attention to the use of power: the metaphors verbalized or seen in visual form and the attitudes/emotions expressed. The task is to understand the dynamics of the system: to examine the central organizing tendencies, the LSP—who is being kept busy with what behavior and for what purpose or goal?

An art experiential that might make these dynamics more comprehensible is to have the family members draw themselves and each other as animals in relation to the problem/conflict that was presented when coming in for therapy (Oster & Gould, 1987). In the processing of the drawings following this art task, the family members are often surprised to find that something very self-revealing happens in their own art. An elephant meant to be the image for Mom is very tiny and hardly visible; a horse meant to represent Dad looks extremely powerful; a snake used as a symbol for the sister slithers around the edge of the paper; a dog to depict the brother looks vicious; the cat for another member looks lazy; the animal for self is a rather large mouse hiding in the corner. Sometimes the artist is not included in the picture and this could be an expression of feeling rejected by the family (Farrell, 1992, unpublished manuscript).

The presenting problem/complaint might be a lack of cooperation among the family members to help out at home, a child with poor grades, a provider with no job, a sexually active teenager, a partner feeling left out, or a very sick child/caregiver. As the family looks at the art they have created, they also begin to trust the process as one that has personal meaning for them.

To elaborate on the use of power: the therapist looks for power in the family's LSP and how that power is maintained, as well as recognizing the power play inherent in the presenting symptom, for example, depression, defiance, or disobedience. Other dynamics that are possible to see in the drawing and/or in the process of drawing might include the issue of intimacy: closeness, distance, isolation, and enmeshment; boundary issues (who is included and who is excluded); and the myths and beliefs that form the lifestyle types that organize the system, such as the need to be "first," "best," "the baby," "the excitement seeker," "the getter," "the martyr," "the aginner," or "the victim" (Mosak, 1977).

ART EXPERIENTIAL: FAMILY SCULPTURE IN CLAY

In this art experiential, clay is used to do a sculpture of the family. This experiential works well with families who have adolescent or teenage children. Family members are told to represent in form the feeling that each family member has for them, including one for themselves (Keyes, 1983; Liebmann, 1986). When the forms are completed, they are told to put them on a board in relation to each other. Two or three adjectives can be used to describe each form. Processing can include looking at the distance between the forms, journaling about what it is like to be a member of this family, wondering what each form might say to the artist and how the artist would answer. The family sculpture can be thought of as a self-portrait. Each form can represent an aspect of the self as well. What in the self is like each member of the family? How does each member influence the way the self relates to the others? What ways of relating to each other are liked or disliked?

The figures can be moved around and put into different positions. Sometimes the artist can recognize strengths and/or weaknesses about self or others. New decisions can be made when the artist is ready to do so. Having an understanding of the messages from other family members can encourage one to make new decisions and expand awareness of the family relationships.

Family members might be protecting an alcoholic member, keeping a member depressed, or maintaining a family myth: "There is no sexual abuse in this family." The family art session reproduces or highlights to a degree the family's everyday pattern of communication/interaction (Kwiatkowska, 1978). The art process, especially when all can come to an agreement and work on the same piece of paper to produce something, seems to promote cohesiveness and cooperation with one another (Dreikurs, 1986). Art can encourage, change, diminish resistance, and lead toward more constructive/ healthy relationships.

THE CONCEPT OF RESISTANCE

Therapy is designed to overcome resistance, but sometimes clients will not do what they have agreed to do. Sometimes the whole family fights against change, thereby defeating the very therapist whom they have asked to help them. Adlerians view resistance as being both positive and negative. On the positive side, resistance can demonstrate integrity and setting up a healthy boundary. But to resist can also mean that one feels powerless and inadequate and might give up by becoming a victim or rebel in ways that are dysfunctional (Sherman & Dinkmeyer, 1987, p. 82).

Sometimes in families, it is not the ordinary therapeutic resistance, or misalignment of goals that the therapist encounters, but a deeply entrenched and dysfunctional family LSP that rigidly resists any insight or change. There is a particular kind of resistance some seriously disturbed families present to a therapist which ignores the pain of an individual family member. Especially in alcoholic or incestuous families, there are mixed messages confusing to all the family members. Family members have rigid roles to play, whether or not they want those roles. These roles are useful in maintaining homeostasis, but do not support the family well-being (Linesch, 1993, p. 13). The therapist sometimes uncovers alcoholism, abuse, violence, or incest which must be contracted to stop, and when necessary reported to authorities. It is also important to acknowledge and address the extremely high levels of emotion and loss that accompany any of these behaviors by first creating a safe place in the art therapy session for this to happen.

In families where there is violence and abuse, the art can help to alter perceptions, modify dysfunctional worldviews, and effect change without requiring insight into the behavior (Riley, 1990). Art is a powerful intervention for those who talk very little or talk too much or who like to intellectualize. Sometimes asking family members to "draw what will make the family relationships better" invites cooperation and reduces resistance.

When there is severe trauma, family members may have no inherent coping skills for surviving the unspeakable loss and grief they are experiencing. The family presents with a state of psychological imbalance in response to the feelings of loss, whether it is of self-esteem, care-taking, self-confidence, or safety. The individual subjective experience of the event (possibly a family member's suicide) needs to be explored and some personal meaning created for the loss. Especially in crisis intervention, the use of art is an ideal method to help with processing the grief and to encourage the family's inner strength (Linesch, 1993).

Sometimes a family member is unwilling to come to therapy. The rest of the family can "draw what it feels like with that missing member" and "how it feels without that member." This can lead to action goals if they are realistic. Then to have the clients draw "what does each of you need to do to make that happen?" indicates the need to concentrate on changing their own behavior before they can expect any changes in the family dynamics.

TERMINATION

Mary Farrell (1992) works in a hospital and reported about the work she does with families in that setting. Her work is basically with adolescents who stay in the hospital only a short time, but then upon their release are joined by their families for a last art therapy session. Her goal is to get the family members communicating in a way that shows respect for one another. She offers the family a tray containing a ring of soft clay with more clay on the side. She instructs them to add or take away or change the shape of the ring without breaking it. The tray containing the circle of clay is rotated every ten minutes so that each family member has a chance to work on all parts of it. The family can enhance each other's work, but are told not to destroy anything the other person created. When the circle is completed, the family decides on a title and discusses their process with the therapist.

By participating in this art task, the parents give indication that they are invested in the adolescent's treatment. The circle can symbolize the family unit working together and having fun for mutual pleasure. This art therapist likes to use "the clay circle" at the end of working with a family because it can stimulate cooperation and the feeling of belonging.

SAMPLE CASE

Here is a sample case that the art therapist recorded when she was an art therapist in a pastoral counseling center. The names and circumstances in this case study have been altered to protect confidentiality.

Informed consent: Written informed consent was obtained for this case study in 1996. However, the file for this family was shredded in 2003 when it exceeded the statue of limitations for saving the file.

There was a lot of noise and shouting going on in the waiting room of the pastoral counseling center. The art therapist opens the door and is surprised to see that it is just one child creating the disturbance by running around the room, up and down the stairs, and occasionally shouting at his mother. The mother responds by harshly telling the child to settle down, to be quiet.

The family is invited into the office. The father, Jim, quiet and unassuming, a son, Peter, age 9, acting much like his father, and the mother, Betty, who continues to deal with David, age 5, all take their places. David, however, jumps up and begins to run around the table where we are seated, much to the mother's increasing exasperation. David is asked if he would like some crayons and paper and he accepts the offer.

In a few brief moments, the therapist finds out that Betty and Jim have been married for 6 years and that David is their child, and that Peter is Betty's son by her first marriage. Jim had never been married before; he is 12 years older than Betty, who is 38. Jim is clearly confused by the situation, but has good intentions and is quite optimistic that everything will be fine if they could ever get David to calm down. Jim is coming to family counseling because Betty has insisted upon it, and he is concerned about her depression. Peter pipes up that he is here for the same reason. Betty complains that both Jim and Peter are totally passive and don't help her with anything, especially with David. However, the three of them agree that it is a family problem, and that they are willing to cooperate in order to have some peace in the family. Can the therapist help them, the family wants to know. David keeps on coloring.

When asked, the parents report that David's disruptive behavior has been going on in the home for quite some time now, a year or more. Peter chimes in that David's unruly behavior has been quite a problem for him as well. Peter plays the cello, is quite talented, and when it's time for Peter to practice, David begins to create an uproar. The same thing happens when Mom is talking on the phone, or Dad is reading the newspaper. Peter wants Mom to stop the problem. At school, however, David is the model student, very bright, able to read and write stories, grasp number concepts, is quite the helpful friend to other students and the teacher, and not one bit of a behavior problem.

The therapist asks, "What sense can you make out of David's behavior?" The parents think it might be to keep them busy with him, or to be in control of the house, that possibly he isn't getting enough attention.

"What would it look like to keep busy with David in a useful way?" After a while, Peter answered, "I could play games with him." When David is asked if he would like that, he just keeps on coloring.

Because David seems to be enjoying the art supplies, the art therapist decides to ask the family if they are willing to draw the family members each doing something at home. Everyone agrees, except David, who now declares he will not participate. He is asked if he is willing to sit quietly while the others work on their drawings. He looks around with amusement.

Betty, Jim, and Peter are in the process of telling each other about their pictures when David erupts, runs around the room, and starts shouting. Betty stops talking about her picture. She takes a black marker and puts a big "X" through her portrait of David, and then underlines it. David grabs the closest crayon and scribbles out the other family figures on her paper. Then he takes a clean sheet of paper and draws himself on it as big as the paper.

The family continues to process their drawings and what they mean to each other. Mother, a frown on her face, has herself closed off in a half circle on the far right side of the paper. Peter is next to her and they are about the same size, then David, and then Jim is on the other side of David (Figure 7.3).

In Jim's picture (Figure 7.4), Peter, playing his cello, and mother, cooking, are boxed off on the right side of the paper; Jim is boxed off in the garage on the left side of the paper. He has a saw in his hand and a smile on his face. David is standing alone in the yard with the words "Excuse me" written next to him. Peter's drawing (Figure 7.1) has father reading the newspaper, mother next to him looking at David with the words "bla, bla, bla" next to him, and Peter, smiling, is on the far left side. David's portrait is of himself (Figure 7.2).

Figure 7.1 Peter's picture.

Figure 7.2   David's picture.

Figure 7.3   Mom's picture

Figure 7.4   Dad's picture.

Through the art task and a few minutes of processing what the drawings mean to each other, it is not hard for any of us to understand that one member of the family is being identified as the problem and is being blamed for causing trouble in the family. We all had as much information as we needed to understand that the family patterns of communication and behavior have been stabilized, creating a "dynamic equilibrium known as *homeostasis*" (Riley, 1990, p. 71). But now what needs to happen to change the dysfunctional family LSP to one that would decrease David's misbehavior and address the symptom of Mom's depression, Dad's and Peter's passivity? How do the family members understand their roles and what issues have been carried over from the families of origin? Can the therapist really expect this family to keep coming for family therapy? This question is asked and the parents reply that they would like to come without the children. The two boys agree to this arrangement with the idea that they might all get together again later on.

In the following session with the parents each of them is asked to "draw yourself as you see yourself and then draw yourself as you think others see you." In processing these drawings it is learned that Jim is a good provider and wants to protect his wife from having to go out to work, but more than that, he expects her to be a stay-at-home mom like his mother. He sees himself as someone who can fix things.

Betty's picture of how she thinks others see her shows her running around taking all the responsibility for the household tasks and feeling tired and depressed. In the picture for how she sees herself, Betty is dressed in a work suit (she had a job she liked before she married Jim), and is moving away from David. She has become increasingly anxious about her ability to be a "good" parent.

Betty carries with her the message/tape from her mother warning her that if she wants to keep her husband she has to learn how to please him at all costs. After all, isn't that why she lost her first husband? To please Jim, in this marriage, means that she has to do all the work that she thinks others don't want to do, and that leaves her with no time to work outside the home. Besides, she suffers from a form of arthritis and is unable to work long hours. When Betty looks at her self-images, she begins to verbally express her anger at the situation, something she was afraid to do before. As Malchiodi and Riley (1996) state, there is an "innate tendency of the art expression to bring emotions more quickly to the surface" (p. 99). Reframing the trait of anger into something useful, that she wants a change in the family dynamics, helps Betty feel validated (Sherman & Dinkmeyer, 1987). Betty is beginning to realize that her arthritis and depression are real physical symptoms brought on by her body's reaction to stress.

Betty and Jim's visual art helps them to recognize more easily some of the consequences of their beliefs/values and the purpose of their behavior. "Drawing what will make the relationship better" helped Betty and Jim begin to change their pattern of interaction with one another and to understand the motives and behaviors that contributed to those patterns. Together they begin to give each other new ideas for working together, "to negotiate their differences" and to design action goals (Sherman & Dinkmeyer, 1987, p. 75). In talking to each other, they begin to recognize how they have each contributed to the family problem and how they each can support the other in useful ways.

Socratic questioning (Overholser, 1993) helps to confront the private logic and to break up the self-perpetuating thoughts and negative behavior. What does it mean to be a "good" parent? What do you look for in a marriage partner? What would it look like if Jim were to help around the house? What will have to happen if Betty wants to work outside the home? These kinds of evaluation questions help Betty and Jim clarify and integrate their thoughts and feelings (Haden, 1984). "The Socratic method works best with intelligent, motivated clients who are looking for assistance to clarify their problems, identify potential solutions, and to understand themselves better" (Overholser, 1995, p. 284).

In time, Betty and Jim are able to establish a relationship based on social equality, one where there is no superior role. They begin to set forth some realistic goals and act on them. A second car is purchased so that Betty can work part-time outside of the home. As Betty and Jim encourage family fun together, David's disruptive conduct subsides. Family meetings are held once a week, communication improves, tasks are divided, and there is a feeling of optimism for the future.

SUMMARY

Family members, especially the parents/caregivers, must be able to model caring for others to the children in the spirit of social interest and social equality. This calls for trust and mutual respect. The concept of social interest, as found in Individual Psychology, does not offer a do-it-yourself prescription. It offers no easy solutions to finding harmony in relationships and a feeling of belonging, but rather offers hope that change is possible.

Creating an art form that has personal meaning provides a symbolic way of understanding self in relation to other family members. With insight, it is then possible for the family members to move from being discouraged to feeling encouraged, to move from being closed down to becoming actively creative. This fits with what Adlerians call the social interest continuum, cooperation for the welfare of self and others, which is positively influenced by the feeling of courage.

REFERENCES

Bitter, J. (1993). Communication styles, personality priorities, and social interest: Strategies for helping couples build a life together. *Individual Psychology: The Journal of Adlerian Theory, Research & Practice, 49*(3 & 4), 330–349.

Carlson, J., Sperry, L., & Lewis, J. (1997). *Family therapy: Ensuring treatment efficacy.* New York: Brooks/Cole.

DeOrnellas, K., Kottman, T., & Millican, V. (1997). Drawing a family: Family Art assessment in Adlerian therapy. *Individual Psychology, 51*(4), 451–460.

Dinkmeyer, D., McKay, G., & McKay, J. (1987). *New beginning skills for single parents and stepfamily parents.* Champaign, IL: Research Press.

Dreikurs, S. (1986). *Cows can be purple: My life and art therapy.* Chicago, IL: Alfred Adler Institute.

Farrell, M. E. (1992). Unpublished manuscript.

Haden, J. (1984). Socratic ignorance. In E. Kelly (Ed.), *New essays on Socrates* (pp. 17–28). Lanham, MD: University Press of America.

Keyes, M. F. (1983). *Inward journey: Art as therapy.* London: Open Court.

Kwiatkowska, H. (1978). *Family therapy and evaluation through art.* Springfield, IL: Charles C. Thomas.

Landgarten,H. (1981). Clinical therapy: A comprehensive guide New York, NY: Brunner/Mazel.

Landgarten, H. (1987). *Family art psychotherapy.* New York: Brunner/Mazel.

Liebmann, M. (1986). *Art therapy for groups.* Cambridge, MA: Brookline Books.

Linesch, D. (Ed.). (1993). *Art therapy with families in crisis: Overcoming resistance through non-verbal expression.* New York: Brunner/Mazel.

Malchiodi, C., & Riley, S. (1996). *Supervision and related issues: A handbook for professionals.* Chicago, IL: Magnolia Street Publishers.

Mosak, H. (1977). *On purpose.* Chicago, IL: Alfred Adler Institute.

Oster, G. D., & Gould, P. (1987). *Using drawings in assessment and therapy: A guide for mental health professionals.* New York: Brunner/ Mazel.

Overholser, J. (1993). Elements of the Socratic method: I. Systematic questioning. *Psychotherapy, 30,* 67–74.

Overholser, J. (1995). Elements of the Socratic method: IV. Disavowal of knowledge. *Psychotherapy, 32*(2), 283–292.

Riley, S. (1990). A strategic family systems approach to art therapy with the individual. *American Journal of Art Therapy, 28,* 71–78.

Sherman, R., & Dinkmeyer, D. (1987). *Systems of family therapy: An Adlerian integration.* New York: Brunner/Mazel.

Sherman, R., Oresky, P., & Rountree, Y. (1991). *Solving problems in couples and family therapy: Techniques and tactics.* New York: Brunner/Mazel.

Sperry, L., & Carlson, J. (1991). The work-centered couple. *Family Psychologist, 4,* 19–21.

CHAPTER 8

Filial Art Therapy
A Rogerian Approach

LINDA L. MCCARLEY

Filial therapy is a Rogerian approach designed to enhance the parent-child relationship, improve communications, increase the awareness of the child, and build the child's self-confidence. An assumption of filial therapy is that parents can learn to take on the role of the therapist and effectively bring about the behavioral and emotional changes they desire in their children. With this approach the therapeutic skills are transferred from the therapist to the child's primary caregivers. It is the parents or caregivers, therefore, who ultimately become the agents of change. Filial therapy may be utilized for individual families and may also be easily adapted for use with multifamily groups (Ginsberg, 1989; B. Guerney, 1964; B. G. Guerney, L. F. Guerney, & M. P. Andronico, 1979; L. Guerney, 1979; L. Guerney & B. Guerney, 1985; L. F. Guerney & B. Guerney, 1994; Landreth, 1991).

As an art therapist in private practice, I have frequently trained parents to facilitate home-based filial art therapy sessions with their children to address their presenting problems (Chapman & McCarley, 2002; McCarley, 1995, 2000; McCarley & Chapman, 2003). The principal strategy of filial art therapy is to bring about positive growth and change in children by establishing a therapeutic home-based art studio to conduct nondirective art therapy. Parents are taught how to provide a safe, empathic environment in which the child can express feelings and thoughts openly and honestly during art-making sessions. Over time and with practice, the parent learns to become more supportive and empathic, and the child becomes more aware of his or her thoughts and genuine feelings. Thus, introducing the home-based art studio to provide filial art therapy brings about a positive shift in the parent-child relationship. This enhancement, in combination with additional behavioral techniques, if needed, generally resolves the child's behavioral and emotional issues that the parents seek to address in therapy. The relationship enhancement approach helps parents gain a sense of competence in their parenting abilities as they begin to see the results from the applications of newly learned skills. After attending a series of skills-training sessions with the art therapist, the parent is prepared to facilitate "special art times." Soon after beginning the sessions at home, the parent begins to transfer and generalize the newly learned skills and apply them as needed to routine family situations. Additionally, behavioral techniques are utilized to help children accomplish appropriate developmental tasks. As parents learn how to recognize and accept the genuine feelings of their children, they also become more insightful in regards to their own emotional issues. As a result, filial therapy often brings benefits, not just for the child who is identified as having the problem, but for all participating family members.

Traditionally, filial therapy has flourished under the domain of child-centered play therapy, which includes setting up a play area with toys as well as with art supplies. Offering art materials rather than toys as the primary medium for filial therapy brings a different dimension to the experience. In most families, art materials, other than crayons and markers, are not made available to children on a regular basis due to the fact they are typically considered to be messy, may need to be supervised, and need to be replenished. If art making is not routinely provided in the home, it may be perceived as a more unique experience and, therefore, more "special" to children. The art materials are to be put away between sessions and saved for a "special art time." Art making offers a natural medium of expression for the child and this mode of communication may help to equalize the power within the family, especially if parents do not consider themselves to be skilled artists. Provision of a few simple art materials allows for the expression of a wide range of human emotion and experience. Structuring the sessions with developmentally appropriate art materials allows for use of a filial approach for children as well as adolescents.

SKETCHES OF LEADING FIGURES

In 1909 Freud reported that changes were brought about in a 5-year-old boy while instructing his father to carry out play sessions at home. In 1949 Dorothy Baruch purported that parents who provided planned play sessions in their homes could enhance their relationships with their children. These early home-based play sessions did not depend upon systematic training or close supervision of the parents by a therapist, rather parents were merely advised to schedule and participate in regular playtimes with their children. Virginia M. Axline's book entitled *Play Therapy* (1969) describes a Rogerian child-centered approach to play therapy. Natalie Rogers was encouraged by her father, Carl Rogers, to read Axline's book and to utilize these child-centered play therapy methods in her own home to help her daughter overcome toilet training difficulties (Landreth, 1991).

The term "filial therapy" was first introduced in 1964 by Bernard Guerney, who conceptualized the idea of enhancing parent-child relationships and reducing parent-child problems by having the parents provide child-centered play therapy in their own homes (L. F. Guerney & B. Guerney, 1994, p. 128). Since then filial therapy models have been given various labels, such as "Child-Parent-Relationship Training (CPR)" (Landreth, 1991, pp. 335–352), and "child relationship enhancement (CRE)" (L. F. Guerney & B. Guerney, 1994, pp. 128–129). Bernard Guerney's interest in engaging the family to treat troubled children by focusing on family relationships can be traced to his earlier participation in the development of structural family therapy (Nichols & Schwartz, 2001).

The work being done by child-centered filial play therapists has inspired the development of a filial art therapy model which has been presented at the American Art Therapy Association annual conferences (Chapman & McCarley, 2002; McCarley, 1995; McCarley, 2000; McCarley & Chapman, 2003). Whereas filial play therapy relies upon the use of a specific list of toys with the inclusion of some art materials and a sand tray, filial art therapy is focused upon the use of developmentally appropriate art media. Filial art therapy is, therefore, applicable for children in the pre-art stage through adolescence.

THEORETICAL FORMULATIONS

Filial therapy evolved from an understanding of psychodynamic, humanistic, and behavioral theories. Although primarily Rogerian, it is also an eclectic approach to family therapy that typically involves and benefits the whole family. Judith Rubin noted in her book (1987) that art therapists have not embraced a purely person-centered approach in their work and suggested that other approaches may need to be integrated to be effective. The benefits of utilizing an eclectic approach have also been demonstrated in art therapy by Wadeson (2001).

The antideterministic perspective of filial therapy recognizes the importance of teaching parents skills so they will be empowered to bring about positive changes in their children. Filial therapy is also, therefore, a psychoeducational approach that recognizes the unique power of parents to positively influence their children. Parents are not seen as the cause of their children's problems, rather they are seen as having good intentions for their children, and merely needing knowledge and skill to help them reach their goals in parenting (Ginsberg, 1989; B. Guerney, 1964; Guerney et al., 1979; L. Guerney, 1979; Guerney & Guerney, 1985, 1994; Landreth, 1991).

Carl Rogers's influence gave rise to the development of filial therapy. He believed that all human beings possess an innate capacity to strive toward self-actualization. Rogers (1980) explained that we are naturally inclined to act in our own self-interest, as well as be affectionate and loving toward others, and that both desires are intrinsic. However, as we strive for love and acceptance of others, we sometimes find it necessary to suppress our natural desires in order to fulfill our cravings for receiving approval and recognition. As a result, we may behave in ways that we perceive others want us to, rather than in the ways we wish. Most people find a way to mitigate the conflict between a need or wish for approval from others and a wish to act in one's own immediate interest. Sometimes, however, there is a conflict between these two goals which causes us to unconsciously deny, repress, or distort our own inner wisdom in search of acceptance, so that we no longer listen to what we know to be true for ourselves. Rogers discovered the value of providing an empathic and accepting relationship which he referred to as an *unconditional positive regard*. This allows for the safe exploration of any repressed feelings so that one can embrace one's own inner truths. Family members were not included in therapy by Rogers because they were not considered to be capable of providing total unconditional regard. Rogers believed that the possibility of disapproval or rejection from a family member in the session might cause the primary client to sacrifice or suppress expression of his or her genuine feelings and inner wisdom in order to win the acceptance and approval of other family members (Nichols & Schwartz, 2001). In 1964 Bernard Guerney (Guerney, L. F. & Guerney, B., 1994) introduced an integrated model in which he taught parents to take the role of the therapist and use Rogerian skills in home-based play therapy with their children.

NORMAL FAMILY DEVELOPMENT

A systemic perspective held by filial therapists is that a child's sense of self and self-development is greatly influenced by the parent-child relationship (Ginsberg, 1989). Filial therapists' view of families through a humanistic lens enables them to think of parents as having good intentions for their children. Children are seen as resilient and capable of overcoming obstacles and adapting to difficult situations. Due to their creative and resourceful abilities, they can normally resolve many of their own problems if they are in a supportive environment and allowed to freely explore their potentiality in a safe and creative way. Children thrive in a nurturing family where their creative spirit is nurtured without risking undue fear of rejection. The opportunity to be creative and have that creativity recognized and validated within an accepting and nurturing family is incredibly important in the process of maturation and self-realization. The filial therapy approach recognizes the good intentions of parents' wishes to enhance their children's creative spirit and build self-esteem. It has been demonstrated that when parents learn more effective ways of relating to their child, the results will be beneficial for the whole family (Guerney, B. G., Guerney, L. F., & Andronico, M. P., 1979).

Ginsberg (1989) purported that children's experience within the relationship of their parents or primary caregivers determines how they develop their own sense of self, as well as how they become socialized, and eventually learn to have healthy and intimate relationships while maintaining a sense of independence and autonomy.

DEVELOPMENT OF BEHAVIOR OR EMOTIONAL DISORDERS

Even though parents have good intentions and love for their children, they may lack adequate skills to deal with the complexities of parenting. Parenting styles that were modeled and learned from previous generations may no longer be adequate for today's complex family life. Families may also experience problems that arise because children's natural tendencies toward self-realization, and their parents' own strivings toward self-actualization, may conflict with counterpressures that arise from the expectations imposed by society. These counterpressures may be further exacerbated by any number of situations, such as economic stress, traumatic events in the family, job or school-related concerns, and requirements of time commitments that limit the available time parents have to spend with each other and with their children. If parents become overwhelmed while trying to manage these pressures, they may become susceptible to feelings of shame, guilt, and self-blame. These feelings of inadequacy multiply and can directly affect they way they feel about their children, negative dynamics between parent and child ultimately affect the development of the child (Landreth, 1991).

Parents who are overwhelmed with stress and counterpressures may fail to provide their children with the patience, recognition, and acceptance they need to develop positively. These deficiencies may cause children to experience insecurity and anxiety and develop defenses that can eventually lead to dysfunction (Ginsberg, 1989).

GOALS OF THERAPY

The purpose of filial therapy is to provide a format for relationship enhancement that will nourish positive development in children. During appointed times, parents practice responding empathically to their child, recognizing and encouraging their child's positive efforts, setting limits appropriately without criticizing, and joining with their child in creative endeavors. In order for the child to achieve creative mental growth, it is imperative for the child to feel completely safe to express thoughts and feelings, and to be free to make choices without undue concern for being judged. Children also need to be anchored to the world of reality by being made aware of responsibilities in relationships and in the world.

The second goal is for parents to learn how to empathize with the child and validate the child's art-making experiences. As the child begins to openly express thoughts and feelings related to her art-making experiences, she will acquire an improved sense of self and mastery, and she'll be better able to articulate and cope with her feelings.

The third goal is for the parent to build confidence in the child by giving the child complete undivided attention during the "special art time." The child's self-confidence will be nourished by having the opportunity to make choices in art materials and by freely selecting creative projects that appeal to her. As she makes her own choices, she will also experience the consequence of her choice and will take ownership for that responsibility. This will eventually lead to making more mature choices which will, in turn, build greater confidence in the child.

Ultimately, Ginsberg reports (1989) that the child's development within the relationship of parents or primary caregivers determines how children develop their own sense of self, become socialized, and eventually learn how to have healthy and intimate relationships while maintaining a sense of independence and autonomy.

CONDITIONS FOR BEHAVIOR CHANGE

In order for change in the child to occur, the primary caregivers must agree to commit to the time required for learning new relational techniques and structuring a home-based art studio on a regular basis. The parent or caregiver must be stable enough to consistently create a safe place for free expression during the "special art times" with the child. Maintaining this structure creates a shift in the family. This coordination often requires greater cohesion and cooperation among family members as well as mutual acceptance of responsibility.

By practicing empathic responding and therapeutic limit setting during the "special art time," the parents gradually begin to generalize and utilize their newly acquired relationship techniques at other times. As intergenerational patterns of relating are replaced with new ones, parents experience a sense of mastery which reduces stress and anxiety within each of the family members and the family as a whole benefits (Ginsberg, 1989).

TECHNIQUES

Engaging Parents as Allies

The goal of the first session is for the therapist to recognize and validate the parents' perspective of the problem and begin forming a therapeutic relationship with the parents. It is essential to establish a good working rapport with the parents as they will become the therapist's primary allies throughout this process. In addition to taking a traditional psychosocial history and setting goals for therapy, it is useful for the therapist to ask parents to describe the positive aspects of their child. The next meeting is a family art therapy session during which the therapist invites the whole family to use the time to make art in many of the ways that they wish. To say to the family that they can make art in any way they like would make it more difficult to set limits if a child or family member were to act out. This meeting may be structured as a nondirective art-making session during which the family dynamics may be observed. A selection of developmentally appropriate art media are made available. During the third meeting the art therapist clarifies previous goals and suggests other goals if indicated. At this time, the art therapist proposes that the parents continue attending sessions to learn special art therapy techniques so they can take over the role of the therapist.

Teaching Techniques to Parents

This psychoeducational phase of therapy begins by providing a rationale and overview of the program. This is followed by a discussion about structuring the home-based art studio in terms of its location within the home, the need for privacy, regularly scheduled uninterrupted times lasting 30 minutes, age-appropriate art materials, and access to water. Practicality issues need to be covered, such as how to oversee the other children during this time. During this session a description of filial art therapy principles, which are adapted from Axline (1969, pp. 73–74) are reviewed.

1. The purpose of the home-based art therapy studio is to enhance the parent-child relationship and to nourish the child's development, creativity, and self-esteem.
2. During the art session, the parent does not attempt to change the child or direct the art making, rather the parent accepts the child and his or her art as is.
3. The parent conveys to the child that he or she is free to express *all* feelings and create art in any way she or he wishes.
4. During the art session, the parent strives to understand the child's feelings and experiences and reflects those back to him or her to help the child gain awareness and to feel validated.
5. The parent provides the child with opportunities to solve his or her own problems during the art session, and respects the child's ability to make changes in her creative efforts and in her life when ready.
6. The parent does not direct the child's art making, actions or verbalizations. Rather, the parent reflects the child's experience as the child takes the lead and the parent follows and conveys a prizing of the child.

7. The parent remains patient and understands that creativity, growth, and change are gradual. The child will direct his or her own change when he or she feels ready.
8. The purpose of limits is to help the child become aware of his or her responsibilities in relationships and in the world.

The next technique introduced is empathic responding with a Rogerian child-centered approach. Worksheets describing potential scenarios that could arise in an art session are provided and parents are asked to write empathic verbalizations. This is followed by role playing with art materials. In addition to completing worksheets the parent practices in a mock art session with the therapist. Homework assignments are given between sessions: (a) notice your child's feelings and experiences, write them down, and bring them back to share in the next parent meeting; (b) practice reflecting and validating your child's feelings and experiences; and (c) practice setting limits. Limit-setting guidelines are reviewed, worksheets are provided, and the parents role-play to learn how to utilize the following three steps as provided by Landreth (1991, p. 223):

A—Acknowledge the child's feelings, wishes and wants.
C—Communicate the limit.
T—Target acceptable alternatives.

Learning these skills takes several sessions, and the therapist will need to continue motivating the parents by expressing faith in their ability and by reminding them of the value and purpose of this approach. After the basic concepts have been covered and practiced, the child attends a session with the parent and the parent observes the therapist providing child-centered art therapy. This is followed by a debriefing, and then the therapist observes the parent providing art therapy to the child.

Implementing the Home-Based Studio

Once the parent is comfortable with these newly learned skills, the parent-child art therapy sessions can begin to take place in the home-based studio. An area of the home is designated where privacy can be maintained. The parent is given a list of developmentally appropriate art materials to provide. While the parents are conducting weekly art therapy sessions at home, they continue to come to therapy appointments for ongoing coaching. During this phase, cognitive behavioral techniques may be introduced to supplement during times other than in the art therapy sessions. As parents begin using more empathic responses in combination with limit setting and behavioral techniques, the need for coaching sessions decreases and appointments are spread further apart until termination.

EVALUATING THERAPY THEORY AND RESULTS

Mr. and Mrs. Martin called for an appointment to discuss concerns regarding their child, a 9-year-old boy named Drake. Mrs. Martin reported that Drake was reluctant to get his homework done each day and that she was upset with herself for not being able to handle the situation and for getting impatient with him. She said every afternoon turned into a power struggle between the two of them. She also said the problem was just between herself and her son. Mr. Martin and Drake reportedly had several fun father-son activities that they enjoyed doing together, but Mrs. Martin felt that her relationship with her son was unfairly focused on the more serious tasks related to getting homework done, getting ready for bed, and also getting ready for school. I explained that I thought filial art therapy might be beneficial. After learning the principles and techniques, Mrs. Martin brought her son to the office and observed me with him in a nondirective art session.

I explained to Drake that he could create art or construct something of his choosing. He was free to use what was available in my studio office. He found a shelf of books with arts and crafts guidelines. His mother observed as I verbally tracked his search for an inspiration. After leafing through several books, he decided to create a large basket of eggs using balloons covered with papier mache. Part of the structuring involved setting out the needed supplies for his chosen project. The project was unfinished at the end of the session, and he agreed to return next week to work on it. During the next session I asked his mother to sit next to him and try noticing him as he created his art piece. We traded places and I became the quiet observer watching the mother take on the role of the therapist. She tracked his actions and reflected his experiences skillfully. Drake then looked at his mother and suggested that they could do this together at home. She agreed and they took the unfinished project home. Following the sessions at home, Mrs. Martin journaled about her sessions so she could share them with me when she returned. Following is an excerpt from her journal.

> Our first "special art time" went very well. Drake was not at all tentative. He made some comparisons to Miss Linda's (the therapist) at first. Our flour container was bigger and so forth. He showed frustration sometimes by growling and giving his project a mean look, but immediately went on. I reflected, "You were frustrated, but you kept on working." He didn't talk much at first except to say he wished we had a whole hour. I reminded him about the fact that we only have 45 minutes. He said, "Yeah, but I still wish it was an hour ... he began telling me in detail about his day at camp, more than he ever had without a lot of prodding questions on my part. During the time he asked if I had ever done papier mache when I was a girl ... When he got his first balloon covered, he spent a couple of minutes holding it (his head was down) just rubbing it and squeezing it. He

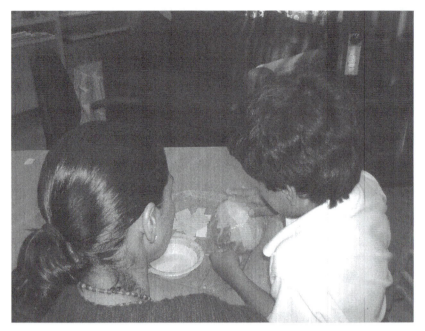

Figure 8.1 Mother and child making art.

also tasted the mixture and then the flour. First he just dipped his finger in and then scooped a bit into his mouth. Of course, a white mist puffed out when he talked (he liked that), and he said it tasted like bread and that he liked bread. He never asked for my help. We both enjoyed our time.

In this first home-based art therapy session, Mrs. Martin was able to realize how to improve her relationship with her son. She was patient and understanding of his wish to spend longer than the planned amount of time, yet she was firm in setting the limits and maintaining the structure. His desire to retreat from the expectations placed upon him by homework and school were satisfied as he relaxed and regressed with use of the fluid mixture of flour and water which was well tolerated by his mother. She praised his effort for working on the project even though he got frustrated at one point, but she did so without making him feel judged. This case demonstrates a nondirective approach that helped Drake feel nurtured, cared for, understood, and accepted by his mother. His freedom to make choices and proceed in a nondirective fashion without judgment allowed him to function creatively and independently. After the session and throughout the week, Mrs. Martin began generalizing her skills by reflecting and accepting Drake's negative feelings about his homework. In the office, Mrs. Martin also learned behavioral techniques to reinforce a positive outcome regarding the struggle with homework.

Filial therapy with the use of toys is well researched with various populations, and it has also been modified for use without toys. However, outcome studies regarding the use of filial art therapy is still limited.

SUMMARY

The filial art therapy home-based studio model gives parents an opportunity to practice new relationship skills by committing to sessions once a week for 30 minutes. The specific methodology format teaches parents to be empathic, patient, and respectful of their children. They also learn how to set limits without losing control. The "special art time" results in the child feeling prized and appreciated, which fosters self-acceptance and self-esteem. The child becomes more independent and mature while the parent gains a new sense of self-confidence. This model is suitable for children and adolescents because the materials are selected with consideration of the child's level of development. The parents become the therapist's allies and the agents of change, while the therapist serves as the parent's partner, educator, and coach.

RECOMMENDED READINGS

Axline, V. M. (1969). *Play therapy.* New York: Ballentine Books.

Landreth, G. L. (1991). *Play therapy: The art of the relationship.* Muncie, IN: Accelerated Development.

Schaefer, C., & Carey, L. C. (Eds.). (1994). *Family play therapy.* Northvale, NJ: Jason Aronson.

REFERENCES

Axline, V. M. (1969). *Play therapy.* New York: Ballentine Books.

Chapman, L. M., & McCarley, L. L. (2002, November). A playful palette: Blending art therapy and play therapy techniques. Workshop presented at the annual conference of the American Art Therapy Association, Inc., Washington, DC.

Ginsberg, B. (1989). Training parents as therapeutic agents with foster/adoptive children using the filial approach. In C. Schaefer & J. Briesmeister (Eds.), *Handbook of parent training: Parents as co-therapists for children's behavior problems* (pp. 442–478). New York: John Wiley & Sons.

Guerney, B. (1964). Filial therapy: Description and rationale. *Journal of Consulting Psychology 28,* 303–310.

Guerney, B. G., Guerney, L. F., & Andronico, M. P. (1979). Filial therapy. In C. Schaefer (Ed.), *The therapeutic use of child's play* (pp. 553–566). New York: Jason Aronson.

Guerney, L. (1979). Play therapy: A training manual for parents. In C. Schaefer (Ed.), *The therapeutic use of child's play.* New York: Jason Aronson.

Guerney, L., & Guerney, B. (1985). *The relationship enhancement family of family therapies.* In L. L'Abate and M. A. Milan. New York: John Wiley.

Guerney L. F., & Guerney, B. (1994). Child relationship enhancement: Family therapy and parent education. In C. Schaefer and L. Carey (Eds.), *Family play therapy* (pp. 127–138). Northvale, NJ: Jason Aronson.

Landreth, G. L. (1991). Filial therapy: Child-parent-relationship training using play therapy skills (CPR for parents). In G. L. Landreth, *Play therapy: The art of the relationship* (pp. 335–352). Muncie, IN: Accelerated Development.

McCarley, L. L. (1995, November). *Incorporating art making in play therapy: A child-centered approach.* Course presented at the annual conference of the American Art Therapy Association, Inc., San Diego, CA.

McCarley, L. (2000, November). Filial art therapy: Transitioning from the clinical setting to the home-based studio. Paper presented at the annual conference of the American Art Therapy Association, Inc., St. Louis, MO.

McCarley, L. L., & Chapman, L. M. (2003, November). A good fit: Play and art therapy models tailored to fit the child. Advanced practice presentation at the annual conference of the American Art Therapy Association, Inc., Chicago, IL.

Nichols, M. P., & Schwartz, R. C. (2001). *Family therapy: Concepts and methods.* Boston: Allyn and Bacon.

Rogers, C. R. (1980). The foundations of a person-centered approach. In *A way of being* (pp. 113–136). Boston: Houghton Mifflin.

Rubin, J. A. (Ed.). (1987). Humanistic approaches. In *Approaches to art therapy: Theory and technique* (pp. 135–137). New York: Brunner/Mazel.

Wadeson, H. (2001). An eclectic approach to art therapy. In J. A. Rubin (Ed.), *Approaches to art therapy* (pp. 306–317). Philadelphia: Brunner-Routledge.

CHAPTER 9

Narrative Art Therapy Within a Multicultural Framework

JANICE HOSHINO AND DANIELLE CAMERON*

INTRODUCTION

Gaining competency in a specialty area, such as narrative family art therapy, requires an art therapist to synthesize substantive volumes of specialized information in relation to an increasingly specialized field. Additionally, art therapists must incorporate how these broad, yet specialized areas of theory and practice are integrated into the clinical setting. Furthermore, it is imperative that the art therapist develops a competent multicultural framework that provides an effective therapeutic environment for a plethora of clients. Sophistication and comfort with art processes and a solid foundation in historical, theoretical, and clinical perspectives within a multicultural framework comprise a strong clinical foundation.

To gain mastery in several areas in art therapy and family therapy incorporating a narrative lens also assumes one's competency in diversity, which may seem daunting, if not impossible. One may question both the necessity and feasibility of this proposal. Our own profession of art therapy has consistently remained overwhelmingly female (91%) and largely White (90%), with the remainder identified as Hispanic American (1.2%), African American (1%), Native American (0.5%), Asian American (0.8%), or multiethnic (1.3%) (Elkins, Stovall, & Malchiodi, 2003). Consider the following demographic in contrast

---

* Danielle Cameron, MA, is a creative arts therapist on the geriatric psychiatric unit at Auburn Regional Medical Center in Auburn, Washington. Danielle graduated with a masters in psychology degree with a specialization in art therapy and mental health counseling at Antioch University Seattle.

to our own field: African Americans now comprise 12% of the total population; Latinos comprise 9%, and Asian Americans comprise 3%, adding up to 25% of the total population (Native American and other groups were not specified in this report) (Roberts, 1995). The need for competency in and diversity among practicing art therapists holds enormous importance, yet it appears that diversity within our profession (6.3%) is not increasing at the same pace as the general population (25%). Notably, the profession of art therapy is not largely different from other mental health professions: ethnic minority art therapists appear to be similar to minority psychologists, whom, according to Hammond and Yung (1993), comprise 5.1% or less of all practicing psychologists.

Each family seeking art therapy has complex and distinctive features that can be simultaneously intimidating and inspiring for the art therapist. Incorporating a multicultural framework that is both expansive and inclusive may help inform the art therapist to more effectively conceptualize and thereby engage with families seeking art therapy. One such model is Hays's (1995, 1996a, 1996b, 1996c, 2001) ADDRESSING framework. Hays presents a "trans-cultural-specific perspective" (1996a, p. 334). The letters in the ADDRESSING acronym draw attention to ten cultural factors and minority groups. They are: Age and generational influences, Developmental and acquired Disabilities, Religion, Ethnicity, Socioeconomic status, Sexual orientation, Indigenous heritage, National origin, and Gender. Such a model may provide a more comprehensive understanding of the psychological ramifications of exclusionary behavior, particularly if the art therapist has lived in the mainstream, White culture of privilege.

In her description of social construction theory, Tracy Ore (2000) notes that, "What we see as real is the result of human interaction" (p. 5). Social construction theory offers an explanation of how exclusionary behavior manifests. Through social construction, "we create aspects of our culture, objectify them, internalize them, and then take these cultural products for granted" (Ore, 2000, p. 5).

Art therapy and narrative family therapy may be particularly effective segues when working with diverse families seeking therapy. Art therapy with families can provide a powerful catalyst to share perceptions, explore dynamics, and identify the desires, dreams, and goals of the family. The creative process may provide the family an opportunity to examine issues both through a realistic viewpoint and a metaphoric lens. Similarly, narrative family therapy incorporates a model of the therapeutic metaphor.

DEVELOPMENT AND HISTORY OF FAMILY ART THERAPY THEORY

Pioneer art therapist Hanna Yaxa Kwiatkowska, is credited as the first family art therapist. Wadeson (1980) noted: "From her pioneering work in the 1960's, others have branched out to adapt her methods and develop new ones for using art therapy with many kinds of families in various treatment settings" (p. 280). Many acknowledged the effectiveness of both systemic thinking and therapeutic intervention, and other schools of thought emerged to grow the profession of family therapy. These included family of origin theory (Bowen, 1978; Framo, 1992; Hovestadt & Fine, 1987; Kerr & Bowen, 1988; McGoldrick & Gerson, 1985; Papero, 1990), strategic family therapy (Madanes, 1981), structural family therapy (Minuchin, 1974), symbolic/experiential family therapy (Napier, 1988; Napier & Whitaker, 1978; Whitaker, 1989) and behavioral family therapy (Jacobson & Gurman, 1986), a general systems framework (Ackerman, 1979; Bertalanffy, 1968; Green & Framo, 1981; Nichols, 1999; Nichols & Everett, 1986; Watzlawick, Bevin, & Jackson, 1967), and multicultural and gender issues (Carter & McGoldrick, 1989; David & Erikson, 1990; Lappin, 1983; McGoldrick, Giordano, & Pearce, 1996; Taffel & Masters, 1989).

The aforementioned schools provided a broad foundation for the family therapy field to grow: "unlike other fields that were relatively homogeneously organized around one theory or approach, family therapy had a wide variety of leaders and theories and drew followers from many backgrounds" (Nichols & Schwartz, 1998, p. 315). Although one cannot negate the contributions of the early schools, Nichols and Schwartz (1998) identify shortcomings in these models. These include inattention paid to ethnicity, race, socioeconomic status, sexual orientation, and families other than two-parent nuclear families. From these early schools, new schools of thought began to emerge in the 1980s and 1990s. These include, but are not limited to, postmodern, social constructionism, solution focused, and narrative therapies. Art therapists (Riley, 1988, 1999; Riley & Malchiodi, 1994; Rubin, 1999; Wadeson, 2000) also began to take notice of family therapy and later how the postmodern movement might be integrated with art therapy.

CORE CONCEPTS OF NARRATIVE THERAPY

Nichols & Schwartz (1998) purport that family therapists appreciated and accepted the notion of social constructionism, as it shifted the focus of family therapy from *changing action* to *changing meaning*. This notion that the therapist's job was to co-create new realities with family, as opposed to more traditional approaches such as advising or directing interventions, was supported with a new academic theory.

Hoffman (2002) asserts that narrative therapy emerged out of post structuralism and deconstruction. Goldenberg & Goldenberg (2004) state:

> *Post structural* thought rejects the notions that there is a deep structure to all phenomenon and that its complexity can be broken down

to its elements. To structuralists, behavior is simply the surface manifestation of deeper elements buried within the individual, these elements can be classified and retrieved, and only by an objective outside expert exploring and interpreting those deeper layers can the "truths" about the meanings of the behavior be revealed. (p. 343)

The development of narrative therapy is largely attributed to the work of Michael White and, second, David Epston. White was largely influenced by the writings of Michel Foucault (1965, 1980), a French intellectual and social critic who wrote extensively about the politics of power. White and Epston (1990) note: "Foucault argues that we predominately experience the positive or constitutive effects of power, that we are subject to power through normalizing 'truths' that shape our lives and relationships" (p. 19). White and Epston may be considered the founders of narrative therapy, but Nichols and Schwartz (1998) identify several other narrative therapists who have expanded narrative therapy in new ways. They include Jill Freedman and Gene Combs, Jeffrey Zimmerman and Vicki Dickerson, Stephan Madigan, Karl Tomm, and Harlene Anderson and the late Harry Goolishian.

Nichols & Schwartz (1998) state, "narrative therapy focuses on understanding how experience creates expectations and how expectations then shape experience through the creation of organizing stories" (p. 397). Freedman and Combs (2000, cited in Goldenberg & Goldenberg, 2004) further distinguish narrative therapy:

> …our sense of reality is organized and maintained through the stories by which we circulate knowledge about ourselves and the world we inhabit. Stories, according to narrative therapists, shape our experiences; the stories we enact with one another are not about our lives, but rather are "our lives". For many family therapists, influenced by this powerful, original, and optimistic approach, the long-standing metaphor of systems has been replaced by the metaphors of language, stories, and their meanings. (p. 343)

Likewise, Goldenberg & Goldenberg (2004) note that the narrative therapist helps the client view life as multistoried, recognizing options and possibilities, but that they do not help clients replace one story with another.

Consider the juxtaposition art therapy and creative process have with narrative therapy. How often has art been a conduit for the clients to organize their thoughts? Indeed, the permanency of art, in and of itself, provides the client an opportunity to create, witness, and reflect upon the image and subsequent story that language may not. Art images also provide numerous stories, and a collection of images may serve as a collage representing the landscape of their lives. Language, in our opinion, has limitations in the therapeutic arena; art may diminish some of the ambiguity inherent in verbal therapy alone.

Narrative therapists work with families towards the goal of "reauthoring" their lives. How these goals are met are through constructs such as externalization of the problem, employing therapeutic questions, seeking unique outcomes, and co-constructing alternative stories. These stories can be done through ceremonies, therapeutic letters, and storied therapy.

Before these constructs are defined, it is important to understand the stance of the narrative therapist. Nichols and Schwartz (1998) provide the following synopsis of the theory proffered by White (1995) and Freedman and Combs (1996):

> 1) take a collaborative, listening position with strong interest in the client's story; 2) search for times in a client's history when he or she was strong or resourceful; 3) use questions to take a non-imposing, respectful approach to any new story put forth; 4) never label people and instead treat them as human beings with unique personal histories; 5) help people separate from the dominant cultural narratives they have internalized so as to open space for alternative life stories. (p. 402)

PROCESS AND GOALS OF NARRATIVE ART THERAPY

Nichols and Schwartz (1998) describe the goals of therapy:

> The goals of narrative therapy aren't modest. Narrative therapists aren't problem solvers. They're interested in awakening people from the trances they've been lulled into by powerful forces of culture, so they can have a full range of choices ... Narrative therapy is designed to transform clients' identities, from flawed to heroic. (p. 407)

White and Epston (1990) further state:

> Insofar as the desirable outcome of therapy is the generation of alternative stories that incorporate vital and previously neglected aspects of lived experience, and insofar as these stories incorporate alternative knowledges, it can be argued that the identification and provision of the space for the performance of these knowledges is a central focus of the therapeutic endeavor. (p. 31)

As noted above, narrative therapists work with clients to externalize the problem, reauthor one's life, employ therapeutic questions, seek unique outcomes, and co-construct alternative stories. The following sections provide the reader with a historical framework relevant to the population used in this chapter in our case study examples, a definition of the therapeutic components of narrative art therapy, case examples of incorporating art making with personal narratives, and potential narrative art therapy directives.

CASE EXAMPLE: A HISTORICAL SYNOPSIS

Incorporated into this chapter are case study examples of how art therapy might work in combination with narrative therapy. These examples are taken from a research project in which four graduate-level art therapy student researchers worked with six elderly Japanese Americans who had been sent to internment camps with their families during World War II. This research project, entitled, "Can image making with elders enhance personal historical narrative?," explored ways in which art making might influence the story told by each participant. The fruit of the research included both participant-generated narrative and artwork created around their internment experience, with results supporting the compatibility and usefulness of combining art therapy with narrative therapy. (Please note that pseudonyms are used to identify participant artworks and narrative.)

Many Americans living in 2005 are unaware that over 60 years ago, in the time leading up to and including World War II, a gross injustice was perpetrated against roughly 110,000 Japanese Americans living in the United States because of their ancestry. Many Japanese Americans remain silent about this time and have not shared their experiences with family and friends, let alone strangers.

The attack on Pearl Harbor shocked most of the Japanese American community, who could not have predicted what would happen next. In February 1942, President Franklin Roosevelt issued Executive Order 9066, which gave military commanders the power to "exclude any and all persons" from military zones. Suddenly Washington, California, Oregon, and Arizona were military zones, and Japanese Americans were the persons who needed to be excluded (U.S. Department of War, 1979). Of the 127,000 persons of Japanese ancestry living in the continental United States, 113,000 lived in Washington, California, Oregon, and Arizona (Thomas & Nishimoto, 1986).

Japanese Americans were forced from their homes in southern Arizona, California, western Oregon, and Washington, in the single largest forced relocation in U.S. history. Without formal charges, evidence, or trials, persons of Japanese ancestry were held in crude prison camps situated mainly in desolate areas of the United States (Burton, Farrell, Lord, & Lord, 2002). Anyone with one sixteenth or more Japanese blood was included (Uyeda, 1995, cited in Burton et al., 2002). Ironically, two-thirds of those interned were American citizens.

Today, many ponder how such a gross injustice occurred, largely supported by numerous systems, including government, businesses, and the public. From a narrative perspective, Michael White cited work by Michel Foucault (1965, 1980). White & Epston (1990) noted that

> Commonly it is proposed that power is repressive in its operations and in its effects, that it is negative in force and character. Power is said to disqualify, limit, deny and contain. However, Foucault argues that we predominately experience the positive or constitutive effects of power. (p. 19)

Further, Foucault saw language as an instrument of power; he insisted that certain "stories" about life, perpetuated as objective "truths" by the dominant culture, help maintain society's power structure and eliminate alternate accounts of the same events (for example, regarding what constitutes normal sexuality, or what behavior should be classified as pathological, or how to react to members of a minority community, or what it takes to be a "real" man). Those with dominant or expert knowledge (politicians, clergymen, scientists, doctors, therapists), according to Foucault, hold the most power and determine what knowledge is held to be true, right, or proper in society (Freedman & Combs, 1996, cited in Goldenberg & Goldenberg, 2004, pp. 346, 347).

Japanese American residents and families were given short notice to leave their homes and relocate to temporary detention camps. Many were forced to sell homes, property, and sentimental belongings for very little. One man would later testify, "We were given eight days to liquidate our possessions. It is difficult to describe the feeling of despair and humiliation experienced by all of us as we watched the Caucasians coming to look over our possessions and offering such nominal amounts, knowing we had no recourse but to accept whatever they were offering because we did not know what the future held for us" (Armor & Write, 1988, p. 4). There followed a 3- to 4-year period of devastating uncertainty and anxiety.

Upon arrival the relocated, disoriented Japanese Americans found that their families were assigned to a 20-foot-square "room" within hastily constructed barracks. The "room" had "a pot-bellied stove, a single electric light hanging from the ceiling, an army cot for each person and a blanket for the bed" (Takaki, 1993, p. 383). Food was inadequate, not so much in quantity, but in quality. Eating was done in a cafeteria setting, with 250 to 300 people sharing a common mess hall (Yatsushiro, 1979). Frequent contamination of food and water caused repeated outbreaks of dysentery, which plagued internment camp residents (Jensen, 1998). All but one of the camps had barbed wire surrounding them. Soldiers with machine guns in guard towers with searchlights guarded the camps, their machine guns and search lights pointed inward (Shelton, 2002).

Historically, subjugated people have been objectified for purposes of social control (Foucault, 1965, 1973, 1979). Additionally, Foucault's (1979) analysis of Jeremy Bentham's eighteenth-century architectural forms for the purpose of social control conveys an interesting historical perspective (see White, 1997, p. 200). This process has more recently been identified as "socially constructed racism" (Ore, 2000).

The Issei (first-generation Japanese Americans) endured extreme adversity and discrimination in order to establish their homes and families in the United States. As a result of the events leading up to and including Executive Order 9066, years of hard work were lost. Families were forced to leave most of their property behind. Further, families became fragmented due to the mounting physical and emotional pressures both from within the camps and the outside world.

Research participants described how their family structure "disintegrated" due in part to the fact that leadership had been taken from the traditional head of the family, the father, "because he had no power to tell us what to do anymore." Structural changes in activities of daily living also altered family dynamics. One simple example of this was mentioned by nearly all of the research participants. Before internment Japanese American families ate meals together. In camps everyone ate in a mess hall, which split children from parents because they could, and did, join their friends for meals, rather than sit with their families.

The stage was set for internment when President Roosevelt signed Executive Order 9066 on February 19, 1942, authorizing military authorities to exclude civilians from any area without trial or hearing. The first exclusion acts to be enforced occurred in Washington roughly one month later. Internment officially lasted three years, through January 1945 when a Supreme Court ruling determined that "loyal" citizens could not be lawfully detained (Densho, 2005). Sadly, thousands of Japanese Americans remained living in camps until August 1946, simply because they had nowhere else to go.

As part of the interviews the student researchers asked participants to create three images around their internment experience. The first art directive was to make an image of themselves and their family during internment. The second was to draw an image that comes to mind of their family during the tumultuous decade following internment. The last art directive was a picture or symbol to represent what wisdom they feel they may have gained from their experience that they would like to share with their children and grandchildren.

A number of recurrent themes became evident from the emerging stories and artworks of the participants. Of relevance to this chapter is the theme of identity, especially the turning point that came individually and collectively through the process of, and, for some, participation in redress.

The historical significance of Taan's first drawing, Boredom at Camp (see Figure 9.1), became clear after reviewing all four interview transcripts and finding references in each to a sudden, unexpected, unwanted abundance of spare time. "Ted" put it like this: "Well, you know they had a lot more time. You've got to remember, these people were mostly hard working, *working* people, mostly farmers, and they were used to working seven days a week and long hours and things like that. So all of a sudden they find themselves with nothing to do, and so they started to do things like ... craftwork, and things like that."

Figure 9.1 Boredom at camp.

EXTERNALIZATION OF THE PROBLEM

Definition

White and Epston (1990) define externalizing as "an approach to therapy that encourages persons to objectify and, at times to personalize the problems that they experience as oppressive. In this process, the problem becomes a separate entity and thus external to the person or relationship" (p. 38).

Goldenberg and Goldenberg (2004) explain that the role of the narrative therapist is to engage the client in *externalizing conversations* so the client may attach new meanings to his or her experiences. The client is therefore able to separate his own identify from the problem, and thereby revise his relationship with the problem, which has had a debilitating influence over the client's life.

White and Epston (1990) purport that, "neither the person nor the relationship between persons is the problem. Rather, the problem becomes the problem, and then the person's relationship with the problem becomes the problem" (p. 40). Goldenberg and Goldenberg (2004) further assert that

> Consequently, no time is devoted to discovering family patterns or exploring family dynamics, nor to searching for critical events in the past that led to the current situation. ... That is, the therapist helps families "externalize" a restraining problem—in effect, by deconstructing the problem as an internal deficiency or pathological condition in the individual and redefining it as an objectified external and unwelcome narrative with a will of its own to dominate their lives. The therapist then encourages the family to unite against that problem. (p. 348)

What is the benefit of separating from a problem? Zimmerman and Dickerson (1996) assert that this may provide a venue for helping people notice other choices for their own behavior and for their expectations of others. White and Epston (1990) further assert that the client may experience the problem as oppressive, and reframing the problem as external to the person or relationship may provide the client an opportunity to view the perceived, fixed qualities of the problem as more fluid and less restrictive.

White and Epston (1990) found that externalization of the problem is helpful to persons in their struggles with problems. Two conclusions about externalization of the problems that seem particularly relevant for the Japanese Americans are that the practice allows for people to cooperate, to unite against the problem, and to diminish its power in their lives. At this point clients may be empowered to live their lives minus the problem's dominant influence. It is important to note that the role of the therapist is to assure that the problem is externalized from the family's world and language (White & Epston, 1990).

Case Study Example

Before a family issue or problem can be externalized, the internalized problem must be identified. Consider the following images and quotations taken from our Japanese American participants. Bear in mind that these were generated some 60 years *after* their internment experience.

In this simple image created by "Tani," shown in Figure 9.2, one can see and feel the sobering, impersonal reality of becoming numbered prisoners forced to live in ramshackle buildings located essentially nowhere.

This image also illustrates one way that the Japanese American culture differs from Western culture. When initially asked to draw her family at the time of internment, Tani resisted, saying she was not an artist. As an alternative we suggested she could represent each family member with shapes and colors, in other words, a geometric family drawing/collage. She depicted herself and her family as variations of the same geometric form, with herself and her sisters as three orange squares, and her parents as two rectangles,

Figure 9.2 Tani's drawing.

larger versions of the girls, one pink and one black. In essence, their similarities outweighed their differences. The image speaks eloquently about her sense of being part of a collective whole. One may also ponder if this image reflects the experience of having been interned: that the squares characterize the internees as nameless, faceless, meaningless individuals, stripped of their individuality and freedom.

Tani also drew the "room" her family lived in (Figure 9.3), which was typical for all internees. It had 5 "beds" (gunnysacks filled with straw), one hanging light, and a pot-bellied stove. This drawing hauntingly depicts the spare slice of interior space allotted to most internees, depending on family size. Each participant commented on their allotted space in the barracks, separated from neighboring families by makeshift curtains only. That she titled it "Minidoka or Puyallup" reflects the fact that all the barracks were essentially identical.

One spoken example of how the humiliation of internment became internalized for many Japanese Americans is evident in the following comment made by one research participant. Taan said, "because we were put into, we were put in *prison* you have this … a feeling of here is something we did *wrong*, you know, and we know it [that perception] was wrong, but for some reason … it is always in the back of your mind that you were arrested and *did* something."

"Sonoko" described the internalization of racism against Japanese Americans this way: "And the melting pot, oh boy, we were part of this melting pot and that resonated so deeply. So, and there was a pain … but we kept quiet … we kind of pushed down that hurt and … there was that sense of inferiority

Figure 9.3 Tani's drawing of a room.

that kind of stayed with me, I know, as a child. And my smallness, my, uh, Japaneseness, you know, all those things."

Close to 30 years after the war many of the previously silent Nisei (second-generation Japanese Americans) began to speak, calling for redress for the more than 110,000 Japanese Americans who had been wrongfully imprisoned, and had lost everything as a result. Another participant, Ted, was a pivotal player in the redress efforts. Although a child at the time of internment, he had lived much of his adult life silently accepting the role of alien in his own birth land, and becoming involved in redress empowered him, and brought forth his voice. In essence, he had begun the process of externalizing the problem, from *himself and the other Japanese Americans*, to the actual problem, which was *the injustice of the internment*.

In a drawing of his lifeline (Figure 9.4), Ted describes himself prior to redress as a "foreiner inhibited (sic)." As a result of his tireless efforts for redress from 1978 on, he established an empowered, assertive self. While describing this drawing, he said (pointing to where he wrote "1978"), "I think during this time was when I really got a lot more confidence in going out and saying, 'Hey, look, something bad happened. We gotta make good on this,' and ask people to help. And I think that got me out of the inhibitions I used to have when I was younger."

Viewed through the lens of narrative therapy, the redress effort allowed Ted and many others to externalize many negative, internalized feelings

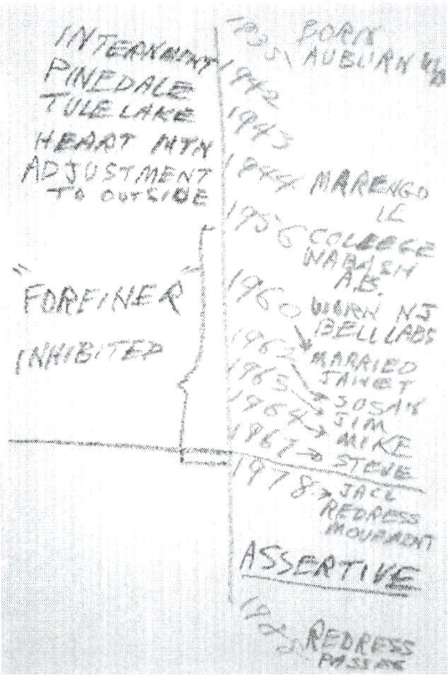

Figure 9.4 Ted's lifeline.

brought on by internment. Compare Taan's description, "a feeling of here is *something we did wrong*" to Ted's "Hey look, *something bad happened.*" These two phrases illustrate a critical shift in perception, the difference between a problem internalized and externalized.

Although it is obvious that the participants had engaged independently on externalizing the problem through such efforts as redress, art making provided a vehicle for the participants to view the problem as separate from themselves.

Art Directives

Externalization of the problem through a tangible, permanent process such as art making seems a natural fit. Carlson (1997) purports: "Having clients draw their problem is a very dramatic way to separate from the problems in their lives. It is externalization in the most literal sense. The act of drawing, however, does not mean that externalization has taken place" (p. 277). To enable the family to separate from the problem, a directive such as, "draw how the problem looks to you," could provide an emotional separation for the family to view and reassess the problem. This, in and of itself, can be enormously helpful; families often struggle with patterns that may be generational and long term, thereby making emotional separation from the problem especially challenging.

Carlson (1997) illustrated externalization of the problem through work with a 14-year-old female living in residential placement for troubled teens. Her self-portraits provided a vehicle for her to recognize the degree to which her anger dominated her life. Through externalizing the anger and its influence on her life, alternative solutions and stories were created. This behavior change shifted the family system to a more productive pattern of dialogue in which the family could then communicate. As her anger diminished, her self-portraits, likewise, appeared less angry.

DECONSTRUCTION, REAUTHORING ONE'S LIFE, AND UNIQUE OUTCOMES

Definitions

Deconstruction, reauthoring one's life, and unique outcomes are three constructs of narrative therapy that are distinctive yet overlap to some degree. We felt it was difficult to completely separate these constructs and that it would be more helpful to combine them within this section.

"Narrative therapy works by helping clients *deconstruct* unproductive stories and reconstruct (reauthor) new and more productive ones" (Nichols & Schwartz, 1998, p. 408). According to Goldenberg and Goldenberg (2004), the term "deconstruction" was introduced by French theorist Jacques Derrida, and is defined as, "disassembling and examining taken-for granted assumptions" (p. 345).

So what is the benefit of recognizing that the problem is the problem, and that the client is not the problem? According to Goldenberg and Goldenberg (2004):

> Narrative therapists use the concept to remind clients that the domi-nance of one meaning or one set of assumptions is an illusion, and that it is possible to have a multitude of meanings or assumptions in understanding the same event or experience. Thus narrative thera-pists help clients reexamine so-called truths about themselves— imposed by others or by the culture and internalized as simply given and unchangeable—and construct new narratives. Deconstruct-ing the power of a dominating, problem-saturated narrative helps empower clients to deal more competently with new views of reality. (p. 345)

White (1993) further notes that:

> Deconstruction has to do with procedures that subvert taken for granted, realities and practices: those so-called truths that are split off from the conditions and the context of their production: those disembodied ways of speaking that hide their biases and prejudices: and those familiar practices of self and relationship that are subju-gating of people's lives (p. 34).

The process of deconstruction is at the heart of narrative therapy. Once the client can externalize the problem and view it as a separate entity, then the client can begin to redefine it, thereby reauthoring his or her life.

Freedman and Combs (2000) note that once the problem is external-ized, the therapist explores with the family experiences or events that do not coincide with the problem, in an effort to begin the process of reauthoring conversations that ultimately aid in the development of alternative stories. The narrative art therapist may also elicit what is coined *unique outcomes*, which can be identified through a historical review of the person's influence in relation to the problem. White and Epston (1990) work with and encourage families to recall "facts" or events that contradict the problem's effects in their lives and in their relationships. Further,

> Although such events are experienced by the persons concerned at the time of their occurrence, the problem-saturated stories of their lives usually rule out the attribution of new meanings to such experi-ences. These historical unique outcomes can facilitate performances of new meanings in the present, new meanings that enable persons to reach back and to revise their personal and relationship histories. (p. 56)

Taan drew this image representing a family conflict over his sister's desire to marry a Chinese man (Figure 9.5). Here is an interesting example of a variation on the theme of discrimination. As it turned out, she did marry the

Figure 9.5 Taan's family.

man and all ended well. So, in this case, the family created a unique outcome, overcoming their own struggle with discrimination by opening their hearts and minds and redefining "family."

Once unique outcomes are developed, the process of reauthoring one's life begins by recognizing how cultural stories influence and shape personal narratives, and provide a framework, or *dominant narrative* that defines the customary or ideal behavior within that particular culture (White, 1995). Goldenberg and Goldenberg (2004) caution: "Bear in mind that clients reauthor their lives, aided by therapists, but that narrative therapists do not reauthor people's lives" (p. 346).

Case Study Example

Perhaps the most profound example of deconstruction that occurred intentionally by and for Japanese Americans in World War II can be found in the remarkable, true stories of Japanese American soldiers who fought for America in spite of internment. Research participant "Bill" put it succinctly: "Talk about ironic, you know, here we are going to be interned, and the [Japanese American] boys are going to fight for their country."

Ted said: "But there are other folks that felt, 'Hey, you know, I'm going to fight for America. I'm an American. And even though I'm being treated badly, I'm gonna go and prove my loyalty.' And so they formed the 442nd Regimental Combat Team, combining it with the 100th Battalion in Hawaii that was all Japanese Americans. (sic) And you know, they went on to become the most decorated fighting unit in American military history."

This was an attempt to counter (deconstruct) in the most dramatic, self-sacrificing manner possible, the untruths being told about Japanese Americans, and to respond, with their lives if necessary, to the injustices they had been dealt. Research participant "Sonoko" wrote numerous poems and prose about Japanese American soldiers in World War II. Following is an example:

> While the Texan Battalion of the 34th Division could not be rescued
> by their own division, the 442nd Combat Team/100th Battalion

broke through the German line: They suffered 814 casualties to save 214 Texans.

Interestingly, Taan, the one study participant who served in the 442nd, barely spoke about it. He did create the image shown in Figure 9.6, however, which depicts a painful scene etched into his memory. While on furlough from the army to relocate his ailing father, Taan was refused service by a railroad employee (pictured here as the larger figure), even though he wore his army uniform. Taan said if the man had been smaller he would have "given him a run for his money."

"Narrative therapists see their work as a political enterprise—freeing clients from oppressive cultural assumptions and empowering them to be active agents in charge of their own lives" (Nichols & Schwartz, 1998, p. 408). This was indeed the case with many of our participants. Japanese Americans who were interned during World War II as children and teenagers are elders now. They repeatedly stressed the importance of telling their stories for the sake of the children and grandchildren. They also emphasized the necessity to educate the community at large about the tremendous injustices that happened to them.

Our participants felt a responsibility to share their stories and opinions about political and human rights issues, because of their internment experience. Following are excerpts from the interviews.

Participant "Meg" stated, "For the sake of all minorities, to uphold the Constitution and say what is right and what should never happen again, and what should, well, like the poor Arabs, you know what's happening now, we have a lot more empathy and understanding for others, and we hope that everybody will have more of that with this coming out to the public. That they can have understanding and want to do what's right, you know."

Figure 9.6 Taan's experience at the railway station.

Participant Ted felt: "But there was a time when people used to make these assumptions and say things that used to hurt a lot, and I wouldn't say anything. And you know all you could say yourself was, 'Oh, here they go again.' But that doesn't happen anymore. And I find myself speaking out on other issues that don't really affect me even if I find that somebody else is being trod on."

In Figure 9.7 Taan depicts the discrimination he encountered upon returning to the United States after having served in the 442nd, while looking for employment.

Taan and his wife Tani played a major part in a legacy that was tangential to having served in the 442nd; the establishment of one nursing home in Seattle, plus an assisted living center, also in Seattle, each designed for disenfranchised Issei parents whose sons who had died in the war.

In our first interview Taan described an incident whereby he went to visit the father of a buddy of his who had died in the war. This man was in a nursing home that accepted state aid patients, which many Issei were by virtue of having lost everything in World War II. Taan described these nursing homes as having a very minimal level of care, a desolate situation made worse by the fact that so many Issei did not speak English. Another of this elderly gentleman's sons was visiting at the same time Taan was there. The son asked Taan if he had any spare change. As Taan reached for his change, the son explained that the staff were more likely to answer the call buttons of patients who could give them some change when they came by, because they were so rushed and busy and because it took longer for staff to understand those patients who did not speak English. Taan said: "…so that, that really, that really pissed me off. So that was my motivation to do something about them."

The first nursing home Taan, his wife and daughter, the Japanese American Veteran's Association and numerous other community organizations developed and sponsored is a 64-unit nursing home. Next, they developed a 50-unit assisted living center.

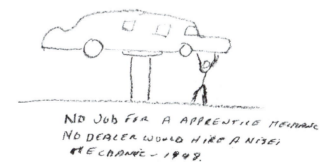

Figure 9.7 Taan's experience looking for employment.

This is the kind of impressive, solid legacy reflective of a culture whose traditions and values have been more oriented toward family and community than toward individual interests and accomplishments, like the United States and other Westernized cultures. This can also be viewed as an example of "rewriting" the end of a story initiated by the dominant culture.

Art Directives

How often do clients find alternative meanings from the images and art they create? Often, the process itself can provide the catalyst for fresh solutions and alternative paths. The narrative art therapist may choose to let the fluid nature of creative process guide the session. Alternatively, the narrative art therapist may find reason to guide the process with directives that assist the client to find new meanings. Regardless of the approach, understanding the process of the client by not imposing one's preconceived agenda onto the client is paramount.

One directive that may aid the client to find alternative meanings is to have the client draw his or her "past, present, and future." This directive is one that at times may be completed in one session and other times may take two or more sessions to complete. It may be a useful directive to give as "homework," to give the time and space sometimes needed to consider unique outcomes. Another simple directive is to have the family draw their ideal world. Questions that narrative art therapists might use to access alternative information and alternative meanings follow.

EMPLOYING THERAPEUTIC QUESTIONS

Regardless if a therapist is a narrative therapist, an art therapist, or a narrative art therapist, it is important to consider the sequence of therapy and the therapeutic conversation. From a narrative lens, this often entails the therapist helping the client access information, using questions to gain information, and subsequently opening new avenues for consideration.

Narrative therapists may question the tension between the dichotomy of fixed surface versus depth descriptions. While it has been common to label underlying traits or personality attributes in more superficial descriptors such as normal/abnormal, functional/dysfunctional, coined *thin descriptions*, White and Epston (1990) argue that therapists should be more mindful of *thick descriptors*, which are more enriched, multistories that are formed in part by personal, historical, and political and cultural forces.

Goldenberg and Goldenberg (2004) note that questions are carefully constructed to open up new pathways of thinking. They state, "White's gentle, respectful, but nevertheless persistent questioning typically is directed at *what* the person is experiencing and *how* the problem was being experienced (p. 349). White and Epston (1990) note that questioning is comprised of two sets: one set encourages clients to map the influence of the problem in their lives and relationships, and the second helps map how they themselves were influential in the life of the problem. The therapist may ask the client or family for a "rich" or "thick" description of the problematic story and later explore alternate stories. Also, these stories may emerge in various ways and be juxtaposed with the stories of others. Cultural discourses might be questioned in the following way: "how do you think society views aggressive and unaggressive men, and what does that say to you about your unconsciousness?"

Goldenberg and Goldenberg (2004) give the following example on how a narrative therapist might differ in his or her questioning techniques from other therapists. A narrative therapist may pose a question to examine how the problem has impacted each member of the family, how the problem has affected the parents, the siblings, and so on. Further, the family may be asked how the problem has affected the relationships and behavior towards each other, everyone's view of themselves, and with others such as friends. This allows the family to gain space from the problem, distance themselves from the story that has shaped their opinions and lives, and allow for the creation of alternative accounts of themselves.

Nichols and Schwartz (1998) provide the following excellent synopsis of the series of questions a narrative therapist might utilize:

Deconstruction questions—externalizing the problem. "What does Depression whisper in your ear?" "What conclusions about your relationship have you drawn because of this problem?"

Opening space questions—uncovering unique outcomes. "Has there ever been a time when Arguing could have taken control of your relationship but didn't?"

Preference questions—making sure unique outcomes represent preferred experiences. "Was this way of handling things better or worse?" "Was that a positive or negative experience?"

Story development questions—to develop a new story from the seeds of (preferred) unique outcomes. "How is this different from what you would have done before?" "Who will be the first to notice these positive changes in you?"

Meaning questions—designed to challenge negative images of self and to emphasize positive agency. "What does it say about you that you were able to do that?"

Questions to extend the story into the future—to support changes and reinforce positive developments. "What do you predict for the coming year?" (p. 419)

Art Directives

White and Epston (1990), as mentioned above, suggested mapping the influence of the problem on themselves and further how they were influential in altering the influence on the problem. Imagine the power in an art directive that asks clients to map visually accessing this information. This kind of image parallels the directive of a lifeline, where a client is asked to map his or her life through the highs and lows of life, in an effort to look at it in its entirety. Through a similar directive of mapping the influence of the problem, the client has *externalized* the problem and may also provide a venue to look at the problem longitudinally. A second map, examining his or her own influence may provide the client with an empowering interconnectedness between the two.

Regardless of the directive there are a few things to keep in mind as a narrative art therapist. The narrative therapist does not assume to be the expert in diagnosing things such as ego strength, motivation, needs, drives, etc. Rather, the therapist consults and collaborates with clients on an equal level, the goal being to aid clients to new and alternative dreams, beliefs, values, and commitments. Goldenberg and Goldenberg (2004) note that,

> The narrative therapist is thus *decentered*—still influential without being at the center of what transpires therapeutically...
>
> An important therapeutic twin goal here is the deconstruction of domineering self-narrative and the re-establishment of freedom, individually and as a family, from the dominant discourses of the culture. (p. 348)

THERAPEUTIC CEREMONIES, LETTERS, AND DOCUMENTS

Description

As mentioned previously, narrative therapists work with families to create richer descriptions of alternative stories, so as to stay connected to the preferred narrative. In an attempt to help the family become more multistoried, the narrative therapist has numerous supplementary practices to achieve this goal. Other practices that expand the repertoire of how to approach families seem to again coincide considerably with art therapy. Some of these approaches include definitional ceremonies, letters, and documents.

Definitional ceremonies are viewed as multilayered and often involve the narrative therapist including a nonjudgmental audience to respond to the new, alternative story, or to a retelling of the story. The audience may be professional, such as a reflecting team, or more personal, such as group members who will witness the alternative stories. Goldenberg and Goldenberg (2004) note:

> It may consist of tellings (by the person who is at the center of the ceremony), retellings of tellings (by the reflecting team or outside witnesses who have observed the tellings), retelling of retellings (again, by the person who responds to what was told by the outsiders), retellings of retellings of retellings (by the first set of outside witnesses or a secondary group of witnesses), and so forth. The point

is to thicken alternative stories, authenticating the person's preferred claims about their lives, and promote the idea of options for actions that the person at the center of the ceremony might not have otherwise considered. (p. 353)

It is always interesting to note the degree to which professions overlap or share similar viewpoints. It is not unusual for an art therapist to assign "homework" with clients or families. Techniques such as journaling and creating art outside of sessions can have rich results. Families may find expressive tasks such as journaling or art making beneficial on many levels; for emotional outlets, to sort through feelings and thoughts, and in a narrative stance, to find new alternative stories and meanings.

Narrative therapists often use letters sent to clients in a variety of therapeutic ways, to supplement and extend therapeutic sessions and keep clients connected to the emerging alternative story. With the client's consent, Epston, in particular (White & Epston, 1990) routinely employs therapeutic letters in summarizing sessions, inviting reluctant members to attend future sessions, addressing the future, and so on. Doing so enables the therapist to extend conversations while encouraging family members to record or map their own individualized view of the sequences of events in their lives over a period of time. Letters, because they can be read and reread days, months, or even years later, have great continuity value; they "thicken" or enrich an alternative story line and help clients stay immersed in the reauthoring process. Epston and White (1995) estimate that a single letter can be as useful as at least four or five sessions of therapy (pp. 353–354).

White and Epston (1990) were instrumental in developing and using letters for numerous reasons throughout the narrative therapy process, and they provide a plethora of letters throughout their book. Following is a very brief definition and description of the use of letters. They include:

1. *Letters of invitation*, which may be used to engage clients in therapy who are reluctant to attend.
2. *Redundancy letters*, which may be used to examine the multitude of roles one may assume. They provide an example of a letter they gave to a son who had taken care of his heroin-addicted mother; the letter asked that he give up his role as "her father" now that his mother was sober (p. 91).
3. *Letters of prediction*, which may be used at the end of therapy for the family's future. These can be written for a short term, such as 6 months.
4. *Counter-referral letters*, which may be written to the client's doctor to report on the progress of overcoming his or her dilemma.
5. *Letters of reference*, which may be used to aid in reinforcing the client or family in progress around finding alternative stories, etc.
6. *Letters for special occasions*, which may be used when a family is struggling with a particular occasion. An example given was the unveil-

ing of a gravestone for a family and how the letter helped the family prepare and put their minds to rest.

7. *Brief letters*, which are sent to socially isolated individuals when the therapist feels they are having a tenuous existence and are particularly at risk.

8. *Letters as narrative*, which may be co-constructed with the family or with other professionals to make sense of recent events, as well as provide a plan of action in the letter.

9. *Self stories*, which are invitations by the therapist to the family or client to record their own stories. This can employ a large range of media, including poetry, as presented in the following section.

Another creative technique employed by narrative therapists such as White and Epston (1990) is the development of various certificates or declarations to celebrate the new stories that are constructed. Examples given are certificates such as "certificate of concentration," "escape from tantrums certificate," and "escape from misery certificate" (pp. 196–198).

Case Example

One research participant, Sonoko, preferred to express herself with poetry, as opposed to art making. Following is a poem she wrote describing the disorienting train ride that took her family away from their home:

> They brought these old trains, where they got them I don't know.
> That squeaked, creaked, and jolted to sudden halts.
> The air inside was stuffy and stale.
> As the trains passed through towns
> The M.P.'s gave orders: "Keep the shades down!"
> For a few brief moments,
> As they traveled through barren lands,
> The M.P.'s allowed internees to pull up the shades.
> Hungry eyes swallowed the world outside.
> Between the slits around the shade and window,
> The sun disappeared beyond the horizon
> And returned at the break of day.

She wrote anther poem, which describes one response she had to the oppression suffered by Japanese Americans. Following is an excerpt:

JAPANESE NAME

> My daughter was ten then:
> "Mommy, why didn't you name me Shigeko or Midori
> Or some other Japanese name? …
> …When my child asked

"Mommy, why didn't you name me
With a Japanese name?"
I could only respond:
"Roberta Lynn is such a pretty name
We chose it especially for you."

And finally, she wrote a poem which is a scathing hypothesis regarding the United States government's possible motivation for Japanese internment:

The Constitution was bent:
Those in power
failed to acknowledge the American soul
of Japanese Americans.
They saw them through the clouded lens of racism.
Their loyalty was questionable—potential saboteurs.
They used "Military Necessity" for their removal.
The Constitution was bent:
Those in power listened to the voices
Of those who would gain
Thousands of acres of land
Made fertile and bountiful
by the hard, weather-beaten hands,
by the long hours and strong backs
of Japanese farmers.

CONCLUSION

The development of narrative therapy provides a new venue in which to work with families to deconstruct old notions and replace them with new and mul-tistoried possibilities. The strong component of social justice, awareness of cultural alternatives, and the cultural context in which stories are constructed blends well with a model such as Hays's ADDRESSING model. Additionally, the reauthoring and co-construction process lends itself to creative process, such as art therapy. Helping the client separate from the problem may be argu-ably most effective through a tangible, permanent means such as art therapy. It may provide the distance needed for the client to recognize that, "the client is not the problem, the problem is the problem" (Goldenberg & Goldenberg, 2004, p. 355).

In this chapter, we sought to provide the reader with not only a narrative framework, but also a comprehensive understanding of the population we chose to work with. We were hopeful that interviews and art making through a narrative lens would provide an opportunity to break the silence that has remained prevalent with this population, perhaps an unspoken trauma:

Silence is a key mechanism by which trauma in one generation is communicated to the next. ... Silence can communicate a wealth of meanings. It is its own map: don't go there; don't say that; don't touch; too much; too little; this hurts; this doesn't. But why the territory is as it is cannot be read from the map of silence. Sometimes silence is total, sometimes it is pocketed with speech. Often parents who have suffered political violence cannot bring themselves—or may be unable—to tell a sequential narrative of the ordeal. Children in families in which speechlessness dominates and few facts have been disclosed may fantasize details to imagine the parental trauma. (Ancharoff, Munroe, & Fisher, 1998; Weingarten, 2003) (Weingarten, 2004, p. 51)

The conclusions drawn by the researchers after examining the participants' artwork and reviewing their narratives supported our hypothesis that image making with elders would indeed be a useful method for both sparking memory and adding depth to their stories. The images created became springboards for discussion around the themes of family, discrimination, and deprivation.

Carlson (1997) noted that narrative and art therapies share certain theoretical beliefs that are consistent with one another. "Among these are the ideas that recapturing hidden aspects of self-expression or lived experience, the principle of co-construction in understanding the therapeutic relationship and the belief in the creative abilities in persons" (p. 275).

ACKNOWLEDGMENTS

The authors acknowledge the contributions of the researchers involved in this project: Kali Kuwada, M.A., Carleen Yates, B.A., Penny Potter, M.A., and professor Jayashree George The authors also express their deepest gratitude and humble thanks to the participants who opened their memories, hearts, and homes so we could better understand their painful journeys, and celebrate their resilience, and generous contributions to all of humanity. Working with them was nothing short of inspirational.

REFERENCES

Ackerman, B. (1979). Relational paradox: Toward a language of interactional sequences. *Journal of Marital and Family Therapy, 1*(5), 29–38.

Ancharoff, M. R., Munroe, J. F., & Fisher, L. M. (1998). The legacy of combat trauma: Clinical implications of intergenerational transmission. In Y. Danieli (Ed.), *International handbook of multigenerational legacies of trauma* (pp. 257–276). New York: Plenum Press.

Armor, J., & Write, P. (1988). *Manzanar.* New York: Times Books.

Bertalanffy, L. von. (1968). *General system theory.* New York: Braziller.

Bowen, M. (1978). *Family therapy in clinical practice.* New York: Aronson.

Burton, J. F., Farrell, M. M., Lord, F. B., & Lord, R. W. (1999). *Confinement and ethnicity: An overview of World War II Japanese American relocation sites.* Seattle: University of Washington Press.

Carlson, T. D. (1997). Using art in narrative therapy: Enhancing therapeutic possibilities. *American Journal of Family Therapy, 25*(3), 271–279.

Carter, E., & McGoldrick, M. (Eds.). (1989). *The changing family life cycle* (2nd. ed). Boston: Allyn & Bacon.

David, A., & Erickson, C. (1990). Ethnicity and the therapist's use of self. *Family Therapy, 17*(3), 211–216.

Densho (2005). Retrieved from http://www.densho.org/causes/default.asp

Elkins, D. E., Stovall, K., & Malchiodi, C. A. (2003). American Art Therapy Association, Inc. 1998–1999 membership report. *Art Therapy: Journal of the American Art Therapy Association, 20*,(1), 28–34.

Foucault, M. (1965). *Madness and civilization: A history of insanity in the age of reason.* New York: Random House.

Foucault, M. (1973). *The birth of a clinic: An archeology of medical perception.* London: Tavistock.

Foucault, M. (1979). *Discipline and punish: The birth of a prison.* Midlesex: Peregrine Books.

Foucault, M. (1980). *Power/knowledge: Selected interviews and other writings.* New York: Pantheon Books.

Framo, J. (1992). *Family-of-origin family therapy.* New York: Brunner/Mazel.

Freedman, J., & Combs, G. (1996). *Narrative therapy: The social construction of preferred realities.* New York: W. W. Norton.

Freedman, J., & Combs, G. (2000). Narrative therapy with couples. In F. M. Dattilio & L. J. Bevilacqua (Eds.), *Comparative treatments for relationship dysfunction* (pp. 308–334). New York: Springer.

Goldenberg, I., & Goldenberg, H. (2004). *Family therapy: An overview* (6th ed.). Pacific Grove, CA: Thompson, Brooks/Cole.

Green, R. J., & Framo, J. L. (Eds.). (1981). *Family therapy: Major contributions.* Madison, CT: International Universities Press.

Hammond, W. R., & Yung, B. (1993). Minority student recruitment and retention practices among schools of professional psychology: A national survey and analysis. *Professional Psychology: Research and Practice, 24,* 3–12.

Hays, P. A. (1995). Multicultural applications of cognitive-behavioral therapy. *Professional Psychology: Research and Practice, 26*(3), 309–315.

Hays, P. A. (1996a). Addressing the complexities of culture and gender in counseling. *Journal of Counseling and Development, 74,* 332–338.

Hays, P. A. (1996b). Cultural considerations in couples therapy. *Women and Therapy, 19,* 13–23.

Hays, P. A. (1996c). Culturally responsive assessment with diverse older clients. *Professional Psychology: Research and Practice, 27*(2), 188–193.

Hays, P. A. (2001). *Addressing cultural complexities in practice: A framework for clincians and counselors.* Washington, DC: American Psychological Association.

Hoffman, L. (2002). *Family therapy: An intimate history.* New York: W. W. Norton.

Hovestadt, A., & Fine, M. (Eds.). (1987). *Family of origin therapy.* Rockville, MD: Aspen Publishers.

Jacobson, N. S., & Gurman, A. (1986). *Clinical handbook of marital therapy.* New York: Guilford Press.

Jensen, G. M. (1998). The experience of injustice: Health consequences of the Japa-
    nese-American internment. *DAI-A*, No. 58/07, p. 2718.
Kerr, M., & Bowen, M. (1988). *Family evaluation.* New York: W. W. Norton.
Lappin, J. (1983). On becoming a culturally conscious family therapist. In C. J. Fali-
    cov (Ed.), *Cultural perspectives in family therapy* (pp. 122–136). Rockville, MD:
    Aspen.
Madanes, C. (1981). *Strategic family therapy* (pp. 122–136). San Francisco:
    Jossey-Bass.
McGoldrick, M., & Gerson, R. (1985). Constructing genograms. *Genograms in family
    assessment* (pp. 9–38). New York: W. W. Norton.
McGoldrick, M., Giordano, J., & Pearce, J. K. (1996). *Ethnicity and family therapy* (2nd
    ed.). New York: Guilford Press.
Minuchin, S. (1974). *Families and family therapy.* Cambridge, MA: Harvard University
    Press.
Napier, A. Y. (1988). *The fragile bond.* New York: Harper & Row.
Napier, A., & Whitaker, C. (1978). *The family crucible.* New York: Bantam.
Nichols, M. (1999). *Inside family therapy.* Boston: Allyn and Bacon.
Nichols, M. P., & Schwartz, R. C. (1998). *Family therapy: Concepts and methods.* Boston:
    Allyn & Bacon.
Nichols, W., & Everett, C. (1986). *Systemic family therapy: An integrative approach.* New
    York: Guilford Press.
Ore, T. E. (2000). *The social construction of difference and inequality: Race, class, gender,
    and sexuality.* Mountain View, CA: Mayfield.
Papero, D. V. (1990). *Bowen family systems theory.* Boston: Allyn & Bacon.
Riley, S. (1988). Adolescence and family art therapy: Treating the "adolescent family"
    with family art therapy. *Art Therapy, 5*(2), 43–49.
Riley, S. (1999). *Contemporary art therapy with adolescents.* London: Jessica Kingsley
    Publications.
Riley, S., & Malchiodi, C. A. (1994). *Integrative approaches to family art therapy.* Chi-
    cago: Magnolia Street.
Roberts, S. (1995). *Who we are: A portrait of America based on the latest U.S. Census.* New
    York: Times Books.
Rubin, J. A. (1999). *Art therapy: An introduction.* New York: Brunner/Mazel.
Shelton, L. (Producer). (2002). After silence [video recording]. Bainbridge Island, WA:
    Foxglove Films.
Taffel, R., & Masters, R. (1989). An evolutionary approach to revolutionary change:
    The impact of gender arrangements on family therapy. In M. McGoldrick, C.
    Anderson, & F. Walsh (Eds.), *Women in families: A framework for family therapy*
    (pp. 117–134). New York: W. W. Norton.
Takaki, R. (1993). *A different mirror, a history of multicultural America.* Boston, MA:
    Little, Brown and Company.
Thomas, D. S., & Nishimoto, R. J. (1986). *The spoilage.* Berkeley: University of Cali-
    fornia Press.
U.S. Department of War. (1979). *Final report: Japanese evacuation from the West Coast
    1942.* New York: Arno Press.
Wadeson, H. (1980). Family art therapy. In H. Wadeson (Ed.), *Art psychotherapy* (pp.
    280–316). New York: John Wiley & Sons.
Wadeson, H. (2000). *Art therapy practice, innovative approaches with diverse populations.*
    New York: John Wiley & Sons.

Watzlawick, P., Bevin, J., & Jackson, D. (1967). *Pragmatics of human communication*. New York: W. W. Norton.

Weingarten, K. (2004). *Common shock: Witnessing violence every day: How we are harmed, how we can heal*. New York: Dutton.

Whitaker, C. (1989). *Midnight musings of a family therapist*. New York: W. W. Norton.

White, M. (1993). Deconstruction and therapy, In S. Gilligan & R. Price (Eds.). *Therapeutic conversations* (pp. 22–61). New York: W. W. Norton.

White, M. (1995). *Re-authoring lives: Interviews and essays*. Adeleine, Australia: Dulwich Centre Publications.

White, M. (1997). *Narratives of therapists' lives*. Adeleine, Australia: Dulwich Centre Publications.

White, M., & Epston, D. (1990). *Narrative means to therapeutic ends*. New York: W. W. Norton.

Yatsushiro, T. (1979). *Politics and cultural values*. New York: Arno Press.

Zimmerman, J., & Dickerson, V. (1996). *If problems talked: Adventures in narrative therapy*. New York: Guildford Press.

CHAPTER 10

Conclusion

CHRISTINE KERR

The family is one of nature's masterpieces.

Santayana

It has been a privilege to bring this book to those clinicians who are interested in family therapy and to those family art therapists who routinely use creative means to engage their client families in treatment. As a practicing clinician, family art therapist, and professor, I am cognizant of the number of therapeutic and educational experiences that I have had the privilege to be a part of, which have shaped my worldview professionally, theoretically, and personally. It has been my pleasure to author three chapters in this book, as well as the introduction and conclusion of this book. I believe these writings reflect the best of my therapeutic work with families. The story of this book seems to have been an in-depth, searching journey, which has resulted in both me and the other authors finding a way to create meaning within the family therapy process. All of these chapters reflect theoretical paradigms and the respective author's subjectivism. Subjectivism is defined as the search for meaning within a particular theoretical construct.

THE FAMILY THERAPY THEORIST AND THE FAMILY ART THERAPIST

The challenge of the family therapy theorist is to speculate and contemplate on a phenomenon of a particular theory, as it relates to how individuals live, work, play, and love together. As family art therapists and family therapists, the objective in treating families is to relieve suffering and anguish. Our primary job is to heal. Notwithstanding, family therapists and family art therapists need to additionally decipher theory. Family art therapists and family therapists should innately feel a personal affinity for a particular theoretical construct, apply those techniques to individual families and, most importantly, sustain a conviction that change within every family may be possible over time. In the chapters that I have authored this has been the main goal of my writing. A second goal in the overall writing of this book has been to assist the family art therapist and family therapist to further their understanding of family therapy theory as it is *successfully* applied to the visual arts. As a group of authors, we as family art therapists have looked at the major theoretical paradigms and methodological issues of different theorists, which include the practical application of the visual arts to treatment. We have tried to separate out the decisive techniques of different family systems, and we have applied case-vignettes to augment the theorist's clinical orientation.

However, the more we talk about theory and technique, the greater the danger of seeing family art therapy as a purely technological enterprise. Family work is far from this. Family therapy and family art therapy requires mindfulness to *seeing* the family constellation within their worldview, their history, their burdens, and their aspirations. It also requires the clinician to remain *mindful*, to remain open to the influences and impositions of his or her *own* worldview.

Collaboration

It is essential to see other professionals in an open and collaborative manner. As family art therapists and family therapists, we must never forget that we are not a *masterpiece* but *a work in progress*. In the following portion of the conclusion, I will highlight the other authors' comments regarding the collaborative efforts in writing this book.

It is important to note that I thought about this type of book many years ago when I first began teaching family therapy. I was focused on my doctoral dissertation, and I met Helen Langarten, ATR, HLM and Shirley Riley, ATR at a conference that was hosted by the university where I am a full-time professor. It was at a dinner in New York City that I began discussing my interest in pursuing this type of book with these two renowned family art therapists. Both of these amazing women gave me their wisdom. They individually advised me and then collaboratively spoke about the pitfalls and joys of publishing. They emphasized the need to network. In reflecting back over the past 12 years, I recall that this is now the moment for moving forward with this book. I am seasoned. I feel grounded. My gratitude goes without saying to both of these renowned family art therapists.

At my first AATA Education Program Approval Board meeting (EPAB), I met the individuals who are now featured in this book. Again, at this first meeting, I felt it was essential *to see* other professionals in an open and collaborative manner. Consequently, this book is the end result of very wonderful family therapists *working together*. To understand the efforts of all those who helped to create this book is perhaps to reiterate a resounding metaphor of mine. This metaphor speaks to all of those who have worked together as authors and who practice with families in crisis everyday. We share the conviction, that the sum of the whole is greater than the parts. Writing this book was a summation of all our efforts and a rich family experience.

Be well.

Janice Hoshino, ATR-BC, LMFT

Every so often unique ideas arise harmoniously and serendipitously. Indeed, this was true with the origin of this book. It was during an EPAB (Education Program Approval Board) meeting in San Diego, California, that I first had the opportunity to work with Chris Kerr. At one point, I glanced across the table at Chris and felt she was engaged in the same parallel thought process to the topic at hand; our connection was immediate, and there was an odd sense that I had known her forever. When she later approached me with the concept of a collaborative writing project, we found one of our mutual interests was in systems theory and family art therapy. When she shared this idea to write a book with the EPAB, many were excited, loved the idea, and expressed an interest in participating in this new endeavor.

At the end of the EPAB meeting, as I looked around the room, I was honored with the opportunity to partner with a group of women I so deeply admired, trusted, and respected; a group of women who would opt for collaboration over competitiveness, would support instead of oppose each other, and would uphold respect over disregard—a refreshing alliance. Of course, this is not to insinuate we did not have to negotiate details and particulars; but the respect, mutual appreciation, and expertise of the collective whole coincided well with system's theory notion that, "the whole is greater than the sum of its parts."

As the project coalesced, another positive dynamic that emerged was the authors' areas of expertise, which were distinctive and diverse. These included Sharyl's expertise in object relations theory, Judy's with Adlerian therapy, and Linda's with filial therapy. Chris and I negotiated how to share and divide our areas of interest, including Bowen, general history, Minuchin, and so forth.

The Journey of Research   Researching art therapy and related articles can be both enlightening and frustrating. It is always informative to peruse not only the literature, but also the authors and their credentials. What was particularly frustrating in this endeavor was the paucity of family art therapy articles that were actually written by art therapists, yet were published in well-respected family therapy journals. I contacted one author who had written on family art therapy and asked where she received her art therapy training. After several e-mails of rather evasive information, she informed me she had received her "training" at an art therapy weekend workshop and had received "supervision" for doing art therapy. She did not respond to further questioning on the credentials of her "supervisor." Perhaps the most impudent article I found was again in a well-respected, family therapy journal. Riley was consistently misspelled "Ribey" and Wadeson was misspelled "Wadison." How this article was accepted with these gross errors conveyed to me several factors: First, it appears that both the authors and reviewers, regardless of how prestigious the journal, are not necessarily trained or particularly knowledge-able about art therapy. Imagine "Bowen" cited consistently as "Bolen"! Second, there is undoubtedly an interest in art therapy by family therapists. However, it's unfortunate that little notice has been given to the qualifications of those authors as art therapists. Hopefully, this book will expand awareness to the non–art therapy community about art therapy, as well as provide a valuable resource for the art therapy community.

Judy Sutherland, ATR-BC

Looking for ways to resolve problems brought about by family patterns has been a life-long interest both personally and professionally. Not that I expected to be my own family therapist, or to "fix the problem," but I hoped to under-stand why certain unwanted problems came up over and over again both in my family of origin and in my family today. Sometimes the problem would not be so obvious, but I could feel it in my body either as a symptom: illness, pain; or an emotion: fear, anger, or depression. Other times there would be open conflict where I would find myself saying things to my parents, my hus-band, or my children that I wouldn't dare say to others. Without thinking, I would find myself repeating these patterns.

As an adult, I gradually learned to recognize that I had to first change my attitudes and behavior before I could expect anything in the family system to change. I began by exploring my responses to past experiences I had as a child and how they shaped and formed a pattern for how I perceive others and the world around me. Certainly I had everything I needed as a child for living life in a family—food, shelter, caring adults, and lots of time to explore my world and to learn. And, of course, some of my experiences were hurtful, and I never did learn how to cope very well with adversity.

At those times, especially, I learned to express myself through art, some-thing I continue to do today. Slowly, I have found ways to change my attitudes and behavior when what I am doing does not lead to resolving the problem at hand.

That's not to say I have gotten rid of all of my problems or painful areas in my life, but I do have a better understanding of how I have shaped and cre-ated the meaning I give to my life. Having self-awareness and knowing that I am responsible for my own happiness, feeling that I can take care of myself, and, most of the time, meet the tasks of life in the spirit of trust and mutual respect, gives me self-confidence and courage.

I had these thoughts in mind when we were all together one day and decided to each contribute to a book on family art therapy. The opportunity seemed to present itself to me at a time when I was ready to write down my ideas and work together to complete this project. Just as we have all had different experiences in life and created our own responses to them, we all have experienced different ways of doing family art therapy. We have taken what has worked best for us and now give it to you. The diversity in these chapters reflects the diversity in our lives and in families around the world. I hope you receive this gift with the idea that you can take some of what you read and make it your own.

Sharyl Thode Parashak, ATR-BC

Upon occasion, professional work in a group gives rise to feelings of camaraderie towards a unified purpose. If conditions are right, each individual contributes to the greater purpose of the group, keeping individual agendas at a minimum so that the work of the group is made possible. As members of that group become closer, each may feel strongly committed to the original stated purpose, but also recognize that something more is being created through the strength of the group.

Virginia Satir wrote of the larger context of families: "Families and societies are small and large versions of one another. They are both made up of people who have to work together, whose destinies are tied up with one another" (1972, p. 290). Unlike families of origin, the writers of this book had a choice in participating on a professional committee and of writing this book; like a family of origin, the writers were each involved with the process of planning, decision making, communication, and support of each other toward a common goal. This involved each member sharing individual experiences and expertise, all of which brought the book together. Conceptualizing, planning, communicating, and supporting mutual efforts of each member of the group, be it authors writing a book or members of a family, brings cohesion and a shared sense of purpose. The authors of this book encountered a parallel experience of a family working towards its highest function.

Linda McCarley, MSSW, LCSW, ATR-BC, RPT-S

Writing the chapter "Filial Art Therapy" has been mixed with hopes and concerns for this author. It was my initial hope that I would be able to convey not only my thoughts about the value of offering a person-centered, home-based family art therapy approach, but also that I might offer readers some useful child-centered techniques that could also be adapted to other modes of art therapy. There are numerous situations in which a child can benefit from making art in the context of a trusting and mutually respectful relationship with an adult who is using the filial art therapy approach (e.g., medical setting, school art therapy, etc.).

Filial art therapy appears very simple at first glance, but in practice it becomes clear to therapists and parents that there are several levels of complexity to master. If one is easily discouraged or unable to focus on the goals, the outcome could be disappointing. However, most parents, in my experience have demonstrated that they desire an improved relationship with their child.

The parents have demonstrated a sincere commitment to learn new skills and practice them during art sessions in their own homes. Usually, they only practice filial art therapy for a few months. Yet they report reaping the benefits of lasting improvements. They also report improved relations and greater sensitivity to other members of the family.

Using this approach has been deeply satisfying for me because I have enjoyed the benefits of developing intimate trusting relationships with the families while they are in the process of enriching their relationships with their children and with each other. It is my sincere hope that descriptions of the home-based art therapy model will be a model that therapists can utilize and adapt with their own client population.

My own professional evolution, which includes a background in social work, play therapy, family therapy, and art therapy, has provided the seeds for developing this approach. My hope for the future is that readers and practitioners will also be inspired to adapt and blend this approach in ways that fit with their own practice. I hope that this chapter will invite research in filial art therapy and encourage practitioners to adapt, blend, and develop new approaches with today's changing families.

REFERENCES

Satir, V. (1972). *Peoplemaking*. Palo Alto, CA: Science and Behavior Books.

About the Authors

Christine Kerr, Ph.D., ATR-BC, LCAT is Associate Professor of Art and the Director of Clinical Art Therapy at Long Island University at C.W. Post. Dr. Kerr has 34 years of clinical art therapy experience. She has a Ph.D. in Psychology and is a board certified licensed art therapist. Her main focus is the clinical application of art psychotherapy in adult populations, including but not limited to, affective disorders, addictions, eating disorders, dissociative disorders, and family therapy. She maintains a private practice in New York.

Janice Hoshino, Ph.D., ATR-BC, LMFT, has been a registered and board certified art therapist for over 24 years. She is a licensed marriage and family therapist in Washington state and a clinical member of the American Association of Marriage and Family Therapy. She founded and chairs the art therapy program at Antioch University Seattle and maintains a private practice in Redmond, Washington.

Linda L. McCarley, MSSW, LCSW, ATR-BC, RPT-S, began conceptualizing a filial art therapy approach while working as a psychiatric social worker and art therapist at a teaching clinic known as the Child Guidance Clinic in Dallas, Texas (now known as the Child and Family Guidance Center). During her years at the clinic, between 1991 and 1996, she received training in various models of family therapy and child therapy. She then went into private practice in Dallas, where she has continued providing filial art therapy to families.

Sharyl Thode Parashak, MAT, ATR-BC, is a board certified, registered art therapist. Sharyl has 23 years of clinical experience in art therapy with individuals aged 14 months to 106 years. Sharyl has taught undergraduate and graduate art, art education, psychology and art therapy for 34 years, including supervision of graduate art therapy students providing services to Head Start and early Head Start. Photography remains Sharyl's creative passion.

Judy H. Sutherland, Ph.D., ATR-BC, is a faculty member and Director of the M.A. in Counseling Psychology: Art Therapy and the Post-Master's Certificate in Art Therapy programs, Adler School of Professional Psychology. She also maintains a private practice in Illinois.

Index